£7-50

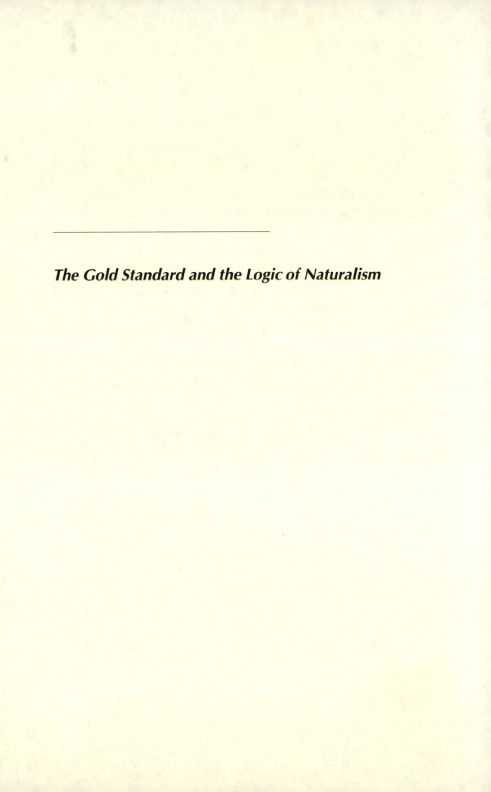

The Gold Standard and the Logic of Naturalism

The New Historicism:
Studies in Cultural Poetics

STEPHEN GREENBLATT, General Editor

1. *Holy Feast and Holy Fast: The Religious Significance of Food to Medieval Women,* by Caroline Walker Bynum
2. *The Gold Standard and the Logic of Naturalism: American Literature at the Turn of the Century,* by Walter Benn Michaels
3. *Nationalism and Minor Literature: James Clarence Mangan and the Emergence of Irish Cultural Nationalism,* by David Lloyd

THE GOLD STANDARD AND
THE LOGIC OF NATURALISM

AMERICAN LITERATURE AT THE
TURN OF THE CENTURY

WALTER BENN MICHAELS

University of California Press
Berkeley / Los Angeles / London

University of California Press
Berkeley and Los Angeles, California

University of California Press, Ltd.
London, England

©1987 by
The Regents of the University of California

Library of Congress Cataloging-in-Publication Data
Michaels, Walter Benn.
  The gold standard and the logic of naturalism.
  (The New historicism : studies in cultural poetics)
  1. American fiction—20th century—History and
criticism. 2. Naturalism in literature. 3. Economics
in literature. 4. Consumption (Economics) in
literature.
5. Production (Economic theory) in literature.
6. Capitalism and literature. I. Title. II. Series:
New historicism.
PS374.N29M5   1987   813'.52'0912   86-14654
ISBN 0-520-05981-6 (alk. paper)
ISBN 0-520-05982-4 (pbk. : alk. paper)

Printed in the United States of America
1 2 3 4 5 6 7 8 9

TO MY MOTHER AND FATHER

Contents

Acknowledgments ix

INTRODUCTION: THE WRITER'S MARK 1

1. *SISTER CARRIE'S POPULAR ECONOMY* 29
2. *DREISER'S* FINANCIER: *THE MAN OF BUSINESS AS A MAN OF LETTERS* 59
3. *ROMANCE AND REAL ESTATE* 85
4. *THE PHENOMENOLOGY OF CONTRACT* 113
5. *THE GOLD STANDARD AND THE LOGIC OF NATURALISM* 137
6. *CORPORATE FICTION* 181
7. *ACTION AND ACCIDENT: PHOTOGRAPHY AND WRITING* 215

Index 245

Acknowledgments

 M any of those who contributed to this book are thanked within: I would like to take this opportunity to thank some who aren't: Kenneth Abraham, Richard Bridgman, Wai-Chee Dimock, Stanley Fish, Barbara Freeman, Stephen Greenblatt, Ruth Leys, Mark Maslan, Franny Nudelman, Richard Poirier, Lynn Wardley. And I would like to acknowledge once more the help of three people without whom these essays could not have been written: Frances Ferguson, Michael Fried, and Steven Knapp.

All the essays in this book with the exception of "The Writer's Mark" and "Action and Accident" have been published elsewhere: "*Sister Carrie*'s Popular Economy" in *Critical Inquiry* 8 (Winter 1980); "Dreiser's *Financier*" in *American Realism: New Essays*, edited by Eric J. Sundquist (Baltimore, 1982); "Romance and Real Estate" in *Raritan* 2 (Winter 1983) and then in *The American Renaissance Reconsidered: Selected Papers from the English Institute, 1982–1983*, edited by Walter Benn Michaels and Donald Pease (Baltimore, 1984); "The Phenomenology of Contract" in *Raritan* 4 (Fall 1984); "The Gold Standard and the Logic of Naturalism" in *Representations* 9 (Winter 1985); "Corporate Fiction" in *Reconstructing American Literary History*, Harvard English Studies 13, edited by Sacvan Bercovitch (Cambridge, 1986). I am grateful to the editors of *Critical Inquiry*, *Raritan*, and *Representations*, and to the editors of the Harvard University Press and the Johns Hopkins University Press for permission to reprint them here.

INTRODUCTION: THE WRITER'S MARK

What kind of work is writing? In Charlotte Perkins Gilman's *Women and Economics* (1898), it is simultaneously paradigmatic of "economic production" and, like production itself, as Gilman understands it, hardly economic at all. "Economic production," she writes, "is the natural expression of human energy"; "human beings tend to produce, as a gland to secrete."[1] In fact, the desire to produce precedes even the desire to consume: " 'I want to mark!' " cries the child, demanding the pencil. He does not want to eat. He wants to mark" (116–17). Not only is production imagined here as the most primitive desire, it is imagined as in some sense more primitive than any desire can be. Children may "want" to mark, but glands don't want to secrete, and insofar as the child marking is like the gland secreting, the child's work seems more a matter of physiology than of psychology.

Gilman's polemical point in insisting on the absolute priority of production is, of course, to emphasize the unnaturalness of an economic system that denies "free productive expression" to "half the human race," i.e., to women. Women who are not allowed to mark are like glands somehow prevented from secreting. In response to the claim that woman's economic role as a "nonproductive consumer" is "natural," Gilman thus appeals to a "process" more natural even than the "process of consumption." But if the analogy between production and secretion effectively forestalls one kind of question— why do women want to work?—it raises at the same time the possibility of another—what exactly does production produce? The child wants to mark because it is natural to want to "make," but when he marks, what is he making?

Women and Economics is largely uninterested in this question; in this text, production is so normal that the notion of secretions as exemplary products seems only a fleeting oddity. But Gilman's famous short story "The Yellow Wallpaper" (1892),

---

[1] Charlotte Perkins Gilman, *Women and Economics*, ed. Carl Degler (New York, 1966), 116. Subsequent page references are cited in parentheses in the text.

although it too has its normalizing tendencies, is more committed to examining the naturalization of production.

From one standpoint it may be misleading to describe "The Yellow Wallpaper" as having normalizing *tendencies*, since, in Gilman's own account, the story is utterly committed to the project of normalization, having been written against S. Weir Mitchell's infamous "rest cure" ("Rest means with me . . . [the] absence of all possible use of brain and body")[2] and in praise of "work, the normal life of every human being." After her "nervous breakdown," Gilman wrote, it was only by rejecting Mitchell's advice "never to touch pen, brush or pencil again" that she saved her sanity. Although a Boston doctor characterized it as maddening to read, "The Yellow Wallpaper" was written, according to Gilman, with a therapeutic motive: "It was not intended to drive people crazy, but to save people from being driven crazy."[3] If Mitchell's rest cure meant, as he himself described it, "neither reading nor writing," Gilman's work cure required that her audience read and, above all, that she herself write.[4]

But while it is perfectly true that the seemingly crazy narrator of "The Yellow Wallpaper" is forbidden by her doctor husband to write, it is by no means the case that she doesn't in fact do a lot of writing. For one thing, the story is told as a kind of diary. And for another, the "dead paper"[5] on which it is written

[2] S. Weir Mitchell, *Lectures on Diseases of the Nervous System* (Philadelphia, 1885), 275.

[3] Charlotte Perkins Gilman, "Why I Wrote 'The Yellow Wallpaper,'" in *The Charlotte Perkins Gilman Reader*, ed. Ann J. Lane (New York, 1980), 20.

[4] It is in this light that Sandra M. Gilbert and Susan Gubar describe the narrator of "The Yellow Wallpaper" as "literally locked away from creativity" and go on to read her escape from behind the wallpaper as emblemizing "the progress of nineteenth-century literary women out of the texts defined by patriarchal poetics into the open spaces of their own authority" (Sandra M. Gilbert and Susan Gubar, *The Madwoman in the Attic* [New Haven, Conn., 1979], 90, 91). Gilbert and Gubar are right, I think, to see the story as a successful search for authority; in my view, however, the narrator is not so much locked away from creativity as locked into it, and the authority she establishes radicalizes rather than rejects a poetics defined more aptly by reference to a market society than a patriarchal one.

[5] Charlotte Perkins Gilman, "The Yellow Wallpaper," in *The Charlotte Per-*

is so strikingly analogized to the "inanimate thing" (7) that is the wallpaper itself, with its "lame uncertain curves" (5), which, violating "every principle of design" (9), may come to seem unreadable as a decorative "pattern" precisely to the extent that they come to seem readable as a kind of writing—or, if that seems too strong, as a kind of marking. For the narrator's two main activities in "The Yellow Wallpaper" are both forms of marking: she makes marks on paper when she writes, and she also makes "a very funny mark" on the wall when she creeps around the room, "a long, straight, even *smooch*, as if it had been rubbed over and over" (15). Marks may be produced either by covering paper or by uncovering it. And in the course of this marking, the "dead paper," "inanimate thing," comes alive; it begins to move, it begins to smell, it begins to mark back—the "smooch" the narrator makes on the wallpaper is doubled by the "yellow smooches" (14) the wallpaper makes on the narrator. Her own body thus takes its place in the chain of writing surfaces, and she herself comes to seem an animated effect of writing; for not only does her body bear the trace of writing but also it is described as having literally emerged from the wallpaper, so that she can end by wondering if those other "creeping women" "come out of the wallpaper as I did" (18). It is as if she has written herself into her body or, more precisely perhaps, written herself into existence. "'I want to mark!'" says the child in *Women and Economics*: "He is not seeking to get something into himself but to put something out of himself" (117). Beginning with the child's desire to put something out of herself, the narrator of "The Yellow Wallpaper" ends by writing herself into herself.

I suggest, then, that the work of writing in "The Yellow Wallpaper" is the work of something like self-generation and that, far from being a story about a woman driven crazy by Weir Mitchell's refusal to allow her to produce, it is about a woman driven crazy (if she is crazy) by a commitment to production so complete that it requires her to begin by producing herself. Weir Mitchell recommended the infantilization of nervous

kins *Gilman Reader*, ed. Ann J. Lane (New York, 1980), 3. Subsequent page references are cited in parentheses in the text.

women; sufferers from "hysterical motor ataxia" were given kneepads and taught to balance themselves on all fours before learning to "creep." After creeping came walking: "following nature's lessons with docile mind, we have treated the woman as nature treats an infant."[6] "The Yellow Wallpaper" repeats and extends this treatment—not only does the narrator creep, but she also ties herself to the bed with an umbilical cord ("I am securely fastened now by my well-hidden rope" [18])— while reimagining the return to infancy as a moment of willed self-begetting.

But to put the point in this way—to characterize "The Yellow Wallpaper" as transforming Mitchell's scene of feminine infantilization into a scene of feminine self-generation, as redescribing feminine helplessness as feminine empowerment— may be to simplify the discourse of "nervous disease" and the logic of work and ownership in which it plays a part. For while Weir Mitchell did indeed think that "the mass of women are by physiological nature more likely to be nervous than are men,"[7] he did not identify this "weakness" of women with an inability to work. Rather, the physiological weakness of women inevitably makes their bodies the site of a certain kind of work. Always in danger of losing "self-control," women must make "repeated efforts" to resist hysteria, with its physical symptoms (paralysis, tremor, spasm) and, even worse, its mental ones (a "nervous" girl in one of Mitchell's novels, for example, develops an "alternate consciousness" and writes shameful love letters to a man for whom the "real" girl feels only respectful friendship).[8] Thus, to be a woman is to confront on a daily basis the physiological labor of "self-conquest."[9] And the "peculiar physiology" of women turns out to require not that they be treated differently from men but that they be treated more like them: "The boy is taught self-control, repression of emotion, not to cry when hurt. Teach your girls these things and you will

---

[6]Mitchell, *Diseases of the Nervous System*, 47.
[7]S. Weir Mitchell, *Doctor and Patient* (Philadelphia, 1887), 137.
[8]S. Weir Mitchell, *Dr. North and His Friends* (New York, 1900), 302.
[9]Mitchell, *Diseases of the Nervous System*, 33.

in the end assure to them . . . interior control."[10] Woman's weakness is the pretext for woman's work, and woman's work only makes visible the efforts required of every self.

The (male) child wants to mark. He wants to work, to "put something out of himself," and, by working, to guarantee control over himself. But the hysteric also wants to mark, to write passionate love letters, for example. The difference is that the hysteric's efforts seem to produce marks not of herself but of some other self. In fact, according to William James in *The Principles of Psychology*,[11] the phenomenon of "hysterical" or "automatic" writing was the "most cogent and striking" proof of the existence of what Mitchell called the "alternative consciousness." Thus Gilman's normal child wants not simply to mark; he wants to make a mark that will be identifiably *his*, for only then does that mark provide the guarantee of identity he is seeking in the first place. If the threat of hysteria is the threat of losing self-control, of sometimes becoming someone else, the point of marking is to produce evidence that you are still the same person. Your mark is a continual reminder that you are you, and the production of such reminders enforces the identity it memorializes. From this perspective, the hysterical woman embodies not only the economic primacy of work but also the connection between the economic primacy of work and the philosophical problem of personal identity. The economic question—How do I produce myself?—and the therapeutic question—How do I stay myself?—find their parallel in the epistemological question, How do I know myself?—or more specifically, as James puts it, How do I know today that "I am the same self that I was yesterday"? What does "consciousness" "mean when it calls the present self the *same* with one of the past selves which it has in mind?" (316).

Phenomenologically speaking, we can tell which past or "distant" selves are ours, James thinks, by the feelings of

---

[10]Mitchell, *Doctor and Patient*, 146.

[11]William James, *The Principles of Psychology* (1890; reprint, Cambridge, Mass., 1983), 202. Subsequent page references are cited in parentheses in the text.

"warmth and intimacy" we experience when thinking about them. These selves bear the "mark" of "animal warmth," and we naturally separate them "as a collection from whatever selves have not this mark, much as out of a herd of cattle let loose for the winter on some wide western prairie the owner picks out and sorts together when the time for the round-up comes in the spring, all the beasts on which he finds his own particular brand."(317). In this analysis, despite the weirdness of its Wild West rhetoric, James thinks that he differs little from what he takes to be the two most common views of personal identity, the "spiritualist" (or Cartesian) and the "associationist" (or Humean). Extending the metaphor of the herd, however, brings out what seems to him a major difference. If our selves are all bound together by common ownership, the question naturally arises as to what sort of thing or self owns them. For the "spiritualists," the answer is a "real Owner," a "pure spiritual entity," a "soul"; for the associationists, who deny the existence of any such entity, there can be no adequate answer, and indeed, the institutions of selfhood and ownership are both mere fictions. According to James, however, the "owner" of the herd of selves is neither an enduring spiritual substance nor a mere fiction. It is instead a "'section' of consciousness or pulse of thought" (319), "namely, the real, present onlooking, remembering, 'judging thought'" (321). This "thought" sorts through the "past facts which it surveys," collecting some and discarding others, "and so makes a unity." And with this account James thinks he has produced a description of the self that explains how we can experience it both as empirical (instead of spiritual) and as real (instead of fictional).

At the same time, however, James acknowledges that there is something disturbingly counterintuitive about this scenario, since it depicts the self continually *making* a unity that common sense tells us must already be there. It is as if for the "thought" (following out the original Lockean metaphor), all the world were always America, and the separate thoughts "wild cattle . . . lassoed by a newly-created settler and then owned for the first time" (321)—whereas common sense tells us that "the past selves never were wild cattle, they were always owned," an objection that, if admitted, seems fatal to the project of avoiding spiritualism and associationism both. For it now seems that the "mere continuity" between thoughts implied by their common mark is insufficient to account for the unity of the self, and we find ourselves forced either to postulate an "arch-ego," a soul, or to assert with Hume that the self is a fiction.

Still, the original difficulties with these positions remain: we have no experience of anything like a soul, and we do seem to have a sense of a real personal identity. How, then, can we account for the way in which the present thought establishes ownership over past thoughts? Our mistake, James thinks, has been to imagine the thought as *establishing* ownership over past thoughts; instead, we should think of it as *already* owning them. The owner has "inherited his 'title.'" His own "birth" is always coincident with "the death of another owner"; indeed, the very existence of an owner must coincide with the coming into existence of the owned. "Each Thought is thus born an owner, and dies owned, transmitting whatever it realized as its Self to its own later proprietor" (322).

While the notion of an inherited title that never lapses thus lies at the heart of the Jamesian economy of selfhood, Gilman's "The Yellow Wallpaper" begins with an explicit challenge to the exact coincidences required by selves in or as an "hereditary estate" (3). For not only do the "ancestral halls" the narrator and her husband are renting for the summer of her breakdown belong to somebody else's ancestors, their very availability for rent is a function of title disputes among the true descendants: "There was some legal trouble, I believe, something about the heirs and co-heirs; anyhow the place has been empty for years" (4). She understands these legalities as spoiling what she perceives as the "romantic" "ghostliness" of the place; but title disputes don't spoil the ghostliness, they *constitute* it: the house is "haunted" by the ghosts of competing claimants. And in this respect, of course, the house is no more than an emblem for the narrator herself, haunted, like all hysterics—and, if hereditary title breaks down, like all selves—by the ghosts of "alternate consciousnesses." The task of achieving "proper self-control" is the task of banishing the ghosts, of legitimating title.

In one version of romance, what Freud called the "family

romance," legitimation was made possible by the discovery of a secret noble line of descent. This is, in fact, the plot of Weir Mitchell's popular historical novel *Hugh Wynne*, whose young Revolutionary War hero discovers while fighting to free the colonies from Britain that he is himself descended from British nobility. The question of what it means to be an American rebel is here neatly answered by the discovery that one is also an English nobleman; the revolutionary battle for a new identity becomes indistinguishable from the reactionary battle to repossess one's old identity. Such plots had been popular in the United States at least since Hawthorne's *The American Claimant*, and it is hardly surprising that in the turmoil of the nineties they should resurface either in Mitchell's historical romance or in James's Western.

In the "colonial mansion" of "The Yellow Wallpaper," however, the moment that James's account of "herdsmen coming rapidly into possession of the same cattle by transmission of an original title by bequest" (321) leaves most opaque (the moment, that is, of the "original" "bequest") is the moment on which Gilman obsessively focuses. More Lockean—which is to say, in this context, more relentlessly bourgeois—even than James, Gilman imagines that the wild cattle really are "lassoed by a newly-created settler and then owned for the first time"; she imagines that the self can only legitimately own itself if it has worked for itself. The story of "The Yellow Wallpaper" is a story of the origin of property and, by the same token, of the origin of the self. Where the herdsman's mark identifies what is his, the writer's mark creates what will be her. In a "nursery" emptied of all children, not just the "ancestral" ones who used to live there but even her own baby ("Why, I wouldn't have a child of mine . . . live in such a room for worlds" [11])—emptied, that is, of all signs of hereditary succession—the narrator enacts her own birth. One's child is a reminder of the facts of reproduction, the inevitability of fathers and mothers, the natural foundation of inherited title. But in a nursery without children—without, that is, any *other* children—what Gilman takes to be the facts of economic life can replace the facts of sexual life: "Economic production is the natural expression of human energy,—not sex-energy at all, but race-energy. . . . Socially organized human beings tend to produce as a gland to secrete: it is the essential nature of the relation" (116). The economy of autoproduction finds its physiological basis not in the sexual organs but in organs of internal secretion, in something like the pituitary gland; the "creative impulse, the desire to make," is the desire to make something out of oneself, to make oneself out of oneself.[12]

But to put the point in this way, in a way that, I have argued, we are driven to put it by "The Yellow Wallpaper," is to suggest also the conceptual (not to mention the empirical) difficulty of Gilman's project. The child who wants to mark "is not seeking to get something into himself but to put something out of himself" (117). In the "organic life of society," "production and consumption" may go "hand in hand," but "production comes first" (116). If, however, the paradigm of production is secretion—making a mark that is not only yours but you—the difference between production and consumption, between making yourself and using yourself up, may come to seem precarious. Thus Weir Mitchell's *Wear and Tear; or, Hints for the Overworked* laments the "expenditure of nerve material" involved in mental labor and reproves the laborers for living off the "interest" of previous "accumulations of power" and for "wastefully spending the capital" as well.[13] People who work too hard

---

[12] It may be worth noting that James, as one illustration of what he calls "alternating personality," cites Mitchell's account of the "remarkable" case of Mary Reynolds. Mary, a "dull and melancholy young woman, inhabiting the Pennsylvania wilderness in 1811," fell into a profound and unnaturally long sleep from which she awoke with a personality changed in two ways: she was "cheerful" instead of melancholy, and she had forgotten everything and everyone, above all her family. Skills like reading and writing she quickly learned (or relearned), but she "never did learn, or, at least, never would acknowledge the ties of consanguinity." For the next fifteen or sixteen years she passed periodically from one state to the other, now becoming her melancholy self again and recognizing "parental" ties, now cheering up and denying that she was anyone's "daughter." Eventually the alternating stopped and she lived out her last twenty-five years in the second state, a "rational, industrious, and very cheerful" schoolteacher (S. Weir Mitchell, "Transactions of the College of Physicians of Philadelphia, April 4, 1888," as quoted in James, *Principles of Psychology*, 359, 360, 361, 362).

[13] S. Weir Mitchell, *Wear and Tear; or, Hints for the Overworked* (Philadelphia, 1891), 13, 8.

are here described as people who don't work at all; the terms of abuse ordinarily reserved for those who consume without producing are directed instead at those who consume by producing too much.

Against Gilman's reading of herself as a priestess of production, one might then read "The Yellow Wallpaper" as undermining the gospel it meant to preach. Marking produces a "smooch" on the paper, a residue of one's own body on the paper that is simultaneously an opening in the paper. Through that opening—itself an opening in a body, since the wallpaper is figured as skin, and the smooch is thus an orifice—emerges another body: or rather, more body, an important difference, since the narrator is giving birth not to her child but to herself. She is making herself out of her secretions, consuming her body in order to produce her body. "The creative impulse, the desire to make, to express the inner thought in outer form . . . this is the distinguishing character of humanity" (116). But when the "outer form" is the very substance of the "inner thought," creating seems less like making a body out of nothing than like reconstituting it by redistributing it, reproducing it by circulating it. Insofar as the paper you mark will turn out to be you (its surface will be the surface of your own body), and insofar as the marks on that paper will involve putting something on it and taking something off it, even, eventually, taking something (yourself) out of it, Gilman's distinction between making and taking (women are "forbidden to make but encouraged to take" [118]) looks pretty shaky. The child wants to mark and not to eat, but in "The Yellow Wallpaper," the desire to mark is the desire to mark oneself, just as the desire to eat, it seems to me, is the desire to eat oneself—which is why the bedstead in that internal cavity, the nursery, is "fairly gnawed" (17) and also why, although her "appetite" is said to be "better," the narrator does not gain weight. Insofar as the self is the common term here, insofar as your mark is you and you eat what you are, marking and eating cannot be understood antithetically. Thus in "The Yellow Wallpaper," marks made by putting something on are "smooches," and marks made by taking something off are "smooches" too. Any exchange of marks between wallpaper and woman simultaneously puts on and takes off. Marking is eating under a different description. If production and consumption are not precisely identical (one's self is not one's skin), they are, in "The Yellow Wallpaper," something more than inseparable.

For Gilman, then, the work of writing is the work simultaneously of production and consumption, a work in which woman's body is rewritten as the utopian body of the market economy, imagined as a scene of circulation so efficient that exchange is instantaneous: products not only exist to be consumed, but coming into existence they already are consumed. My point here is not to insist on the utopian character of this description (although given the prolonged crisis of what in the eighties and nineties was universally understood as "overproduction," the term *utopian* is hardly inappropriate) but to emphasize the importance for Gilman of the feminine body, understood not only as an object to be exchanged—as when the newly professionalized mothers of *Women and Economics* sell their maternal skills[14]—but as the very site of exchange. In "The Yellow Wallpaper," being oneself depends on owning oneself, and owning oneself depends on producing oneself. Producing is thus a kind of buying—it gives you title to yourself—and a kind of selling too—your labor in making yourself is sold for the self you have made. There can be no question, then, of the self entering into exchange; exchange is the condition of its existence. Producer and consumer, buyer and seller, the narrator of "The Yellow Wallpaper" need not leave her nursery to follow the other creeping women out into the market; her nursery already is the market. Her nervous breakdown marks for Gilman the triumphant omnipresence of market relations.[15]

[14]For an excellent discussion of the changing status of domestic labor, see Susan Strasser, *Never Done: A History of American Housework* (New York, 1982). Like "the early home economists who were her contemporaries," Strasser writes, "Gilman recognized the fundamental historical tendency that had turned women from producers into consumers; unlike most of them, she understood that the process was continuing, as yet incomplete" (221).

[15]In her important account of Gilman's design projects, Dolores Hayden quotes the antifeminist Laura Fay-Smith's argument that "if nature had intended women to be feminists, then women of the future . . . would be born

To read "The Yellow Wallpaper" in this way, then, is to read it as narrating the genesis of the marketplace or, more specifically, the birth of what historians have come to call (with varying degrees of disapproval) the "culture of consumption." That culture, as Richard Wightman Fox and T. J. Jackson Lears have powerfully described it,

> is more than the "leisure ethic," or the "American standard of living." It is an ethic, a standard of living, and a power structure. Life for most middle-class and many working-class Americans in the twentieth century has been a ceaseless pursuit of the "good life" and a constant reminder of their powerlessness. Consumers are not only buyers of goods but recipients of professional advice, marketing strategies, government programs, electoral choices, and advertisers' images of happiness. Although the dominant institutions of our culture have purported to be offering the consumer a fulfilling participation in the life of the community, they have to a large extent presented the empty prospect of taking part in the marketplace of personal exchange. Individuals have been invited to seek commodities as keys to personal welfare, and even to conceive of their own selves as commodities.[16]

---

with 'money as their only standard of value'" (Hayden, *The Grand Domestic Revolution* [Cambridge, 1981], 201). For Fay-Smith, as for Gilman herself, feminism was essentially a market phenomenon.

[16] Richard Wightman Fox and T. J. Jackson Lears, Introduction to *The Culture of Consumption*, ed. Fox and Lears (New York, 1983), xii. I cite Fox and Lears here and Alan Trachtenberg and Ann Douglas below not because they seem to me particularly egregious instances of the genteel or Progressive tradition in American cultural history but—just the opposite—because they are exemplary in their attempts to imagine alternative views of American culture. Which makes it all the more striking that they do not finally dissent from the genteel/Progressive view of important works of art as in some sense transcending or opposing the market. My further point here is that American literary criticism (even more than American cultural history) has customarily understood itself and the objects of its admiration as being opposed to consumer culture— and, with a few exceptions, continues to do so. No doubt the newly politicized proponents of "oppositional" criticism would reject this assimilation of their work to the genteel tradition. But transforming the moral handwringing of the fifties and sixties first into the epistemological handwringing of the seventies and now into the political handwringing of the eighties does not seem to be much of an advance. (It should go without saying that gentility flourishes on

From this perspective, the value of American cultural productions is understood to consist in what Lears calls their "subversive" potential, their attempt to resist "incorporation in the dominant culture."[17] The "radical critics" in whom Lears is interested "viewed consumption as a seduction, a form of captivity."[18] Moving from Veblen in the late nineteenth century to the counterculture of the 1960s, he and Fox point out that there have always been some who "rejected high level consumption and cultivated Spartan self-sufficiency."[19]

Fox and Lears are by no means alone in their sense of the fundamentally critical relation between consumer capitalism and the most powerful works of American culture, between, in effect, consumption and culture.[20] In his wide-ranging and important *The Incorporation of America*, Alan Trachtenberg laments, for example, the increasing dependency of late-nineteenth-century city dwellers on "what was marketed," a dependency that changed them from "active participants" in the culture to "passive spectators" of it, while he celebrates the "residual forms" of a production-based economy whose sur-

---

the right as well as the left; distaste for consumer culture transcends what passes for politics in academia.)

[17] T. J. Jackson Lears, *No Place of Grace* (New York, 1981), xiv.

[18] Fox and Lears, *The Culture of Consumption*, x.

[19] Ibid.

[20] Thus in his interesting and ambitious "The Consuming Vision of Henry James," Jean-Christophe Agnew sets out to argue that James's career reveals "a deepening awareness of the commodity world, an awareness that becomes by the end of his life wholly critical *and* wholly complicit," but in the event Agnew produces readings of *The Portrait of a Lady* and *The Golden Bowl* that choose criticism over complicity in the usual way. Isabel Archer "recovers a serenity that has become hers by virtue of an act of self-conscious renunciation, an act that raises her above the sorts of exchange to which she is, in form, submitting by her marriage to Osmond." And Maggie Verver, heroine of "the first fully achieved literary expression of an American culture of consumption" also ends on "a note of renunciation," a note echoed by James himself who, "having realized in *The Golden Bowl* what he called the 'best' and the 'solidest' of his visions, . . . like Shakespeare's Prospero, renounces it" (Agnew, "The Consuming Vision of Henry James," in Fox and Lears, *The Culture of Consumption*, 84, 86, 91, 100). As long as the best thing to do with consumer culture is renounce it, literary criticism will be happy.

vival "represented resistance to the emerging culture of the marketplace."[21] In the fictions of realism and naturalism, he writes, a "ragged picture" emerges, "of lost hopes, hypocrisy, narrowed and constricted lives, grinding frustrations of poverty and isolation. The report is relieved . . . by acts of courage, a surviving residue of older ways. . . . But the major picture included a keen lament for the passing of an older, more secure and reliable way of life, one based on ingrained assumptions about the possibilities of freedom."[22] And in *The Feminization of American Culture*, from a perspective much narrower than, but in my view not much different from, those of Lears and Trachtenberg, Ann Douglas attacks the literature of a class (ministers and middle-class women) "defined less by what its members produced than by what they consumed."[23] In terms that reproduce the contempt of Lears's radical critics and the nostalgia of Trachtenberg's realists, she contrasts "sentimental," "consumerist" writers like Harriet Beecher Stowe to the "more serious" writers of the Calvinist tradition, interested in "producing, not consuming."[24]

But these terms do more than repeat Lears and Trachtenberg —they replicate Charlotte Gilman. In *Women and Economics*, consumption is equated with powerlessness, or "economic dependence" (109), and production is equated with power: the spirit of "personal independence" that Gilman sees embodied in the "new woman" of the nineties is a function of her economic independence, what Lears calls "self-sufficiency." If, then, Charlotte Gilman plays a role in the emergence of consumer culture, that role seems to be critical. Her feminist critique of "masculinist" culture should thus be read as an exemplary act of "subversive resistance," repudiating the "dominant" consumer culture before it even had the chance to become dominant. In Gilman's proto-Progressive paean to pro-

[21] Alan Trachtenberg, *The Incorporation of America* (New York, 1982), 121, 122.

[22] Ibid., 201.

[23] Ann Douglas, *The Feminization of American Culture* (New York, 1977), 10.

[24] Ibid., 9.

duction we find the roots of the current post-Progressive critique of consumption.

The difficulty with this reading is that Gilman's texts, at least as I have described them, resist consumer culture only in ways allowed by their radical acceptance of a logic of consumption. Their commitment to production is a commitment to production in the market—production (cooking, cleaning, mothering) *for sale*. The domestic identification of production with "self-sufficiency" or "autonomy" provokes in Gilman a kind of agrarian dread: "On wide Western prairies, or anywhere in lonely farm houses, the women of to-day, confined absolutely to this strangling cradle of the race, go mad by scores and hundreds. Our asylums show a greater proportion of insane women among farmers' wives than in any other class. In the cities, where there is less 'home life,' people seem to stand it better"(267). The city—Trachtenberg aptly calls it "the universal market"—makes production bearable because it makes production for consumption possible. Farmers' wives do not go crazy because they cannot work; they go crazy because the work they do cannot become the empowering work Gilman wants them to do. Without consumption, no production; without the market, no power. Gilman rewrites the autonomy of self-sufficiency as the autonomy of free trade. The difference between the strangling cradle and the marking paper is the difference between a society where nothing is for sale and one where everything is.

From this perspective, it seems much more plausible to describe "The Yellow Wallpaper" as an endorsement of consumer capitalism than as a critique of it, and indeed, it is just such a description (albeit of *Sister Carrie* instead of "The Yellow Wallpaper") that lies at the heart of the first essay in this series, "*Sister Carrie*'s Popular Economy." That essay was written not out of any particular interest in the cultural history of the period (I had been working mainly on epistemological questions in literary theory) but out of an isolated admiration for *Sister Carrie* and especially out of irritation with those critics who read it as an indictment of American culture and who understood Carrie's career as progressing from its preoccupation with the material life of Chicago department stores to the "serious" theater of the "ideal" imagined for her by the young engineer, Ames. For Ames, the culture of consumption is "so much show," [25] as indeed it is for many critics who think of great literature as committed essentially to transcending it, and as it is, in some degree, even for its own historians, who think of great works of culture as committed to opposing it. But not, I argued, for Dreiser, at least not in *Sister Carrie*; *Sister Carrie*, I wrote, involved an "unequivocal endorsement" of what I called the "unrestrained capitalism of the late nineteenth and early twentieth centuries."

Almost as soon as that essay was published, however, I began to feel unhappy with this aspect of its argument. While the notion that Dreiser approved of consumer capitalism seemed to me a good deal more plausible than the reverse, finally neither notion seemed very plausible at all. Not because, as Rachel Bowlby puts it, my claim that *Sister Carrie* is "not anti-capitalist" is only "broadly true," since "behind the attractive images of consumption, it clearly shows up some of the peculiar disparities created by" consumer capitalism.[26] Bowlby is surely right about this, but my own unease had nothing to do with a sense that I had overstated my claim—what bothered me was the "endorsement" itself, not whether it was "unequivocal." What exactly did it mean to think of Dreiser as approving (or disapproving) consumer culture? Although transcending your origins in order to evaluate them has been the opening move in cultural criticism at least since Jeremiah, it is surely a mistake to take this move at face value: not so much because you can't really transcend your culture but because, if you could, you wouldn't have any terms of evaluation left—except, perhaps, theological ones. It thus seems wrong to think of the culture you live in as the object of your affections: you don't like it or dislike it, you exist in it, and the things you like and dislike exist in it too. Even Bartleby-like refusals of the world

[25] Theodore Dreiser, *Sister Carrie*, ed. Donald Pizer (New York, 1970), 236. Subsequent page references are cited in parentheses in the text.

[26] Rachel Bowlby, *Just Looking: Consumer Culture in Dreiser, Gissing, and Zola* (New York, 1985), 61.

remain inextricably linked to it—what could count as a more powerful exercise of the right to freedom of contract than Bartleby's successful refusal to enter into any contracts? Preferring not to, he embodies, like Trina McTeague, the purest of commitments to laissez-faire, the freedom in contract to do as one likes.[27]

These points are no doubt obvious. Nevertheless, they were useful in making me realize that I needed to transform an argument about the affective relation of certain literary texts to American capitalism into an investigation of the position of those texts within a system of representation that, producing objects of approval and disapproval both, is more important than any attitude one might imagine oneself to have toward it. In other words, Dreiser didn't so much approve or disapprove of capitalism; he desired pretty women in little tan jackets with mother-of-pearl buttons, and he feared becoming a bum on the streets of New York. These fears and desires were themselves made available by consumer capitalism, partly because a capitalist economy made it possible for lower-class women to wear nice clothes and for middle-class men to lose their jobs, but more importantly because the logic of capitalism linked the loss of those jobs to a failure of self-representation and linked the desirability of those women to the possibility of mimesis. Carrie is desirable, in this reading, because she herself desires—"to reproduce life" (117), to make herself into a representation. And this insatiable appetite for representation Dreiser identifies with sexual promiscuity, corporate greed, and his own artistic practice.

Putting the point in this way makes clear what was wrong with the project of assessing Dreiser's attitude toward capitalism: it depended on imagining a Dreiser outside capitalism who could then be said to have attitudes toward it. But it also makes clear (and for the same reason) why any effort to bracket the question of Dreiser's (or Gilman's or Norris's) attitude could

---

[27] For a different view, see Brook Thomas, "The Legal Fictions of Herman Melville and Lemuel Shaw," *Critical Inquiry* 11 (September 1984): 24–51. According to Thomas, "Poor as he might be, Bartleby's persistent 'I would prefer not to' undermines the contractual ideology that dominated nineteenth century law" (36).

be only partially successful. It is easy (and essential) to stop worrying about whether Dreiser liked or disliked capitalism. But the minute you begin to think about what Dreiser did like and dislike, it becomes, of course, impossible to keep capitalism out—not only because capitalism provides the objects of fear and desire but because it provides the subjects as well. For every commodity created (on, say, the Chicago futures market), a desire can be created (in advertising, by art); for every worthless bit of paper that can be transformed into an object of desire (greenbacks), some impersonal entity can be transformed into the subject that desires it (corporations). Indeed, one must go a step further and say that the logic of capitalism produces objects of desire only insofar as it produces subjects, since what makes the objects desirable is only the constitutive trace of subjectivity those objects bear—what Dreiser calls "the voice of the so-called inanimate" (75), the exchangeability of the hog, the mark on the paper.

"The voice of the so-called inanimate"—if commodities could talk, this, according to Marx, is what they would say: "Our use-value may be a thing that interests men. It is no part of us as objects. What, however, does belong to us as objects is our value. Our natural intercourse as commodities proves it. In the eyes of each other, we are nothing but exchange values."[28] Marx's point here is not that commodities have no use-value—nothing can have *any* value "without being an object of utility"[29]—but rather that their value as commodities depends on something more than the "physical relation between physical things" that marks their value in use. The "qualities" of commodities "are at the same time perceptible and imperceptible by the senses";[30] hence, while pearls and diamonds, for example, have "physical" "qualities" that make them industrially or aesthetically useful, their value as exchangeable commodities is "physically imperceptible": "So far no chemist has

[28]Karl Marx, *Capital*, trans. Samuel Moore and Edward Aveling, ed. Frederick Engels (New York, 1906), 95.
[29]Ibid., 48.
[30]Ibid., 83.

ever discovered exchange value either in a pearl or a diamond."[31]

The commodity is thus an example of a thing whose identity involves something more than its physical qualities, but it is
by no means the only example. What else, for instance, is
money, which (as opposed, say, to gold) cannot be reduced to
the thing it is made of and still remain the thing it is? What else
is the corporation, which cannot be reduced to the men and
women who are its shareholders? Or, to go beyond the economic subjects of texts like *McTeague* and *The Octopus* to their
mode of literary expression, what else is that mode of expression, writing? For writing to be writing, it can neither transcend
the marks it is made of nor be reduced to those marks. Writing
is, in this sense, intrinsically different from itself, neither material nor ideal. And the drama of this internal division, emerging generally in a thematics of writing and, more particularly, in
what Michael Fried has called a thematics of "the *materiality* of
writing," is, as Fried has shown in his readings of Thomas Eakins and Stephen Crane, one of the most urgent concerns of
artistic representation in the half-century between the end of
the Civil War and the beginning of World War I.[32]

But to describe writing in these terms is not merely to indicate its appropriateness as a more general emblem of the
problematic of internal difference in money and corporations;
it is also to point the way toward a still more general formula-
tion of that problematic: the relation of bodies to souls, the
problem of persons. When, for instance, Carrie, thrilled by
Ames's description of the "pathos" of her "natural look"
(355)—the "shadow" about her eyes, the "peculiar" pout of her

[31] Ibid., 95.

[32] Michael Fried, *Realism, Writing, Disfiguration: On Thomas Eakins and
Stephen Crane* (Chicago, 1987). Much of the reading of Gilman presented here
was worked out in the context of an Institute on American Realism conducted
by Michael Fried and me in the summer of 1985 under the auspices of the National Endowment for the Humanities. I am grateful to the NEH for their support, to the participants in the Institute for their critical interest, and to Michael
Fried for his invaluable help in working through this material that summer and
for reading several months later the penultimate draft of this essay.

lips—longs "to be equal to this feeling written upon her countenance" (356), her longing marks what Dreiser appears to
think of as a constitutive discrepancy within the self. The desire
to live up to the look on your face (to become what is written
on your face) is the desire to be equal to oneself (to transform
that writing into marks). It is, in the logic of the gold standard,
the desire to make yourself equal to your face value, to become
gold. But really to achieve that equality is to efface both writing
as writing and money as money; it is to become not Carrie but
Hurstwood, a corpse in a New York flophouse. This is why the
discrepancy is constitutive—when the self becomes equal to its
body, as Dreiser sees it, it dies.

And by the same token, when William James begins his discussion of self-consciousness by asking about our bodies—
"are they simply ours, or are they *us*[?]" (279)—only to conclude that there can be no principle of personal identity utterly
independent of the body or utterly identical to it, he too is committed to the difference of the self from itself. Ordinarily, James
writes, we think that a "thing cannot appropriate itself; it *is* itself; and still less can it disown itself" (323). But in James's own
account of the self as the continual transformation of owner
into owned, to be itself at all the self must always be appropriating itself. Our body is *neither* us (a material thing that is itself) *nor* ours (making "us" some other *im*material thing that is
itself); it is instead a figure for the irreducible fact of ownership, for a selfhood that consists neither in having a body nor
in being a body but in being embodied.

Ownership for James is thus an internal relation required
by the impossibility of understanding the self as a single, undi-
vided entity, as either a body or a soul. And from this standpoint it might be argued that the discourse of naturalism, as I
characterize it, is above all obsessed with manifestations of internal difference or, what comes to the same thing, personhood. Continually imagining the possibility of identity without
difference, it is provoked by its own images into ever more
powerful imaginations of identity by way of difference: Hurstwood's satisfied body is rewritten as Carrie's insatiable one;
hogs that can exist only in one place at one time are sold many
times on the futures market before they seem to exist at all;

gold turns into money; Royce's theologized communities of insurance and interpretation become Norris's monstrously human Pacific and Southwestern Railroad.

Along these lines, as along others, hysteria is an exemplary disease. With hysteria, as Carroll Smith-Rosenberg has pointed out, doctors were confronted with apparently real physical symptoms without, however, any "organic lesions": "The hysteric might mimic tuberculosis, heart attacks, blindness or hip disease, while lungs, heart, eyes and hips remained in perfect health."[33] Some doctors were thus inclined to dismiss hysteria as a moral (i.e., nonmedical) problem, while others (more sympathetic to their patients or more ambitious for their profession, or both) searched for the "organic explanation" that would, as Smith-Rosenberg acutely puts it, "legitimate hysteria as a disease."[34] On the one hand, then, we have the description of hysteria as a moral problem instead of a disease because it has no place in the body; on the other hand, we have the attempt to legitimate it as a disease by finding it a place in the body after all—the uterus, the central nervous system, or the cerebral cortex. Hysteria thus provides the doctor with the familiar opportunity to dismiss its symptoms as false representations (like *trompe l'oeil* money) or to find them a material equivalent (like gold or paper).

At the same time, however, what was most fascinating about hysteria was precisely the way it resisted the familiar reduction, since it seemed to be *in* the body (it produced real physical symptoms) without being *of* the body (the symptoms were unaccompanied by real organic damage). Thus, despite the efforts of men like Mitchell to discover the organic origins of hysteria, his own writings suggest that what interested him about hysteria was its actuality not so much as a disease of the body but as a disease of embodiment. For example, in what is apparently Mitchell's first publication, a short story called "The Case of George Dedlow," a young medical student fighting in the Civil War loses (by amputation) all his limbs and on recov-

[33] Carroll Smith-Rosenberg, "The Hysterical Woman: Sex Roles and Role Conflict in 19th Century America," *Social Research* 39 (Winter 1972): 664.
[34] Ibid., 666.

ery begins to experience not only the expected depression but some unexpected "physical changes": "I found to my horror that at times I was less conscious of myself, of my own existence, than used to be the case."[35] Understood as a purely physical phenomenon, his situation makes a certain grim sense. Having lost, as he puts it, about half the "sensitive surface" of his body (the skin), he has lost about half of himself; hence his "deficiency in the egoistic sentiment of individuality"[36] corresponds to an actual physical state of affairs, a correspondence that is simultaneously confirmed and disconfirmed by the story's horrorshow slapstick ending. Invited to a "New Church" séance, the narrator somewhat skeptically observes the usual cast of spiritualist characters summoning the spirits of dead relatives until his turn comes and he is seized with a "wild idea." He requests what turn out to be two spirits who, when asked "how they are called in the world of spirits," rap out numbers instead of letters. Called on for clarification, the spirits finally rap out some letters too: "UNITED STATES ARMY MEDICAL MUSEUM, Nos. 3486, 3487." " 'Good gracious!' " the no-longer skeptical narrator cries out, " 'they are *my legs! my legs!* ' " and, having thus temporarily reacquired most of the rest of him, he experiences a "strange return" of "self-consciousness" that enables him to amaze his companions as he rises and staggers for a minute or two about the room "on limbs invisible to them or me."[37]

"Reindividualized" by the return of his legs, George Dedlow recovers himself by recovering his body—but the body he recovers is "invisible." Thus the séance both confirms and disconfirms the identification of self with body. On the one hand, the whole point of the story is to insist that the self does not essentially consist in anything like pure spirit; if it did, no loss of skin could ever amount to loss of self. On the other hand, as the ending also makes clear, no body can exist as body alone. Legs packed in alcohol in an Army Medical Museum live also in

[35] S. Weir Mitchell, "The Case of George Dedlow," *The Atlantic Monthly,* July 1866, 8.

[36] Ibid.

[37] Ibid., 11.

the "spirit world"; selves have spirits, and body parts have spirits too. As a rehearsal for hysteria, "The Case of George Dedlow" denies the possibility of an utterly organic etiology for the disease and instead establishes the condition of personhood—the nonidentity of self with either body or soul—that will make the hysteric's loss of "self-control" possible: "I have so little surety of being myself," the narrator concludes, "that I doubt my own honesty in drawing my pension."[38] The possibility of being oneself here depends on the possibility of not being oneself, which alone enables the project of "self-control" to emerge.

Mitchell thus imagines the loss of self-control that constitutes hysteria (like the transfer of self-control that constitutes the cure for hysteria, the rest cure) as a disease to which the healing physician is himself highly vulnerable. This remains true even in Mitchell's later writings, like the popular novel *Characteristics*, which begins with its doctor hero's temporary paralysis in the war: "For several months I lay quite powerless, all that there was of me within control of my will being the head and its contents."[39] The near indistinguishability of disease and cure is here paralleled by a near indistinguishability of patient and physician. Thus, although it is essential to acknowledge the social conditions that made it possible for men like Mitchell to rewrite their own fears on the bodies of women, it is essential also to note that Mitchell never really thought of hysteria as an exclusively feminine disease. After women, he wrote in *Wear and Tear*, "manufacturers and certain classes of railway officials are the most likely to suffer from neural exhaustion."[40] Perhaps we should regard hysteria as a disease not of women or even of doctors but of the middle-class market to which doctors and women (especially women writers), manufacturers and railway officials all belonged. "I belong to a profession," says Mitchell's Dr. North (also, like Mitchell, a writer), "I sell that which no man can weigh or measure."[41] Like the exchange

[38] Ibid.
[39] S. Weir Mitchell, *Characteristics* (New York, 1892), 6.
[40] Mitchell, *Wear and Tear*, 63.
[41] Mitchell, *Characteristics*, 70.

value of a pearl or diamond, the physician's services and the railroad officer's managerial skills are embodied without being reducible to a body. Like the writer's mark, they are bodies for sale. To be a hysteric is to be always and in principle on the market.

For Marx, the double nature of objects for sale—their perceptible use-value and their imperceptible exchange-value based on labor—was the crucial feature forgotten by classical economics, only to return, distorted and repressed, as "commodity fetishism." If we take the physical properties of commodities as determining their value, he thought, we will never understand the role played by human labor; if, however, we think of commodities in themselves as something more than their physical qualities, we find ourselves transforming a "social relation between men" into the "fantastic form of a relation between things." Commodities come to look neither like things as such nor like things that represent human labor but like things that are somehow human: "This I call the Fetishism which attaches itself to the products of labor, so soon as they are produced as commodities, and which is therefore inseparable from the production of commodities."[42]

Commodity fetishism involves ascribing to things the attributes of persons. For writers like Mitchell and Gilman, however, fetishism cannot consist in an extension of personhood to commodities, since the only way a person can get to be a person in the first place is by articulating in his or her nature the double nature of the commodity. And it is in this articulation that what I take to be the characteristic concerns of naturalism appear: appropriation, legitimation, the need to end representation, and the desire to represent. I use the term *naturalism* here rather than the more general term *realism* not to help breathe new life into the old debate over what naturalism is and how exactly it differs from realism; indeed, I hope to avoid that debate entirely and, if possible, some of the fundamental as-

---

[42] Marx, *Capital*, 83. The relevance of commodity fetishism to the more general question of the relation of objects to persons was suggested to me by Elaine Scarry's discussion of Marx in *The Body in Pain: The Making and Unmaking of the World* (New York, 1985), 243–77.

sumptions that govern it. Insofar as naturalism has been continually (and plausibly) defined as a variant of realism, it has been caught up in endless theorizing about the nature and very possibility of realistic representation: do texts refer to social reality? if they do, do they merely reflect it or do they criticize it? and if they do not, do they try to escape it, or do they imagine utopian alternatives to it? Like the question of whether Dreiser liked or disliked capitalism, these questions seem to me to posit a space outside the culture in order then to interrogate the relations between that space (here defined as literary) and the culture. But the spaces I have tried to explore are all very much within the culture, and so the project of interrogation makes no sense; the only relation literature as such has to culture as such is that it is part of it. If, then, I speak of the logic of naturalism, it is not to identify a specific relation between literature and the real, or even a specific ideological function of literature in relation to the real. I want instead to map out the reality in which a certain literature finds its place and to identify a set of interests and activities that might be said to have as their common denominator a concern with the double identities that seem, in naturalism, to be required if there are to be any identities at all. And if "The Yellow Wallpaper" is for me an exemplary text, it is not because it criticizes or endorses the culture of consumption but precisely because, in a rigorous, not to say obsessive, way, it *exemplifies* that culture. The nervous breakdown of its narrator may well be, as I have suggested, a function of her involvement in a certain political economy of selfhood, but even if, as I have also suggested, that breakdown is not a gesture of resistance to the economy, it would surely be odd to construe it as an endorsement of the economy. After all, is it not as if the narrator *likes* thinking of the self as permanently under construction; she just thinks it is. And "The Yellow Wallpaper" shows us exactly what it would mean to think that.

This is not finally to say, however, that her likes and dislikes don't matter. The child wants to mark, and in Gilman's economy of selfhood, that desire is not incidental. The desire to mark—to maintain the self by producing the self and to produce the self by consuming the self—is the primitive like that

makes the institution of selfhood possible. This very desire produces modern production and consumption; it produces,
above all, the dissemination of subjectivity intrinsic to naturalism as a mode of writing. For what Gilman's child wants is to
mark. His means of inscription into consumer culture is the desire for inscription itself, as if the very category of subjectivity—
the possibility of being a subject—were an effect of writing, as
indeed, in "The Yellow Wallpaper," it is.[43] Hence the impossibility of conceiving the desire to mark as simply the desire of a
preexisting subject. And hence the point of the question, what
kind of work is writing? Gilman's own answer is production,
and in insisting on herself as a writer she means, as we have
seen, to insist on the possibility of women transforming themselves from consumers into producers. But, as we have also
seen, in radicalizing writing Gilman reimagines the distinction
between producing and consuming, so that if the difference
between them does not entirely disappear, the possibility of
choosing between them does. What kind of work is writing? It
is the work of at once producing and consuming the self or,
what comes to the same thing, work in the market. What makes
"The Yellow Wallpaper" exemplary for me is thus its determination to see the self through on its own terms, as a commodity, a subject in the market. And it is the transformations that
that subject may undergo, its likes and dislikes, its various ways
of making its mark, that are themselves the subjects of the following essays.

[43]To speak of the self as an effect of writing is to speak in terms made
newly available in the last twenty years by Jacques Derrida. It is often said that
the "new historicism" opposes deconstruction, in the sense that deconstruc-
tive critics are "against" history and new historicists are "for" it. Neither of
these descriptions seems to me to have much content. In any event, the de-
constructive interest in the problematic of materiality in signification is not intrinsically ahistorical, and my own account of Gilman as obsessed with the production of marks and hence with writing as the condition of personal identity
is meant to be a historical one. If it is wrong, in other words, it is wrong not
because I have the wrong account of language but because I have the wrong
account of Gilman.

1. SISTER CARRIE'S POPULAR ECONOMY

*T*here is a remarkable passage in Dreiser's *Sister Carrie* just after the famous scene in which Carrie first accepts money, "two soft, green, handsome ten-dollar bills,"[1] from the drummer Drouet. "The true meaning of money," Dreiser suggests here, "yet remains to be popularly explained and comprehended." Dreiser then goes on to give two accounts of what this "true meaning" is. He says first that money "stands for . . . stored energy" and hence should be "paid out . . . honestly" and "not as a usurped privilege." When this is understood, "many of our social, religious, and political troubles will have permanently passed" (48). He then emphasizes what he calls "the relative value of the thing," invoking the example of the wealthy traveler stranded on a desert island, where all the money in the world has "no value" because there is nothing to buy and no one to buy from.

These two accounts are similar but not entirely compatible, and it is perhaps worth exploring their implications in a little more detail. Why, for example, does Dreiser think that the recognition of the "true meaning" of money as "honestly stored energy" would put an end to social and political troubles? The answer seems to be that he is here embracing a labor theory of what the economist David Ricardo called "real value," a theory that, at least since Marx, has been one of the cornerstones of socialist economics. One of its first and most lucid expositions can be found, however, in Adam Smith's remark that "labour alone . . . never varying in its own value, is alone the ultimate and real standard by which the value of all commodities can . . . be estimated and compared. It is their real price; money is their nominal price only."[2] Money, in other words, is the symbol of labor; labor is the determinant of value. In an economy in which all commodities were exchanged at their "real value" (the amount of labor required to produce them), labor would

---

[1] Theodore Dreiser, *Sister Carrie*, ed. Donald Pizer (New York, 1970), 47. Subsequent page references are cited in parentheses in the text.

[2] Adam Smith, *The Wealth of Nations*, 2d ed., 2 vols. (Oxford, 1880), 1:34. For an excellent account of theories of value in Smith, Ricardo, and Marx, see Maurice Dobb's *Theories of Value and Distribution Since Adam Smith* (Cambridge, 1973).

always be rewarded "honestly"; "usurped privilege," the unequal exchange of labor and commodities, would be impossible.

But Dreiser's second assertion about money, that it has a
"relative value," is not exactly on all fours with the first vision
of money as symbolic of labor and especially of the value of labor as fixed. For the value of money to become relative, either
money must be divorced from labor or, infinitely more disturbing, the value of labor itself must be seen as relative. To quote
Adam Smith again, although "equal quantities of labour are always of equal value to the labourer, yet to the person who em-
ploys him they appear sometimes to be of greater and sometimes of smaller value. He purchases them sometimes with a
greater and sometimes with a smaller quantity of goods."[3] Here
labor is itself conceived as a commodity, whose value, furthermore, varies according to conditions. Marx, of course, main-
tained that the value of labor was constant, but he distinguished between the "value of labour-power" and the "value
which that labour-power creates."[4] The capitalist pays the
worker the subsistence wage he is worth; he pays, in other
words, for "the labour-time necessary for the production, and
consequently also the reproduction, of this special article,"[5] labor itself. But, controlling as he does the means of and hence
the access to production, he forces the laborer to work additional time, a full day, say, instead of the half-day required for
the "daily sustenance of labour-power." Thus, in a capitalist
economy labor itself can be bought cheap, or, as Marx put it, a
certain amount of labor goes "unpaid." In such cases the value
of the commodities labor produces is greater than the value of
the labor itself. This is the phenomenon that Marx called "surplus value"—the "unpaid labor" "commanded by capital."[6]

The difference between Dreiser's two "true" accounts of
money and value can thus be expressed as the discrepancy be-

[3] Smith, *The Wealth of Nations*, 1:34.
[4] Karl Marx, *Capital*, trans. Samuel Moore and Edward Aveling, ed. Frederick Engels (New York, 1906), 215–16.
[5] Ibid., 189.
[6] Marx, *Theories of Surplus-Value*, pt. 3 (Moscow, 1971), 82.

tween the real value of labor and the price at which the laborer can be forced to sell it. This discrepancy, understood as the "unequal exchange" between capitalist and laborer, was, in Marx's analysis, the "source of profit" and hence the essence of capitalism.[7] Equalizing the exchange, eradicating the discrepancy, might, from this standpoint, be seen as the central task of an anticapitalist economy. But Dreiser doesn't even seem to notice that there is a discrepancy.

The reason he doesn't notice is that, however different these two accounts may seem—in contrast to what he calls Carrie's "popular" and utterly mystified understanding of money—they might as well be the same. According to Dreiser, Carrie's definition of money as "something everybody else has and I must get" (48) completely fails to grasp the relation between either value and production or value and exchange. Money for her is "power in itself"—if she were left alone with her twenty dollars on the desert island, she would never come to recognize the "relative value of the thing"; she would be led to reflect only on "the pity of having so much power and the inability to use it." Thus her almost sensual attitude toward those "two soft, green, handsome ten-dollar bills"; their value for her is not symbolic but intrinsic.

But Dreiser in his own semiphilosophical reflections on money doesn't take the popular definition as literally as Carrie does and so fails to notice an interesting peculiarity in that definition. For the popular account—"Money: something everybody else has and I must get"—defines money not simply as a thing that confers power but as a thing that you want and don't have. Carrie's definition of money, like everything else about her, includes the element of desire; money for her is never simply a means of getting what you want, it is itself the thing

---

[7] Ibid., 80. Marx put it this way: "The labour . . .which the capitalist *pays* for the production of the commodity and the labour which is necessary in order to *produce* the commodity are entirely different. Their difference constitutes the difference between the value advanced and the value earned: between the purchase price of the commodity for the capitalist and its selling price. . . . If this difference did not exist, then neither money nor commodities would ever be transformed into capital. The source of profit would disappear together with the surplus-value."

you want, indeed, it is itself your want. Carrie thus seems to begin with what we might call a principle of discrepancy, an imbalance built into the very possibility of definition—if money, by definition, is the desire for money, then money can never quite be itself. And if money can never succeed even in being itself, how can it ever become what Carrie also thinks it is, "power in itself"? These are the central economic questions posed by *Sister Carrie*.

In the market analysis espoused here by Dreiser and echoed later in the novel, on a moral plane, by the young electrical engineer Ames, the equation of power with desire makes no sense. You are not powerful if you *want* money; you are powerful if you *have* money. You are not happy if you want more than you have; you are happy if you are satisfied with what you have. "The world," as Ames says, "is full of desirable situations, but, unfortunately, we can occupy but one at a time. It doesn't do us any good to wring our hands over the far-off things" (355). Dreiser himself remarks on the at least "seemingly alien" quality of this "observation," but readers of *Sister Carrie* have been less circumspect in understanding Ames to articulate here and elsewhere a vision that Dreiser customarily calls "ideal" and that his readers have, almost without exception, understood to point the moral of *Sister Carrie*. Thus Ellen Moers, one of Dreiser's best critics, calls Ames an "intellectual Midwesterner brought on near the end of the novel to express Dreiser's own opinions,"[8] opinions that, according to Moers, centrally involve an ultimate contempt for the models of "success" represented in the novel by characters like Drouet, Hurstwood, and, to some extent, Carrie herself. For Moers, Hurstwood in particular epitomizes the "shallowness of . . . metropolitan success."[9] She sees his career as a progress from "sham celebrity to fatal anonymity," and the function of Ames is to mark Dreiser's own distance from such unabashed "success worship." Another recent reader, Donald Pizer, is even more explicit; in his view, Ames serves not only to criticize the

[8] Ellen Moers, *Two Dreisers* (New York, 1969), 109.
[9] Ibid., 103.

ethos of material success but also to help Carrie realize that "material comforts do not bring inner peace and happiness and that her spirit demands a higher calling."[10]

Although the moralism of these interpretations may seem at times a little implausible, it is important to remember that they derive from a model that is not at all implausible. Indeed, it is from the standpoint of this model that Carrie's equation of power with desire seems so naive. The model is an economy of scarcity, in which power, happiness, and moral virtue are all seen to depend finally on minimizing desire. Wringing our hands over far-off things can serve only to perpetuate discontent; the Amesian ideal is satisfaction, a state of equilibrium in which one wants only what one has. The enemy, then, is a conception of desire as disrupting this equilibrium, desire that, exceeding and outstripping any possible object, is in principle never satisfied. Carrie's "popular understanding" of money is, of course, a version of this more general economy of excess, and as such it is an explicit repudiation of the Amesian "ideal" and of the humane values of equilibrium and moderation that accompany that ideal. I should like to suggest here that Carrie's economy of desire involves an unequivocal endorsement of what many of Dreiser's contemporaries, most of his successors, and finally Dreiser himself regarded as the greatest of all social and economic evils, the unrestrained capitalism of the late nineteenth and early twentieth centuries. The power of *Sister Carrie*, then, arguably the greatest American realist novel, derives not from its scathing "picture" of capitalist "conditions" but from its unabashed and extraordinarily literal acceptance of the economy that produced those conditions.

One way, perhaps, of clarifying what I mean here is by contrasting Dreiser's practice in *Sister Carrie* with the practice of his realist predecessor, William Dean Howells. This contrast is, of course, from a certain standpoint one of the most familiar in American literary history and has usually worked to the detriment of Howells, whose own realism, as Vernon Parrington noted years ago, has always seemed "wanting" to generations

[10] Donald Pizer, *The Novels of Theodore Dreiser* (Minneapolis, 1976), 65.

"bred up on Theodore Dreiser."[11] What Parrington called Howells's "obtrusive morality, his genial optimism, his dislike of
looking facts in the face,"[12] in short, his gentility, made him an
easy target for the second generation of American realists,
Mencken, Sinclair Lewis, and Dreiser himself. But, as Parrington also noted, the Howells of the eighties and nineties—who
spoke out almost alone among American intellectuals to pro-
test the manifest injustice of the Haymarket anarchist trial and
who, in the wake of the verdict and of his own renewal of social
concern, wrote his friend Henry James that he could hence-
forth only "abhor" civilization "and feel that it is coming out
all wrong in the end, unless it bases itself anew on a real
equality"[13]—this Howells hardly deserved the moral portrait
Lewis drew of him as "a pious old maid whose greatest delight
is to have tea at the vicarage."[14] In fact, emphasizing his commitment to social justice and his opposition to "sentimentality"
in the novel, Moers has gone on to claim an essential kinship
between Howells and Dreiser; Howells, she says, "was the
ideal reader for whom Dreiser wrote when he became a novelist, a realist, at the end of the nineties."[15]

The depths of Howells's own commitment to realism were
readily apparent at least as early as 1885 in *The Rise of Silas Lapham*, which traces the social, economic, and emotional careers
of a New England paint manufacturer and his family attempting
to make their impact on Boston society. The romantic subplot
of *Silas Lapham* is a particularly complicated one, involving the
love of both his daughters, the beautiful Irene and the clever
Penelope, for an aristocratic young man named Corey who un-
wittingly convinces the Laphams that he cares for the pretty
one when, in fact (in the best Jane Austen tradition), he is desperately in love with the clever one. When they discover their

[11] Vernon Louis Parrington, *The Beginnings of Critical Realism in America,
1860–1920* (1930; reprint, New York, 1958), 241.
[12] Ibid., 242.
[13] Howells quoted in Moers, *Two Dreisers*, 50.
[14] Lewis quoted in Henry F. May, *The End of American Innocence* (Chicago,
1959), 8.
[15] Moers, 55.

mistake, the Laphams are thrown into confusion: Irene's heart is broken, and Penelope, although she returns Corey's love, is racked by guilt and convinced that nothing can ever make their love "right," a prophecy that she does her best to make self-fulfilling by refusing to have anything more to do with the young man. The sentimentality of these proceedings is, of course, self-evident and is indeed highlighted by Howells's implicit comparison between his own romance and the plot of an imaginary sentimental novel much discussed by his characters. The Tennysonian title of the novel is *Tears, Idle Tears*, and, in the words of a certain Miss Kingsbury, "It's perfectly heartbreaking . . . there's such a dear old-fashioned hero and heroine in it, who keep dying for each other all the way through, and making the most wildly satisfactory and unnecessary sacrifices for each other."[16] Boston society, in general, agrees in regarding such novels as frivolous but harmless, with the notable exception of the minister, Mr. Sewell, who thinks them "immoral" because, interestingly enough, they are insufficiently realistic. "The novelists might be the greatest possible help to us," he says, "if they painted life as it is, and human feelings in their true proportion and relation," but novels like *Tears, Idle Tears* are "monstrous" in their "disproportion" (183). According to Sewell, what is particularly "noxious" about these novels is their glorification of pointless "self-sacrifice," and when, sometime later, the Laphams come to him in search of advice on the romantic predicament of their two daughters, the pointlessness of self-sacrifice is precisely the sermon Sewell preaches them. Irene is suffering because Corey loves Pen instead of her; Pen is suffering because she feels responsible for her sister's suffering; Corey is suffering because Pen, out of loyalty to Irene, refuses to see him. This situation seems all wrong to Mr. Sewell. Corey and Pen cannot be held responsible for Irene's unhappiness—that she should suffer is inevitable, but their suffering is an excessive tribute to what he calls "the false ideal of self-sacrifice," an ideal that "comes from the

---

[16]William Dean Howells, *The Rise of Silas Lapham* (New York, 1963), 182–83. Subsequent page references are cited in parentheses in the text.

novels that befool and debauch almost every intelligence in some degree" (223). The Laphams' "duty," Sewell insists, is to let "one suffer instead of three." "That's sense, and that's justice. It's the economy of pain which naturally suggests itself, and which would insist upon itself, if we were not all perverted by traditions which are the figment of the shallowest sentimentality" (222). The goal of realism, literary and moral, is thus to minimize excess: in literature, to replace the monstrously disproportionate role played in the sentimental novel by love with a more balanced vision of "human feelings in their true proportion and relation" (183), and in ethics, to teach people that their duty lies in following the natural economy of pain, in refusing unhappiness that is the product not of a real cause but of a "false ideal."

But perhaps more important than the link between these two forms of realism, literary and moral, is their common opposition to what is in most respects the novel's central concern, what Howells took to be the sudden development of American capitalism in the late nineteenth century. For nothing is more remarkable in *The Rise of Silas Lapham* than the identification of realism with a morality and an economy that are themselves represented in principle as anticapitalist. The main plot of the novel, the story of the conversion of the Laphams' paint business from cottage industry to major manufacture and of Lapham's consequent attempt to establish himself in Boston society, insists on this antipathy at every step of the way.

The business originates in a combination of accident and family piety—Lapham's father discovered the paint and was convinced "there was money in it"; Lapham and his brothers can't see it, and when their parents die, the brothers go off to make careers for themselves while Silas stays behind, holding on to the "old farm, not because the paint mine was on it, but because the old house was—and the graves" (9). And when he discovers that there is indeed money in the paint, Lapham and his wife run the business on a mom-and-pop basis, as if it were less a paint factory than a paint farm. But the Civil War changes all that. On his return, Lapham finds that he has "got back to another world":

The day of small things was past. . . . My wife was at me all the time to take a partner—somebody with capital; but I couldn't seem to bear the idea. That paint was like my own blood to me. To have anybody else concerned in it was like—well, I don't know what. . . . Well, I had to come to it. I took a partner. . . . He had money enough . . . but he didn't know anything about paint. We hung on together for a year or two. And then we quit. (18)

The changed world that Lapham comes back to after the war is a world where capital has become essential, but from the start Lapham thinks of this capitalism not as an opportunity but as, at best, a compromise and, at worst, a violation of the old ways and of the family itself. The paint is like his "own blood"; taking on a partner is like bringing a stranger into the family. The formation and the dissolution of this partnership turn out, in fact, to be the source of almost all their subsequent troubles, and the fact of partnership remains for them always something more than what Lapham tries to convince himself it was, a mere "business chance." It remains for them so fraught with moral implications that finally, when they have lost almost everything, they agree in regarding their fate as a fair reward. Lapham has been brought low as just punishment for becoming a capitalist.

In the long run, then, the taking on of capital is responsible for Lapham's failure; in the short run, however, it makes him extremely successful, albeit in a way that makes success itself the mechanism of eventual failure. Their early career had been given to what Howells calls "careful getting on Lapham's part, and careful saving on his wife's" (25). But this careful balance and distribution of labor in the domestic economy is threatened when, "suddenly," a critical mass is achieved and the money begins to "come so abundantly" that Mrs. Lapham "need not save," and then "they did not know what to do with it." They first attempt to cope with this superabundance by giving more generously than ever to the church and spending a lot of money on horses, clothes, and so forth, by "living," Howells says, "richly to themselves" (27), creating an expensive facsimile of the self-sufficient, almost endogamous existence they enjoyed back on the farm. But eventually the pressure of having literally more money than he knows what to do with tempts Lapham into what Howells saw as the quintessentially capitalist gesture—speculation. This speculation takes two forms, social and financial, both of which involve further deviations from the anticapitalist ideals of personal (or familial) and economic identity. By attempting to buy their way into society instead of continuing to "live richly to themselves," the Laphams risk their own conception of themselves as a family unit, and by speculating in stocks ("gambling," Persis calls it), Lapham jeopardizes the fortune he has made from paint. The potential rewards of such speculation are apparently great—a place in the social world of Boston and an income vastly disproportionate to the amount of labor invested. But these rewards are for Howells only social and financial versions of the "false ideals" advertised by the sentimental novel, just as the precapitalist domestic economy is the equivalent of the realist's natural "economy of pain."

Thus the novel ends with a vindication of realism and domesticity both, at the expense of speculation. Lapham goes bankrupt, but his bankruptcy is not a sign of ruin and disgrace; it becomes instead the vehicle of his final redemption and return to the precapitalist (and in most respects the anticapitalist) ideals of his beginnings. The first step in this return is restitution to his creditors, restitution made possible by a renewal of his business acumen. "The prudence, the good sense, which he had shown in the first years of his success, and of which his great prosperity seemed to have bereft him, came back" (324). And every dollar he makes goes to pay his debts; "he had been no man's enemy but his own . . . he had come out with clean hands" (333). Coming out with clean hands also involves, of course, repudiating "all hope of the social success for which people crawl and truckle" (330), involves finally asserting the autonomy of what Howells calls "character." Character resists fluctuation; never "the prey of mere accident and appearance," it goes "for something" (270). The value of character is like the "values" of contrast in pictures—"rents, stocks, real estate—all those values shrink abominably," but "you never hear of values in a picture shrinking" (89).

This painter's aesthetic is essentially, for Howells, the aesthetic of realism. It is by definition hostile to capitalism not because it necessarily exposes the miserable conditions that a capitalist economy creates (indeed, *The Rise of Silas Lapham* does not) but because it is identified with a fundamentally agrarian, anticapitalist vision of the world. The popular novel, with its "monstrously" disproportionate emphasis on love and self-sacrifice, turns out, surprisingly enough, to be the literary equivalent of the greedy and heartless stock market, which produces wealth out of all proportion to labor or merit. Realism, however, is Howells's literary equivalent of the Laphams' domestic economy and of the Reverend Sewell's "economy of pain." All three stand in precarious opposition to the excesses of capitalism and the sentimental novel or, rather, to the excessiveness that is here seen to lie at the heart of both the economy and the literature.

The closest anyone comes in *Sister Carrie* to articulating this Howellsian vision of literature and morality is, of course, the midwesterner Ames, with his Sewell-like contempt for sentimental novels (especially *Dora Thorne*), his respect for "serious" drama, and his conviction that too much wealth is positively injurious to happiness. A man like that, Carrie thinks wonderingly to herself, "probably could be happy . . . all alone" (237). And, as we have seen, the self-sufficiency of a man alone is, for Howells, not only the guarantee of happiness, it is "character" itself. The character of Carrie, however, is defined very differently by Dreiser. The "one stay of her nature," he writes, was "her craving for pleasure. . . . She would speak for that when silent on all else" (24). Where Howells identifies character with autonomy, Dreiser thus identifies it with desire, ҡ an involvement with the world so central to one's sense of self that the distinction between what one is and what one wants tends to disappear. Ames naturally disapproves of what seems to him this vulgar consumerist aspect of Carrie's personality, reminding her, as noted earlier, that although the world may be "full of desirable situations . . . we can occupy but one at a time. It doesn't do us any good to wring our hands over the far-off things." And it is partly by thinking of remarks like this as Dreiser's own that critics have managed to convince themselves of Dreiser's fundamental hostility to the burgeoning consumer economy he depicts. While Carrie's career progresses, Ames is said to represent an "ideal," what Julian Markels calls "Carrie's final attainment, the knowledge that if she lives only to satisfy herself she will lose herself."[17]

But it is worthwhile noting that this vision of salvation through an end to desire is not what Carrie herself sees in Ames. In fact, she sees just the opposite. She had first been attracted to him, Dreiser says, "because at that time he had represented something which she did not have" (354). Meeting him a second time, she is rather surprised to find herself a little bored, not because Ames has changed but because she has; she now has the career that Ames, at their first meeting, had helped her to want. But Ames succeeds very quickly in making himself interesting again, urging her to get out of musical comedy and go in for tragedy instead, putting an end to her self-satisfaction by creating for her a new desire. "If I were you," Ames tells Carrie, "I'd change" (357), closing their conversation with an account of identity ("If I were you, I wouldn't be you") that replaces Howells's "something" of character, resisting speculation, with a nothing of desire that makes character itself speculative. What you are is what you want, in other words, what you aren't. The ideal that Ames represents to Carrie is thus an ideal of dissatisfaction, of perpetual desire.[18] And in fact, in *Sister Carrie*, satisfaction itself is never desirable; it is instead the sign of incipient failure, decay, and finally death.

The logic of this fear is repeatedly exemplified by Dreiser in a pattern that enacts what he seems to think of as the almost structural impossibility of equilibrium. We are told on the very first page of the novel, for example, that "when a girl leaves her home at eighteen, she does one of two things. Either she falls into saving hands and becomes better, or she rapidly assumes the cosmopolitan standard of virtue and becomes worse. Of an

---

[17] Julian Markels, "Dreiser and the Plotting of Inarticulate Experience," in Dreiser, *Sister Carrie*, ed. Pizer, 538. (Originally published in *Massachusetts Review* 2 [Spring 1961].)

[18] Fred G. See makes a similar point in a different context when he remarks that although "Ames has pointed the way to a higher desire," it is "in no sense ultimate" ("The Text as Mirror: *Sister Carrie* and the Lost Language of the Heart," *Criticism* 20 [Spring 1978]: 147).

moral narrative

intermediate balance, under the circumstances, there is no possibility" (1). What is presented here as a particular moral phenomenon—coming to the city, eighteen-year-old girls get better or worse—turns out, however, to have much wider implications, since its logic is repeated at other very different but nonetheless important moments in the novel. When, for example, Carrie has become from at least one point of view markedly worse—after, that is, she has moved in with Drouet—she is represented as simultaneously wanting to marry him and realizing that she doesn't much care for him. "She really was not enamoured of Drouet. . . . In a dim way, she was beginning to see where he lacked. If it had not been for this, if she had not been able to measure and judge him in a way, she would have been worse off than she was. She would have adored him" (72). What is important here is not simply that Carrie has outgrown Drouet but that the logic of her involvement with him repeats the logic of her moral encounter with the city. Just as the young girl coming to the city must get either better or worse, Carrie must either love Drouet too much or not love him at all. An "intermediate balance" of affection is as impossible here as an intermediate moral balance is for the young girl coming to Chicago. Love is either excessive—when it becomes adoration—or nonexistent. And Dreiser does not confine this denial of equilibrium to Carrie; it describes the progress of Hurstwood's career as well. "A man's fortune or material progress is very much the same as his bodily growth. Either he is growing stronger, healthier, wiser, as the youth approaching manhood, or he is growing weaker, older, less incisive mentally, as the man approaching old age. There are no other states" (239). Manhood appears here only as the impossible balance, the vanishing point youth approaches and old age falls away from.

Manhood is thus one version of the myth of equilibrium, of satisfied desire. There is nothing mythical, of course, about the notion that desires can be satisfied; the myth is that satisfaction can be distinguished from death. Dreiser associates Hurstwood's decline, conventionally enough, with what he calls a "lack of power" (161), but this lack of power is not a function of Hurstwood's inability to get what he wants, it is a function of his inability to want badly enough. He is unable to convince

Carrie to run away with him not because she has moral scruples but because he is lacking what Dreiser calls "the majesty of passion." In New York, no longer "subject to" the "burning desires of youth," he becomes increasingly "addicted to his ease" (267), content to read in the newspapers about the world he had once been a part of. His decline, in effect, inverts the morality of ascesis. Wanting less, needing less, he finds himself not, like Lapham, saved from the indignities of capitalist "truckle" but condemned instead to the breadline and the flophouse. Old age is a failure not of ability but of desire.

Instead of seeing satisfaction as the necessary and appropriate goal of desire, Dreiser seems to see it only as an inevitable but potentially fatal by-product. Desire, for him, is most powerful when it outstrips its object; indeed, it is the very fact of this excessiveness that fuels *Sister Carrie's* economy—which is one reason why Carrie is right to think of money ("something everybody else has and I must get") as "power itself." The economy runs on desire, which is to say, money, or the impossibility of ever having enough money. Nothing is more characteristic of Carrie than her ability to "indulge" in what Dreiser calls "the most high-flown speculations" (22), rocking in her chair and spending in "her fancy" money she hasn't yet earned. Fancy or imagination is the very agent of excessive desire for Carrie, enabling her to get "beyond, in her desires, twice the purchasing power of her bills" (48). When Drouet suggests to her that she has dramatic ability, "imagination," as usual, "exaggerated the possibilities for her. It was as if he had put fifty cents in her hand and she had exercised the thoughts of a thousand dollars" (118).

Art itself, according to Dreiser, is the "outworking of the desire to reproduce life" (117), and Carrie's own ambitions and desires as an artist are a function of what he calls her "naturally imitative" bent (79). Having perceived "the nature and value of those little modish ways which women adopt when they would presume to be something" (78), Carrie attempts to make "something" of herself by imitating the mannerisms of others, the "graceful carriage" of one, another's way of dressing. And the kind of art that she finds attractive is thus what Dreiser calls the theater of "ideal conditions," "drawing-room concoctions in which charmingly overdressed ladies and gentlemen suffer the pangs of love and jealousy amid gilded surroundings. . . . Who would not grieve upon a gilded chair? Who would not suffer amid perfumed tapestries? . . . Grief under such circumstances becomes an enticing thing," Dreiser writes; "Carrie longed to be of it. She wanted to take her sufferings, whatever they were, in such a world, or failing that, at least to simulate them under such charming conditions upon the stage" (228).

Of course, Carrie's taste in art, like her definition of money, is "popular" and thus profoundly at odds with the realism demanded by Howells in *The Rise of Silas Lapham* and so often in later years by Dreiser himself. The plays she attends and then performs in are theatrical equivalents of the sentimental novel *Tears, Idle Tears*, frivolously ignoring the realist responsibility to "paint life as it is." What Howells deplored in such productions, however, was not simply their frivolity but their danger as models, a danger that takes two forms. The first, and most obvious, is that the models are bad ones. The second, and more serious, is the very notion of art as model; where realism imitates life, painting it "as it is," the sentimental novel, presenting itself as model, seduces its readers into lives lived in imitation of art. Realism, defined by its fidelity to things as they are, can never in principle serve as a model, good or bad, since only when art is *not* like life can life attempt to become like art. The true scandal of sentimentality is thus its inversion of the proper relation of life to art, an inversion made possible only by the introduction of a discrepancy between the two terms.

But it is, of course, precisely this discrepancy and the consequent inversion that constitutes for Carrie the "charm" of the theater, awakening in her what Dreiser elsewhere calls the "old, helpful, urging melancholy" (225) of desire. The play she goes to see with the Vances, Matthews and Jessop's *A Gold Mine*, seems intensely "real" to her, not as a representation of existing realities but as a representation and indeed creation of hitherto unimagined possibilities. In fact, the effect of all art on Carrie is to arouse in her "longings for those things which she did not have" (77). And if, in Carrie's popular economy, these "longings" are themselves money (currency and commodity both), then the theater is indeed a gold mine, and the economic function of art is the production of desire.

Realism, by the same token, appears in *Sister Carrie* only under the sign of economic decline. When Hurstwood returns, for example, from his ill-fated venture as a strikebreaker in Brooklyn, he settles into his rocking chair and loses himself in the evening papers. The iconography here is quite explicit. For Carrie, the rocking chair has been the site of the sentimental imagination, the location of capitalist dissatisfaction; "rocking to and fro," she has "longed and longed and longed" (87). For Hurstwood, however, it is a "comfortable" refuge (313); the stories he reads in "the 'World' " offer depictions not of "ideal conditions" but of his own experience. " 'Strike Spreading in Brooklyn,' he read. 'Rioting Breaks Out in all Parts of the City.' " The newspaper here is the paradigmatic realist text, painting life as it is and producing not desire but "wonderful relief." Hurstwood "read and read" (315), Dreiser says, and this reading marks one of the crucial stages in the slow waning of his fortunes. Realism in *Sister Carrie* is the literature only of exhausted desire and economic failure.

This conception of art and the relation between art and desire is, of course, very different from Howells's in *The Rise of Silas Lapham*, where art, like character, was seen as a kind of still point, a repository of values that resisted the fluctuations and inequalities of industrial capitalism. And it is different also from another, more recent reading of nineteenth-century fiction that has found perhaps its most brilliant articulation in Leo Bersani's *A Future for Astyanax*. According to Bersani, "desire is a threat to the form of realistic fiction" (a judgment in which Howells would have concurred). "Desire can subvert social order";[19] hence, "realistic fiction serves nineteenth-century society by providing it with strategies for containing (and repressing) its disorder" (63). The central example in Bersani's analysis is Balzac's *La Peau de Chagrin*, a text of more than passing interest to readers of *Sister Carrie*, since Dreiser is known to have

---

[19]Leo Bersani, *A Future for Astyanax* (Boston, 1976), 66. Subsequent page references are cited in parentheses in the text.

read it (at the Carnegie Library while working on a newspaper in Pittsburgh) several years before undertaking *Carrie*.[20] "The message in *La Peau de chagrin*," Bersani says, "is simple: desire disintegrates society, the self, and the novel" (70). The "lesson" of Balzac is thus that "desire destroys," and the "task" of the novelist "is consequently to castrate desire" (72)—"the containment of desire is a triumph for social stability" (73).

This is a view that, in a curious way, Bersani himself endorses, albeit with the polarities reversed. Like Balzac, Bersani is committed to a vision of desire as fundamentally subversive and to a concomitant sense of the irreducible opposition between desire and social power. Unlike Balzac, he is committed not to repression and sublimation but to a project of "desublimating desire" (6), a "deconstruction of the self" that would rescue repetition from derivation. It doesn't seem to me necessary to trace the ramifications of Bersani's subtle and sophisticated argument here; what is important for our purposes is his insistence on the opposition between desire and what he perceives as the capitalist economy of realism. And nowhere in his reading of Balzac is the strength of this insistence more apparent than where it begins to seem most implausible. The economy of *La Peau de chagrin*, Bersani rightly reminds us, is "dependent on speculation and the accumulation of debts" (74). As such, it "glamorizes the speculator," making him its "hero." And yet, he insists, "the real fate of speculative desire in capitalistic society" and in realistic fiction is failure. "The most successful profiteer" turns out to be not the "speculator" or "gambler" but the "hoarder," whose "nondesiring egoism profits from the speculative investment of others" (74). This account is peculiar in that to maintain the opposition between industrial capitalism and desire Bersani is forced to see the "gambler" and the "speculator" as threats to the "capitalistic economy" and the nondesiring miser as the quintessential cap-

[20]This encounter is recorded in Robert H. Elias's invaluable *Theodore Dreiser: Apostle of Nature* (Ithaca, N.Y., 1970), 74. Elias's reading of Balzac is not as bold as Bersani's, but it operates in the same register; he sees the story as a parable of moderation and notes that Dreiser seemed "somehow to disregard" its moral: "Raphael had his wishes, but also paid his price, slowly killing himself with his desires."

italist. But in fact, gambling and speculation are integral features of a capitalist economy, and the miser's hoard, at least according to Marx, is by definition not capital: "for so long as the hoard remains in the condition of a hoard, it does not function as capital, does not take part in the process of creating surplus value." Indeed, Marx says, the "process of hoarding" "figures as an end in itself only in the undeveloped, pre-capitalist forms of . . . production."[21] In his attempt to identify capitalism with a realist hostility to desire, Bersani thus finds himself constructing a precapitalistic fantasy of capital itself, a fantasy that interestingly enough, corresponds closely to what I earlier called Howells's domestic economy. Bersani thinks of this economy as capitalist; for Howells, more accurately, it is anticapitalist; for both, realism is its perfect moral expression. The dream of realism is the end of desire. But where Howells regarded desire as capitalist and disapproved it, Bersani regards it as anticapitalist and approves it.

Dreiser's view, at least as I have begun to sketch it, is different from both of these. For him, as for Howells, capitalism is an economy of desire, but the utopian alternative, the refuge from want that Howells found so attractive, represents to Dreiser only death and disaster. And the "disruptive" element in desire that Bersani finds attractive is for Dreiser not subversive of the capitalist economy but constitutive of its power. Nevertheless, it might be argued that this identification of power with desire that seems to distinguish Dreiser so sharply from realism's repressive fear of desire turns out in the end to mask a subtle strategy for enforcing that very repression. The career of Hurstwood, for example, portrayed by Dreiser as a working out of the inexorable cycle of rising and falling desire, might from this standpoint plausibly be seen as an attempt to contain desire by naturalizing the limits upon it, by invoking what Bersani calls the "biological alibi" implicit in every naturalism. In this reading, society's interest in containing and repressing desire effaces itself only to return triumphantly disguised as nature. And, in fact, Dreiser appears to adopt just such a view when, commenting on the course of Hurstwood's career, he writes:

[21]Karl Marx, *Capital*, ed. Frederick Engels, 3 vols. (New York, 1967), 2:83.

"If each individual were left absolutely to the care of his own interests, and were given time enough in which to grow exceedingly old, his fortune would pass as his strength and will. He and his would be utterly dissolved and scattered unto the four winds of the heavens" (239–40). Hurstwood's decline thus becomes the second balancing term of Dreiser's "equation inevitable," the story of the failure, in Richard Lehan's words, that is "built into the pursuit of success."[22] In the end, the difference between the terms reduces biologically to zero.

But the equation, balancing success with failure, wealth with poverty, is not as inevitable as it first appears. There are, according to Dreiser, two possible ways out: die young or become very rich indeed. The advantage of dying young is obvious—you escape the long, slow diminution of desire. But Dreiser's account of the advantage of extreme wealth is a little more problematic, since it doesn't involve what one might expect, the possession of an amount of money so great that it will outlast you no matter how long you live. In fact, the whole point of the passage cited above is to suggest that it is in principle impossible for anyone to make enough money to provide permanently for himself. But if saving for the future is a strategy that, no matter how much you save, is doomed to failure, how can the rich man save himself from Hurstwood's fate? He saves himself, simply enough, by hiring young men. His fortune "becomes allied with young forces," with "young men drawn to it by salaries" (240). Thus the "process of accretion is never halted," the fatal "balancing stage is never reached" (239). What the rich man buys with his money is the young man's desire. And that desire confers upon his fortune, if not upon his person, a kind of ever-expanding capitalist immortality. Money resists biology, resists naturalization.

Dreiser's sense that a man's fortune must continue to grow or else begin to decline is only one of the more extreme examples of his consistent repudiation in *Sister Carrie* of any form of equilibrium. From a political standpoint, it is a rather striking example, since it closely parallels both the early-

---

[22]Richard Lehan, *Theodore Dreiser: His World and His Novels* (Carbondale, Ill., 1969), 51.

nineteenth-century economists' fear of a "stationary state" and the early-twentieth-century Marxist critique of imperialism, what Lenin was to call in 1916 "the highest stage of capitalism" (by which he meant the last stage). In this analysis, the concentration of capital had led inexorably away from free competition and toward monopoly; monopoly in turn had found its most perfect expression in the imperialist export of capital, creating that paradigm of "parasitic or decaying capitalism," the "usurer state."[23] All these developments were inevitable, given what one writer, paraphrasing Rosa Luxemburg's The Accumulation of Capital, calls the "economic disequilibrium," the continual need for expansion at the heart of "pure capitalism."[24] This disequilibrium is inscribed, as we have seen, in the definition of money with which this essay began: "something everybody else has and I must get. . . . Power in itself." This definition of money as the desire for money has built into it the impossibility of satisfaction so central to Dreiser; the equation precisely does not balance, and out of this imbalance is generated the "power" of the capitalist economy. The economic term for this imbalance and for the powerful excess it generates is, of course, profit, a "surplus," as contemporary economists define it, "in excess of the value of all the inputs."[25]

From this standpoint, it isn't hard to see that Howells's hostility to capitalism derived not so much from the amply documented humanitarian horror he felt in the presence of capitalistic excesses of wealth and poverty as from his fear of the principled commitment to excess he correctly sensed at the core of even the most moderate and benign capitalism. His commitments to "realism" and especially to "character" are exemplary in this regard. We are, for example, so accustomed to identifying capitalism with some form of rugged individualism that it is extraordinarily difficult for us to see what Howells saw

[23]V. I. Lenin, Imperialism: The Highest Stage of Capitalism (Peking, 1975), 150.

[24]Tony Cliff, as quoted in Rosa Luxemburg's The Accumulation of Capital: An Anti-Critique, trans. Rudolph Wichmann, ed. Kenneth J. Tarback (New York, 1972), 28.

[25]Dobb, Theories of Value and Distribution, 60.

quite clearly and what *Sister Carrie* exemplified—that the capitalism of the late nineteenth and early twentieth centuries acted more to subvert the ideology of the autonomous self than to enforce it. It is a curious and not insignificant irony that the critics who have recently been most active in attending to the deconstruction of the self have characteristically seen themselves as heralding the death of a certain bourgeois mystification when in fact they are merely arriving at an account of self that was already implicit in the writings of Adam Smith and David Ricardo.

Howells himself, as is well known, was a socialist, albeit so genteel a one that his own generation felt no discomfort in enshrining him as "dean" of the literary establishment, while the next generation dismissed him contemptuously as the "pious old maid" of American literature. But it is worth noting that this same generation of younger radicals greatly admired and were greatly influenced by Thorstein Veblen, whose sudden rise to intellectual prominence can be largely attributed to the two favorable reviews Howells wrote of *The Theory of the Leisure Class* in 1899. The two men were in many ways very different; Veblen's corrosive sarcasm alone would seem enough to exempt him from accusations of piety. But, in fact, Veblen and Howells held almost identical views of the American economy; indeed, Veblen's account of the creation of that economy reads like a generalized version of the career of Silas Lapham. Following a tradition inaugurated by the French Physiocrats, Veblen identified the crucial moment in economic development as the shift from the "struggle for subsistence," when the community is able to produce only as much as it needs to consume, to the point where "industrial efficiency is . . . carried to such a pitch as to afford something appreciably more than a bare livelihood to those engaged in the industrial process."[26] This "something more" the Physiocrats called the *produit net*, and they made it the cornerstone of their vision of the uniquely productive and beneficial role of agriculture. But where the Physiocrats thus tended to regard surplus-value as, in Marx's words, "a gift of

[26]Thorstein Veblen, *The Theory of the Leisure Class* (New York, 1953), 35.

nature,"[27] Veblen regarded it as tantamount to original sin. It was the very existence of this surplus that made possible the existence of a nonproductive leisure class and hence that undermined the productive "instinct of workmanship" with the dissipating principles of "conspicuous consumption" and "waste." For Veblen, as for Howells, excess was the enemy.

In dismissing Howells for his gentility, critics have usually meant that, despite his socialism, he was insufficiently critical of the social and economic world he inhabited. In praising Dreiser for his lack of gentility, we have usually meant that he was in his work and his life an uncompromising opponent of bourgeois morality and economy both, of what he himself loved to call "convention." What I have been trying to suggest is that there is something radically wrong with these scenarios, not simply with their view of Dreiser and Howells but with their account of the whole question of literary economy and with the theoretical assertions that seem to me to follow from this account. Howells's gentility consisted not in being insufficiently critical of his society but in being scandalized by it, a response whose contemporary currency is undiminished. For if the scandal of nineteenth-century gentility was excess, the scandal of gentility today is power. Capitalism, the economy of powerful excess, is scandalous both times. Thus, even those critics like Bersani who have been quickest to recognize the inevitable involvement of literature with political and economic structures of coercion have continued to insist on its peculiarly skeptical relation to those structures. According to Bersani, "literature," unlike "propagandistic writing," is "an exercise of power which self-destructively points to the impossibility of its claim to power-generating knowledge."[28] After all, Bersani reminds us, there is "a crucial difference between capitalistic excess in the strictly verbal economy of literature and capitalistic excess on, say, the world oil market."[29] This is the difference between

[27] Marx, *Theories of Surplus-Value*, pt. 1, as quoted in Dobb, *Theories of Value and Distribution*, 40.

[28] Leo Bersani, "The Subject of Power," *Diacritics* 7 (Fall 1977): 11.

[29] Leo Bersani, "Rejoinder to Walter Benn Michaels," *Critical Inquiry* 8 (Au-

"literary and nonliterary exercises of power," between the "power of language" and the "power of effective physical realizations." And the irony "intrinsic to literature" is nothing more or less than its awareness of this difference, its modest confession that "the emptily limitless power of language severely restricts the authority of the writing and reading of literary texts."[30]

Thus, according to Bersani, realism's fear of desire is in effect a fear of literature, for it is only in literature that desire can be truly excessive. Literature, in fact, is the scene of "desire's omnipotence." Why? What is the difference between literature's excessive desire and the excessive desire of capitalism? Bersani's simple but powerfully suggestive answer to this question is that economic desires are physical, they are embodied and hence finite, whereas desire in literature has no physical reality, it is disembodied and hence infinite. The terms of literature's irony, then, what one might even call its self-mockery, and the terms of its claim to constitute a site for the critique of capitalist power are identical: literature, disembodied, is incapable of physical coercion but also, for the same reason, immune to physical coercion—it is empty but emptily limitless.

For reasons that emerge most clearly in his and Ulysse Dutoit's remarkable writings on the representation of violence, Bersani finds tremendous critical potential in this emptily limitless character of language, literature, and art in general. Works like the Assyrian wall reliefs, notorious for what Bersani and Dutoit call their "profusely gory detail," and Pier Paolo Pasolini's *Salò*, a film "transcription" of the Marquis de Sade's *The 120 Days of Sodom*, have a moral interest for Bersani and Dutoit, who argue that their refusal of narrative, mimesis, and pyschology constitutes a celebration of the "psychic dislocation of

---

tumn 1981): 161. This essay was written in response to the version of "*Sister Carrie*'s Popular Economy" that *Critical Inquiry* published in 1980, and it was followed by an essay of my own, "Fictitious Dealing: A Reply to Leo Bersani." I remain grateful to Bersani for the seriousness and intelligence of his rejoinder, which, along with some of his other writings (noted below), helped me to extend and, I hope, clarify my own argument.

[30]Ibid., 162.

mobile desire" in preference to a "destructive fixation on anecdotal violence." Hence, for example, *Salò* "almost neglects the orgasm."

> [Pasolini] makes us into more willing, less purposeful spectators than his sado-fascistic protagonists. In a sense, this means that we never tire of being spectators; but it is the very limitlessness of our aestheticism which constitutes the moral perspective on sadism in *Salò*. The saving frivolity with which we simply go on looking creates a consciousness of looking as, first, part of our inescapable implication in the world's violence and, secondly, a promiscuous mobility thanks to which our mimetic appropriations of the world are constantly being continued *elsewhere* and therefore do not require the satisfyingly climactic destruction of any part of the world.[31]

Sex is short but art is long. What we find dramatized in Bersani and Dutoit is not the fear of desire but the fear of desire's end—of orgasm or death.

This vision of art as a device for prolonging desire by indefinitely deferring orgasm (like slowly counting backward from ten or silently reciting the entire starting lineup of the 1947 Brooklyn Dodgers) may seem a little odd, but its relevance to Dreiser can hardly be doubted. Where Bersani, however, emphasizes art's potential for "resistance" to capitalist power, Dreiser seems to have understood the immortalization of desire as a central capitalist strategy. The paradigm of immortality in *Sister Carrie* is, as I noted earlier, the rich man's fortune, which, "allied with young forces," avoids the failure of desire and the inevitable death of the rich man himself. What may seem bizarre in this evocation of immortality is Dreiser's notion that money can provide a continuity of personal identity sufficient to warrant his sense that a single entity is surviving. After all, what provides the identity of a "fortune" if not the identity of the man who owns it? And if all men are mortal, it seems rather fanciful to call a fortune immortal. But, in fact, there is nothing at all fanciful about this depiction of an everlasting cap-

---

[31] Leo Bersani and Ulysse Dutoit, "Merde Alors," *October* 13 (Summer 1980): 31–32.

italist life. Its model is the corporation, and the question of whether or in what sense corporations were immortal was much debated throughout the nineteenth century. As the California writer John Proffat noted in 1876, Chief Justice Marshall thought they were, but the great British jurist Kyd denied that "a body framed by the policy of a man, a body whose parts and members are mortal, should in its own nature be immortal." But if the "artificial bodies" of corporations had, as Kyd points out, no souls and so were not in principle immortal, they nevertheless could (unlike the bodies of "natural" persons) live, under imaginable circumstances, forever, achieving a de facto if not a de jure immortality. Hence Proffat himself endorsed the conclusion of moderate writers like Angell and Ames: "When it is said . . . that a corporation is immortal, it must be understood *theoretically*; and we can understand nothing more than that it *may* exist for an infinite duration."[32]

More could obviously be said about the ontology of corporations, but the salient point for my purposes is that nineteenth-century finance capitalists were, as was Dreiser himself, less impressed by the distinction between the infinite "verbal" and the finite "physical" than we might have supposed and a good deal more disposed to see the infinite power of (in this case, legal) language not as a threat to capitalism but as an essential part of its technology. The production of "artificial bodies" is one way of immortalizing desire thematized by Dreiser, but I think one must see the end of *Sister Carrie* and even the choice of Carrie as a central character in the same light. The novel ends with Carrie rocking her way to new desires, but, of course, it needn't have. It could have ended with the far more dramatic scene of Hurstwood's death (as indeed, in an earlier draft, it did) or with a vision of Carrie moralized, renouncing desire in favor of an Amesian self-sufficiency. Both these alternate endings would have made the novel more genteelly anticapitalist by bringing it to terms with the facts of physical life (death, the limits of desire) in which writers like Howells sought an ideological refuge from the new facts of economic life. Ending as he does, however, with a blatant gesture of dis-

[32] John Proffat, *The Law of Private Corporations* (San Francisco, 1876), 38.

regard for these facts, Dreiser makes use of the verbal forms of fiction to commit himself to the physical forms of capitalism. Beautiful girls grow old and die, but beautiful girls in novels need not; rich old men, despite their riches, also die, but corporations, growing ever richer, need not.

Sister Carrie provides an even more striking example of the capitalist exploitation of fictionality, however, in its narrative of a man's ability to represent himself as a woman or, more precisely perhaps, of a man's ability to represent (his) desire in a feminine mode. There is a marked difference, in this respect, between the valorization of desire that I have characterized as typical of *Sister Carrie* and the aestheticization of desire described by Bersani. The "psychic mobility" that Bersani values takes the form of an "appetite for formal representations" unappeased by a "satisfyingly climactic destruction." This is an aesthetic of consumption proposed in what I take to be characteristically masculine terms, desire emptied of what Bersani calls its "deadly seriousness" and thus immortalized. Dreiser's is also an aesthetic of consumption, but his terms are significantly different. For the model of promiscuity that Dreiser valued is feminine, a promiscuity that is, like the corporation, theoretically infinite and to which the orgasm offers no intimation of mortality. Carrie, for Dreiser, embodies insatiability. Carrie's body, infinitely incomplete, is—literary and economic, immaterial and material—the body of desire in capitalism.

I do not mean to suggest that there is no representation of masculine desire in *Sister Carrie*; in fact, the desire of the man is represented in a form very similar to the one described by Bersani and Dutoit in the passage cited above. Drouet, in particular, is a version of the "tireless" spectator; his way of "looking after stylishly dressed or pretty women on the street," appreciating "their little feet, how they carried their chins, with what grace and sinuosity they swung their bodies," is the "unhindered" expression of the "passion that was in him" (76).[33] Why "unhindered"? Because Dreiser depicts the scene of his passion in a way that values observation over possession, the

---

[33] I owe my sense of the importance of this passage to Hilary Radner.

exercise of a voyeuristic "habit" limited only by the number of pretty women on the streets of Chicago. This aestheticization of desire does not, however, produce the effect in *Sister Carrie* that it apparently does in *Salò*. In *Sister Carrie*, the nonconsuming passion of the man serves primarily to provoke the consuming passion of the woman. "'Did you see that woman who went by just now?'" Drouet asks Carrie on the first of their walks, "'Fine stepper, wasn't she?'" Carrie looks and agrees, "a little suggestion of possible defect in herself awakening in her mind. If that was so fine, she must look at it more closely." The woman's closer look replaces the aestheticizing "distance" of the man's gaze. Or, more powerfully, it makes use of that aesthetic for its own ends. Drouet's unhindered, nonmimetic appreciation of the "fine stepper" produces in Carrie, for Carrie, a "desire to imitate" her. The logic of feminine desire culminates not in a disdain for representation but in the desire to be what you see. "Surely," Carrie thinks, "she could do that too."

Feminine sexuality thus turns out to be a kind of biological equivalent to capitalism or, rather, in the slipperiness of its own biology, a figure for capitalism's ability to imagine ways out of what appear to be biologically immutable limits. One of these ways, as I have noted, is suggested by Dreiser's invocation of the corporation's immortal "artificial body." Another, not mentioned in *Sister Carrie* but central to Dreiser's Cowperwood trilogy and perhaps more revelatory for the relations between literature and economics at the turn of the century, was the futures market. With the rise to economic prominence of the commodities exchanges after the war, the term "fictitious dealing" entered the American vocabulary as a way of describing the activities of commodities traders who had no interest in ever actually taking possession of any commodities. The basic mechanism of this activity was the futures contract, which made it possible to sell commodities you did not own and to profit from utterly arbitrary fluctuations of the market. Farmers, of course, disapproved of such speculation and of the "predatory parasites" who practiced it. It particularly infuriated them that, say, on the grain exchange one bushel of wheat could be "bought and sold on paper contracts . . . of the Chicago gambling hell fourteen times over" before ever going to market—before, perhaps, ever being produced.[34] They were infuriated, in other words, by the scandalous excess that the fiction in fictitious deals made possible. And their outrage led the farmers continually to remind the public of what they took to be the irreducible difference between the physical and the fictional. *Sister Carrie*, throwing in its lot with the Chicago gamblers, reminds us not only that fictions may approve capitalism but also that the difference between the physical and the fictional is not so irreducible after all and that the production of a fictional excess has been one of capitalism's most successful strategies for transforming the economic reality its fictions claim only to represent. To the extent, then, that *Sister Carrie* is itself structured by an economy in which excess is seen to generate the power of both capitalism and the novel, neither the agrarian insistence on the material nor the genteel insistence on the ideal can rescue the text from its own identification with power. From this standpoint, even Dreiser's personal hostility to capitalism comes to seem like only the first of what would be many failed attempts to make his work morally respectable. Or, to put it another way, beginning with Dreiser himself, the task of his critics has been to defuse Carrie's "popular understanding" of money and of the textual, social, and moral economies that accompany that understanding. But *Sister Carrie* has resisted being defused; it has remained powerful by remaining popular.

[34]C. S. Barrett, in House Committee on Agriculture, *Future Trading*, 66th Cong., 3d sess., 1921, 63.

2. DREISER'S FINANCIER: *THE MAN OF BUSINESS AS A MAN OF LETTERS*

*W*here Nature hath in store
Fowle, Venison and Fish,
And the Fruitfull'st Soyle,
Without your Toyle,
Three Harvests more,
All greater than you wish.

Michael Drayton,
"To the Virginian Voyage"

*T*he difference between a wife and a mistress, according to Dreiser, is the difference between a woman who gives her love in a "sweet bond of agreement and exchange—fair trade in a lovely contest"[1] and a woman who loves without thought of return; "sacrificial, yielding, solicitous," she is motivated only by "the desire to give" (173). In *The Financier*, the wife is Lillian Semple, the mistress Aileen Butler, and the general description of wives and mistresses is, at least to some extent, a report of their respective personalities. Aileen is excessive in everything; her innate love of "lavishness" leads her particularly to admire the "rather exaggerated curtsies" (88) the nuns teach her in convent school. She wears "far too many rings" (137), and her choice of clothes is always "a little too emphatic" (124). Lillian's charm, by contrast, is "phlegmatic"; where Aileen's excesses are the products of a "burning vitality," Lillian's fundamental characteristic is "indifference" (47). These psychological differences between the two women naturally extend to their relations with Cowperwood. The mere thought of losing him causes Aileen to announce with a "passion" that makes him "a little afraid" that if he deserts her, she will "go to hell" (291). Lillian, however, reacts to Cowperwood's actual infidelity with comparative equanimity: "Hers was not a soul that ever loved passionately," Dreiser says, "hence she could not suffer passionately" (243). Having risked little, she has little to lose.

Many critics have questioned the relevance of *The Financier*'s love story to its primary subject, the American businessman, complaining, in Donald Pizer's words, about Dreiser's

---

[1]Theodore Dreiser, *The Financier*, with an introduction by Philip Gerber (1927; reprint, New York, 1974), p. 211. Subsequent page references to this edition are cited in parentheses in the text. Reference will occasionally be made, however, to the original 1912 text; these occasions will be footnoted. I have chosen whenever possible to cite Gerber's reprint of the 1927 revision not for aesthetic reasons but because it is currently the only edition available to most readers. And, while I am on the subject, I would like to thank Jane Tompkins for finding a copy of the 1912 original for me and for commenting along with Howard Horwitz on some of the problems raised by my readings of Dreiser in this essay.

"frequent practice of devoting alternative chapters or parts of chapters exclusively to each of these subjects."[2] Pizer himself thinks that the problem is more than merely formal; "the subjects themselves are incompatible," and Dreiser cannot keep Cowperwood's "two lives, that of the world and that of the spirit,"[3] from contaminating each other. Such a reading presumes, of course, the usual hierarchy between spirit and world and also, in Richard Lehan's words, a vision of Dreiser as unable to "reconcile the selfish and altruistic motives that fought within himself."[4] Whatever the ultimate merits of this critical contrast between love and money, Dreiser's account of the fair-trading wife and the freely giving mistress should help us begin to see that, in his view anyway, Cowperwood's sentimental relations are hardly incompatible with his financial ones. In fact, the sentimental for Dreiser is already financial. I would therefore like to begin this essay by exploring some of the ways in which wife and mistress provide paradigms for the major competing accounts of value in *The Financier*'s general economy.

Cowperwood's courtship of Lillian Semple, for example, takes place in an atmosphere marked by extraordinary financial turbulence, the panic of 1857, which, as Cochran and Miller have written, put an end to a "decade . . . of unprecedented prosperity in the United States."[5] During this decade, Frank Cowperwood had established himself as a successful stockbroker, but the panic and subsequent slide into depression dramatize for him "what an uncertain thing the brokerage business was." He begins to think about getting out of "stock-gambling" and into "bill-brokering, a business which he had

[2] Donald Pizer, *The Novels of Theodore Dreiser* (Minneapolis, 1976), 170.
[3] Ibid.
[4] Richard Lehan, *Theodore Dreiser: His World and His Novels* (Carbondale, Ill., 1969), 100. Other useful discussions of *The Financier* include Robert H. Elias, *Theodore Dreiser: Apostle of Nature* (Ithaca, N.Y., 1970), 152–76; F. O. Matthiessen, *Theodore Dreiser* (New York, 1951), 127–58; Henry Nash Smith, "The Search for a Capitalist Hero," in *The Business Establishment*, ed. Earl F. Cheit (New York, 1964), 77–112; and Wayne Westbook, *Wall Street in the American Novel* (New York, 1980), 155–58 and passim.
[5] Thomas C. Cochran and William Miller, *A Social History of Industrial America*, rev. ed. (New York, 1961), 90.

observed to be very profitable and which involved no risk as long as one had capital" (48). At the same time, he finds himself attracted by marriage in general—the "home idea" seems to him society's "cornerstone" (62)—and in particular by Lillian, whose "lethargic manner" and "indifference" convey to him a sexually charged sense of "absolute security" (64).

Marriage to Lillian is thus represented as a kind of emotional bill-brokering, where "you were dealing in securities, behind which there was a tangible value not subject to aimless fluctuations and stock-jobbing tricks."[6] This equation of security and securities with "tangible value" enforces a parallel between the "home idea" and the idea of production. Children, obviously, play a role in this parallel (Cowperwood thinks of having babies as if it were a form of capital accumulation—"he liked it, the idea of self-duplication. It was almost acquisitive" [61]), but much more important is the stability guaranteed by what Dreiser calls the primacy of "fact." The "fact" of marriage allows "no possibility of mental alteration or change" (65), whereas the problem with the stock market is that it is "all alteration" because "buying and selling must be, and always was, incidental to the actual fact—the mine, the railroad, the wheat crop, the flour mill" (43). Cowperwood imagines himself a producer and imagines in production a refuge from risk; the vision of value that emerges here might almost be called agrarian, an economy shielded from fluctuation by the joint facts of marriage and of commodities themselves.[7]

Yet the appeal of Aileen, as we have already begun to see, involves values very different from those represented by Lillian. Dreiser himself insists on the financial implications of this

---

[6]Theodore Dreiser, *The Financier* (New York, 1912), 88–89.

[7]Cedrick B. Cowing (following Hofstadter) uses the term *agrarian* to designate not only farmers but all those "who, for various reasons, endorsed the pre-industrial, pro-agriculture rhetoric" (*Populists, Plungers, and Progressives: A Social History of Stock and Commodity Speculation, 1890–1936* [Princeton, N.J., 1965], 4). I will use the term in a similar fashion but with an even more extended application, because part of my point is that the ideological hostility toward speculation and an economy of fluctuation was as central to many industrialists and indeed to many artists as it was to the staple crop growers and their political champions.

contrast by juxtaposing Cowperwood's growing attraction to Aileen's "vitality and vivacity" (90) with his almost unconscious return to "an atmosphere of erratic and [as it initially seems] unsatisfactory speculation" (94). Entering into an agreement with the Philadelphia city treasurer, George Stener, Cowperwood undertakes to drive a large issue of city loan certificate to par essentially by creating a false demand, buying initially from the city for the city, and thus misleading investors as to the strength of the market. The real attraction of the plan, however, one that makes Cowperwood forget all his reservations, is that as long as the city will "ultimately get par for all its issues," he and Stener can make an extra profit for themselves by speculating in the certificates: "Having the new and reserve issue entirely in his hands, Cowperwood could throw such amounts as he wished into the market at such times as he wished to buy, and consequently depress the market. Then he could buy, and, later, up would go the price" (104). The point here is that the instability Cowperwood fears when thinking of himself as a potential producer of commodities is the phenomenon that makes his success as a speculator possible. "Speculation," as one financial writer defined it in 1909, "is the act of taking advantage of fluctuations in the price of property."[8] Cowperwood, however, not only takes advantage of these fluctuations, he goes one step further; he creates them—they *are* his commodities, the source of his profit. Instead of wheat or steel, the financier produces "fluctuations," "manufactured" by "manipulative tricks" (104).

To speak of Cowperwood as manufacturing fluctuations is, of course, to translate production into an unsettlingly abstract vocabulary, but Dreiser makes it clear that this love of abstraction is central to the financier's career. Cowperwood's first job is in the commission business, brokering flour and grain, but he decides early on that "there was no real money in it," which turns out to mean not simply or even primarily that trading commodities does not provide sufficient opportunity to make big profits. The trouble with commodities, he thinks, is that

[8]Horace White, "The Hughes Investigation," *Journal of Political Economy* (October 1909), 530.

they are not "mental enough." He has no interest in flour or grain: "Money was the thing—plain money, discounted, loaned, cornered, represented by stocks and bonds—that interested him."[9] The financier's dislike of stability thus emerges even more explicitly as a distaste for commodities, and the opposition between the phlegmatic wife and the passionate mistress, between stability and alteration, finds itself reinscribed in the difference between values that are "tangible" and those that are "mental."

Put in these terms, the conflict between wife and mistress can now be understood as a version of the more general conflict over how, exactly, the value of things will be determined. Is value a function of production or of speculation? In America, in the late nineteenth and early twentieth centuries, this question was dramatized most spectacularly in the rapid development of the commodities exchanges after the Civil War and in the subsequent battles—in many respects not yet resolved—over whether and how they were to be regulated. Some economic historians have represented the commodities exchanges simply as "technological advances" in marketing, "bringing buyers and sellers into immediate contact, standardizing quality, codifying trade practices and developing systems of business ethics that speeded all transactions."[10] But it was always clear both to producers, especially farmers, and to speculators that the primary technological advance, the futures contract, could be used for radically different purposes. The mechanism of the futures contract was simple: it allowed the producer of a commodity to sell the commodity on an exchange for future delivery; it allowed him, in other words, to sell a product that he did not yet have, and allowed the consumer of a commodity (for example, a flour miller or a cotton manufacturer) to buy a product before he actually took possession of it. In theory, then, the futures contract permitted the producer to insure himself against a sudden drop in the price of his product before (or when) it actually went to market and to spread his sales out over the year, while permitting the consumer to insure himself

[9] Dreiser, *The Financier*, 55.
[10] Cochran and Miller, *A Social History of Industrial America*, 151.

against a sudden rise in the price of the product and to distribute his purchases over the year.

In practice, however, the futures market, in the eyes of producers and consumers both, seemed mainly to provide a source of profit for a whole new class of middlemen who neither produced nor consumed commodities but speculated in them. Thus, agrarian interests seeking to reform the exchanges characteristically distinguished between two "classes" of future contracts. One, which they approved, involved situations in which (as one witness before the House Agriculture Committee put it) "you do have the grain and you do expect and intend to sell grain. You may not have it at this instant in your possession. It may not be raised yet . . . [but you] expect and intend to deliver the grain."[11] The other class, of which they disapproved, involved the sale of a contract "by a party who does not have the grain and does not expect to have it and does not want to have it, selling to a party who does not want the grain, does not expect to get it, and does not intend to get it, and in fact, does not get it."[12] Contracts of this kind were denounced as nothing more than bets on the price of grain, placed in the same spirit as bets on cock fights or horse races.

Such "fictitious dealings" thus aroused the ire not only of agrarian interests but also of many who were disinterestedly concerned with the protection of American morality. The producers were infuriated by the ability of speculators to manipulate prices for their own ends, offering large quantities of, say, "non-existent" wheat and so temporarily depressing the market "in order to buy cheap from the farmer and later sell dear to the miller." Moralists in general were concerned about the difficulty of distinguishing between hedging (as a form of insurance), legitimate speculating, and outright gambling. The difference between the desire to insure oneself against "uncertainties" and the desire "to get rich without labor" was startlingly difficult to define.[13]

---

[11]Clifford Thorne, in House Committee on Agriculture, *Future Trading*, 66th Cong., 3d sess., 1921, 993.

[12]Ibid., p. 992.

[13]White, "The Hughes Investigation," 533. There is a particularly illuminat-

The source of this difficulty was, of course, the futures contract itself, which, for better or worse, institutionalized and facilitated the selling of property that one did not own. One of the more immediate and, to the producers, dumbfounding consequences of this practice was that, as Cedric Cowing notes, the "number of bushels and bales traded on the exchanges exceeded the annual production from 1872 on and in several years toward the end of the century amounted to sevenfold the annual crop."[14] The farmer could only grow so much wheat, but speculators, selling short, seemed able to bypass the physical conditions of production and even the fundamental laws of identity. What Cowing calls "the physiocratic bias against those who produced no primary products" and in favor of what Dreiser called "tangible value" was at its most intense when confronted with the tricks made possible by the abstract nature of money. And it is these tricks that constituted, in Dreiser's words, the "arts of finance" as practiced by innovators like Cowperwood, who knew

> instinctively what could be done with a given sum of money—how as cash it could be deposited in one place, and yet as credit and the basis of moving checks, used in not one but many other places at the same time. When properly watched and followed this manipulation gave him the purchasing power of ten and a dozen times as much as his original sum might have represented. (109–10)

The art of finance is the production of money by "pyramiding" and "kiting" instead of investing. The financier recognizes in money a quirk of identity that makes it possible to transcend the limitations of any "actual fact." Money can be in two, three, even four places at one time. Seeing this quirk of identity as a principle of productivity, the financier makes ten or twelve times what he has to start with. From the standpoint of the pro-

---

ing exchange on this subject between Thorne and Congressman Edward Voigt of Wisconsin in which Voigt maintains that "there can not be hedging without there being gambling" and Thorne disagrees but is unable finally to give any reasons for his disagreement (*Future Trading*, 997).

[14]Cowing, *Populists, Plungers, and Progressives*, 5.

ducer (the *real* producer) of wheat, oil, or whatever, money's ability to reproduce itself seems to mark its scandalous difference from the material commodity. Money may be cash and credit both, but a bushel of wheat is no more or less than a bushel of wheat. And yet what is truly terrifying about money and the financier's use of it is not finally its difference from real commodities but its similarity to them. For the scandal of the futures market and of the fictitious dealing it makes possible is that, sold as futures, bushels of wheat, like dollars, can be in more than one place at a time. Indeed, as we have just seen, it was precisely this principle of excess—seven times more wheat bought and sold than was actually produced—that infuriated the agrarian interests.

"Money was the thing." Conceived by the producers of primary products as a convenient symbol of the value of those products, it seemed, to producers and speculators both, to take on a life of its own. More "mental" than wheat or oil, it was able to flout ordinary conceptions of identity, producing its own harvests and determining the value of products whose worth it was intended only to symbolize. But at the same time that it was insufficiently material, it was too material—"mental," but a mental "thing." Hence the development of a national money market and of money exchanges, as if money were "real," a commodity to be marketed like any other. Shocking by its immateriality and its materiality both, money seems finally to point to something problematic in the very notion of a commodity and thus to question the opposition between producer and financier with which we began. For if the financier, creating money, is a kind of producer, is not the producer, exchanging his product in trade, a kind of financier?

The force of collapsing these two terms into one another may become clearer if we recognize that, despite the rhetorically strident opposition between producer and speculator that dominates so much of the financial dialogue of the period (and that, as we have seen, has its place in Dreiser's *Financier*), some of its most crucial economic battles were fought on rather different terms. We have only to remember that, as important as the futures market was, certainly the greatest advance in finance technology in the nineteenth century was the development of the trust: the overwhelming fact of American economic life at the turn of the century was the monopoly. In certain respects, of course, the controversies over the trusts repeat some of the central features of the disputes over the commodities exchanges. The heroes of Ida M. Tarbell's *History of the Standard Oil Company*, for example, have a distinctly agrarian cast. The affection of these oil producers and independent refiners for their "oil farms" and refineries is like that of a man for his children, the "fruits of his life": "The thing which a man has begun, cared for, led to a healthy life, from which he has begun to gather fruit, which he knows he can make greater and richer, he loves as he does his life."[15] And the career of the independents' great enemy, John D. Rockefeller, was marked from the very start by the financier's distaste for production. Allan Nevins, his biographer, tells of the thirteen-year-old Rockefeller lending $50 at 7 percent interest and digging potatoes for 37½¢ a day; when the borrower paid him his interest, "John was impressed by the fact that capital earned money more easily than muscle did."[16] More important, Rockefeller decided early on that the production of oil was the one aspect of the business with which he would never have anything to do.

It would, however, be a mistake to see the struggle between the oil producers and the Standard as a version of the conflict between producers and speculators and, in particular, to see Rockefeller in any simple way as a version of Cowperwood. Indeed, one might say instead that Rockefeller and Cowperwood actually embody two very different models of the accumulation of wealth. Psychologically, they are almost complete inversions of one another. Rockefeller was raised in what Nevins describes as "an atmosphere of hazard and dubiety." His father, "Big Bill" Rockefeller, was a brilliant but erratic man, a moneylender, a pitch man selling patent medicines (mainly oil!), an accused horse thief. The impact of his example, Nevins

---

[15] Ida M. Tarbell, *The History of the Standard Oil Company*, 2 vols. (New York, 1904), 1:155.

[16] Allan Nevins, *John D. Rockefeller: The Heroic Age of American Enterprise*, 2 vols. (New York, 1940), 1:68. In addition to being an extraordinarily informative and readable biography of Rockefeller, this is an invaluable text for the study of American social history.

thinks, was to produce in John "a profound desire for certainty and dependability; for a stable home, stable earnings, stable resources, a stable place in society."[17] Dreiser represents Frank Cowperwood's father very differently; the "soul of caution" (2), he was "content to be what he was" and so destined to be only "moderately successful" (10). Along the same lines, Rockefeller was particularly proud of his self-control ("I never had a craving for tobacco, or tea and coffee. I never had a craving for anything")[18] and his ability to accumulate capital by saving, whereas Cowperwood never saves a dime. "It was not his idea that he could get rich by saving," Dreiser writes; "from the first he had the notion that liberal spending was better, and that somehow he would get along" (19).

Given this portrait of Rockefeller, it may seem anomalous that he, like the speculators in grain futures and like Cowperwood himself in his battle against the eponymous iron-manufacturer Skelton C. Wheat, should have found himself opposing the oil farmers. If Rockefeller embodied the wifely virtues of production, how was it that his bitterest enemies were the producers? The answer to this question is that in Rockefeller's astute judgment, oil production was not a source of "tangible value" but was instead a form of speculation. The "curse" of the oil business, he thought, was the "terrific unpredictable fluctuations in prices, the alternations of glut and shortage."[19] And the cause of these fluctuations was the producers' inability to control production, to regulate the flow of oil and so stabilize the market. This failure made the producers speculators against their will, and the establishment of oil exchanges turned both shortage (due to the normal perils of oil-

---

[17] Ibid., 1:90.

[18] Ibid., 1:111.

[19] Ibid., 1:177. The potential profits of speculation in oil were almost as spectacular then as now. Nevins tells the story of "Uncle Russell Sage," who held oil certificates for fifty thousand barrels at 60¢ and then sold them near the end of the oil boom of 1895 at $1.30. Not near enough the end, however—had he waited just another week, he could have sold them at $2.70, increasing his profit by another 250 percent. When prices broke, the Standard intervened, "sustaining the market during some tense days in which an excessively rapid drop would have ruined many producers and refiners" (2:326).

drilling—fires, dry wells, etc.) and glut (due to what Rockefeller denounced as "unlimited competition") into opportunities for the speculator. Echoing the agrarians, Nevins writes that the oil industry had become nothing but "a new form of gambling." Production and speculation were thus seen by Rockefeller as two variations on the same theme, and the job of the refiner, as monopolist, was to regulate the market, controlling the producer and eliminating the speculator. Hence the Standard Oil Trust.

What the example of the oil industry demonstrates, however, is not only that production could be seen as a form of speculation but also that the producers were their own worst enemies. For the greatest threat to oil prices was, just as Rockefeller said, unlimited competition resulting in tremendous overproduction, which in turn resulted—as even the producers acknowledged—in depression for the entire oil industry. In a situation like this, production, especially from the standpoint of the producer, takes on a rather equivocal status. It is, of course, the means of his livelihood, the source of his wealth, but it is a source that requires always a vigilant control, because production carried too far produces not wealth but poverty. One might even say that in a certain sense the competition that gave rise to the trusts was imagined not only as competition between producers but as competition between the producer and his product, or between the producer and what Tarbell called "nature."

"Nature," Tarbell writes, "has been in the oil game."[20] In this scenario, the goal of the producer is actually to regulate nature, to keep her from knocking the bottom out of the market with a glut of oil, wheat, or whatever. The temptation is to moralize this process as nature's revenge on business and profit. Thus, describing one of the periodic failures of the oil producers to control their output, Tarbell writes: "It seemed as if Nature, outraged that her generosity should be so manipulated as to benefit a few, had opened her veins to flood the earth with oil."[21] Production here lashes out against the economy that has

[20] Tarbell, *Standard Oil Company*, 2:157.
[21] Ibid., 1:125.

produced it. The oppositions internal to business—between producer and regulator, regulator and speculator—are absorbed by the great opposition between business and nature herself. Producing commodities—making them, mining them, even growing them—ceases now to guarantee economic virtue and becomes instead the primary form of economic exploitation. In Tarbell's text, this is a particularly dramatic moment, since her own affection for the producers is based largely on their structural proximity to nature, a proximity that nature herself repudiates in the moment of overproduction, exposing *all* businessmen—speculators, manufacturers, farmers—as manipulators.

This very literal naturalization of production is by no means unique to Tarbell. Nature, in the form of the wheat harvest, plays an almost identical role in Frank Norris's *The Pit*, where Curtis Jadwin's bravura attempt to corner the wheat market is broken not by opposing "brokers, traders, and speculators" but by the "wheat itself" and the "very earth herself": "The new harvest was coming in; the new harvest of wheat, huge beyond the possibility of control; so vast that no money could buy it, so swift that no strategy could turn it."[22] The effect of Jadwin's failure is, of course, disastrous, not just for Jadwin but for the wheat farmers and for all the investors who had their money in the rising market. But the final victory of Jadwin's enemies in *The Pit* also makes clear a fact that Tarbell's account of the oil industry never really confronts—nature's uncontrollable bounty does *not* punish every businessman, indeed, it positively favors a few. For the crash in prices caused by nature's cornucopian excess punishes producers and monopoly-inclined regulators—Rockefeller, Jadwin—while paradoxically rewarding those whom Nevins calls "speculators in depression," the short-selling bears.

There were, of course, two kinds of speculators, bulls and bears; bulls bet on a rise in prices, bears bet on a fall. Jadwin,

---

[22]Frank Norris, *The Pit* (New York, 1903), 374. There is an even more lurid example of nature's opposition to regulation in Norris's *The Octopus*, where the railroad agent S. Behrman is murdered at a climactic moment by some hostile wheat.

the "Great Bull," is trying to buy the entire wheat crop; owning it all, he will be able to drive prices as high as he wants. The bears, selling all they have and almost invariably more than they have, want to drive prices down; they count on being able to buy, or buy back, what they sold at prices much lower than those at which they sold. The general public, as virtually every commentator on the subject has noted, is always overwhelmingly bullish, investing for a rise and regarding the great bull traders as, in Cowing's words, "builders" and "doers" with "great dreams of the future." The bears, on the other hand, were "the manipulators whom the public feared and resented." Cowing represents this distaste primarily as a consequence of their "dour personalities," but naturally there were also more substantive reasons.[23] Foremost among these was, no doubt, the profit that the bears made from everyone else's financial distress. A small ring of speculators profits from Jadwin's failure, but the collapse of his corner also starts off a "long train of disasters," sweeping away hundreds of "little fortunes" and culminating eventually in a return of "hard times."[24] By the same token, Cowperwood's "great hour" is one of "widespread panic and disaster" (492); "selling as high as he could and buying as low as he could on a constantly sinking scale" (498), he makes a fortune in the panic of 1873, which ushered in the longest depression (six years) of the nineteenth century.

But more sinister even than this vision of the bear as vulture profiting from the misfortune of others is the vision of the bear presiding over the uncanny juxtaposition of material plenty with financial distress. Hard times are seen here as a function not of scarcity but of overproduction, and so the bear acquires his particularly awful character because he marks the inversion of traditional economic values. The historian Daniel Rodgers has pointed out how many businessmen in the late nineteenth century began to "worry that there were too many factories for the economy to absorb." "Production," Rodgers notes, "had long been the chief of the economic virtues. . . . But if the in-

[23] Cowing, *Populists, Plungers, and Progressives*, 36–37.
[24] Norris, *The Pit*, 419.

dustrial cornucopia could easily spill out far more goods than the nation was able to buy, what then was the place of work?"[25] The bear here, emblemizing the simultaneity of increased productivity and of hard times, is a figure for the irrelevance or even counterproductivity of work; not only does he profit from the labor of others, he succeeds in turning their labor against them, in converting it into the agent of their misfortune.

Yet even this analysis does not quite succeed in accounting for the fearsomeness of the bear. For not only does he profit from the misfortune of others, not only does he wizard their own hard work into the *cause* of their misfortune, he does all this in conjunction with nature! The bear reveals that nature at her most productive and the unproductive speculator—neither growing nor making anything, not even, when he sells short, *owning* anything—are collaborators. The bear's world is a nightmare version of the American dream in which the promise ("Three Harvests more") of unprecedented plenty has turned into the threat ("All greater than you Wish") of overproduction. The land so bountiful no one need work becomes a land whose bounty succeeds somehow in starving instead of feeding its inhabitants. The bear now emblemizes an economy in which the source of production is so uncontrollable, so indifferent to human interests, that labor consists only in betting on what nature will do. The bear puts his money on nature's generosity.

Such an alliance between speculation and production helps explain what would otherwise seem some peculiar inconsistencies in *The Financier*. We have already noted, for example, Dreiser's identification of marriage with an agrarian commitment to production and "tangible value" while at the same time noting his identification of the mistress with the speculator's "mental" manipulations. But when, in more general terms, he attacks marriage and defends the philanderer, he seems to invert the argument, representing the mistress as a physiocrat and the wife as a manipulator of artificial "conventions": "One life, one love, is the Christian idea, and into this sluice or mold it has been endeavoring to compress the whole

[25] Daniel T. Rodgers, *The Work Ethic in Industrial America 1850–1920* (Chicago, 1978), 27–28.

world. Pagan thought held no such belief . . . and in the pri-
meval world nature apparently holds no scheme for the unity
of two beyond the temporary care of the young" (146). Cowperwood's finances may be as divorced as possible from the
physiocratic, but Dreiser still relies on nature to justify his sexual practices. Hence, when the "sweet bond" of marital "exchange" becomes "the grasping legality of established matri-
mony" (197), it is contrasted not simply to the love between
man and mistress but to the single most powerful paradigm of
natural affection, the love of a parent for his or her child,
"broad, generous, sad, contemplative giving without thought
of return" (211).

But what the example of the bear makes clear is that this
juxtaposition of Cowperwood as speculator, profiting from utterly artificial stock fluctuations, with Cowperwood as pagan
lover, flaunting nature in the face of Christian law, is not a simple contradiction. For the mistress and the parent are cornucopian lovers; disdaining "exchange," "giving without thought
of return," they produce affection with the disruptive and inhuman power of nature making commodities. And if what
unites the speculator with nature is precisely the attraction of
the cornucopia, what unites the wife and the producer is the
fear of unlimited production, be it of wheat, oil, or love. The
hostility of wife to mistress thus turns out to be a version of the
producers' mistrust of nature. The mistress, a figure for unproductive manipulation, is also (by nature's illogic of excess) a figure for infinite productivity.

In a certain sense, of course, this naturalization of the "industrial cornucopia" is as dramatic an example of economic
mystification as one can imagine. Rockefeller drew attention to
the sentimentality of this myth when, responding to Tarbell's vision of "Nature" outraged by the profiteering of the Standard
and avenging herself with an oil glut, he remarked that "nature
would not have opened her veins if the producers had not
compelled her to do so."[26] But the sense of nature as producer
does not serve simply, or even primarily, to disguise the role of
the real producers and to relieve them of responsibility for

---

[26]Nevins, *John D. Rockefeller*, 429.

their actions. Rather, as we have seen, it testifies, first, to their frustration at seeing agrarian virtues become the instruments of speculative vice and, second, to their general sense that the economy was completely out of control. What is most natural about production is ultimately its refusal to respond to human intentions. Nature here comes to represent capitalism itself— not, however, as an immutable and exploitative social order but as the principle of mutability, the omnipresence and irre- ducibility of risk.

The Financier illustrates nicely the double-edged character of this naturalization of the economy. Nothing about Dreiser is better known than his susceptibility to Spencerian "physico- chemical" explanations of human behavior. And nothing in Dreiser's work provides a better example of this susceptibility than the allegory of the lobster and the squid that opens The Financier and, from an intellectual standpoint, clears "things up considerably" for the young Frank Cowperwood. The "heavily armed" lobster gradually devours the weaponless squid, answering in the process a question that had long trou- bled Frank: "How is life organized?" (5). "Things lived on each other—that was it." The moral of this story, as Cowperwood and Dreiser come to see it, is the irrelevance of anything but strength in a world "organized" so that the strong feed on the weak. Such a moral is, of course, congruent with the Spencer- ians' social Darwinist tendency to find in natural law a justifi- cation for the robber-baron practices of the most predatory American businessmen. But it is curiously inapplicable to the events of The Financier itself, which persistently exhibit nature not primarily as an organizing force dedicated to the survival of the fittest but as the ultimate measure of life's instability, the "mystic chemistry" that embodies the "insecurity and uncer- tainty of life" (211).

Along these lines, Dreiser presents both the Chicago fire of 1871, which temporarily ruins Cowperwood, and the panic of 1873, which restores his fortunes, as inexplicable and unpre- dictable *lusūs naturae*. Events like the fire, "unheralded storms out of clear skies—financial, social, anything you choose," make wise men "doubt the existence of a kindly, overruling Providence" (226). Part of his point is that nature can be cruel, bringing "ruin and disaster to so many," but more important is what we might think of as nature's ability (and propensity) to be unnatural. Thus, Dreiser's language here anticipates the headlines proclaiming Jay Cooke's failure (Cowperwood's great opportunity) in 1873: "A financial thunderclap in a clear sky"; "No one could have been more surprised . . . if snow had fallen amid the sunshine of a summer noon" (491). Nature, in *The Financier*, is most herself when she is least like what she usually has been. Hence, the business crisis, understood by Dreiser as an essentially natural phenomenon, cannot be mastered or even predicted by any system of thought, any account of life's "organization"—theological, scientific, even economic. "It was useless, as Frank soon found out, to try to figure out exactly why stocks rose and fell" (40). The financier is a gambler "pure and simple."

The financier's inability either to master or confidently to predict events in the economic world around him turns out to have more general implications in the drama of judgment that dominates the last few hundred pages of the novel. The emotional and, as it turns out, legal question raised by these pages is one of what Dreiser calls "control," the relation between intentions and consequences. Charged by Aileen's father with having ruined her life and urged by him to make her do what is right, Cowperwood proclaims his impotence. If "you know anything about love," he tells Mr. Butler, "you know that it doesn't always mean control" (383). His "intentions" toward Aileen were "perfectly good": "if this panic hadn't come along," he had planned to divorce his wife and marry her. His legal defense against the charge of having stolen sixty thousand dollars from the city is identical: his "intentions were of the best" (385), but the unexpected severity of the panic prevented him from restoring the money to the city treasury before he failed.

Neither Butler nor the State Supreme Court buys this defense, arguing in effect that the consequences of Cowperwood's act constitute the best evidence of the "fact" of his intent. Only the dissenting Judge Rafalsky is convinced, and his agreement is articulated in such a way that its force, like that of the natural economy, is double-edged. The effect of upholding

Cowperwood's conviction, Rafalsky writes, is to extend "the crime of constructive larceny to such limits that any business-man who engages in extensive and perfectly legitimate stock transactions may, before he knows it, by a sudden panic in the market or a fire, as in this instance, become a felon" (397). There is, in other words, no necessary relation between inten-tion and consequence, and the court, in convicting Cowper-wood, is punishing him for something he never meant to do, making him responsible for events that he did not, in his own words, "create": "I did not create this panic. I did not set Chi-cago on fire" (264). But to put the argument this way is, in Dreiser's terms, to expose its weakness. For what does the fi-nancier create? His "harvest" (199) depends not on hard work, not even finally on his "subtlety," but on his happening to be in the right place when a crisis comes. If the financier has nei-ther "earned" nor "deserved" (271) his success, then the fact that he has not created the conditions of his failure ceases to count as a mitigating circumstance. Rafalsky is right. The court's decision reduces the difference between the business-man and the thief to a matter of "accident"; judicially deter-mining guilt and innocence is only "glorifying *chance*." But, of course, Cowperwood's whole career is a glorification of chance, and the constant lesson of The Financier is that acci-dents will happen.

In an economy where nature has taken the place of work, financial success can no longer be understood as payment for goods or services. It becomes, instead, a gift, and for Dreiser this economy of the gift functions at every level. We have al-ready seen how it characterizes the love of a parent or mistress and how it also characterizes the winning and losing of specu-lative fortunes: "Who is it that can do anything it was not given him to do? All good things are gifts."[27] The literal force that Dreiser attaches to this claim cannot, I think, be overestimated. Love and money are gifts; personal identity ("Who by taking thought can add one cubit to his stature? Who can make his brain better?")[28] is a gift; even art, although explicitly disso-

[27] Dreiser, The Financier, 479.
[28] Ibid.

ciated from the making of money, participates in the general economy of the gift.

Of course, there are no artists in *The Financier*, a fact consistent perhaps with the absence of producers in general. But there is a good deal of art, procured for Cowperwood by an art dealer whose "fiery love of the beautiful" does duty for a less commercial version of the artistic temperament and awakens in the financier a desire "to make a splendid, authentic collection of something."[29] He begins with furniture, buying, "after the Georgian theory," "a combination of Chippendale, Sheraton, and Hepplewhite modified by the Italian Renaissance and the French Louis."[30] The inventory of brand names is appropriate here: Dreiser lists the objects without describing them—what interests him is accumulation. Cowperwood's "passion" for art takes the exclusive form of a desire "to possess" it, and his way of developing an understanding of it is "by actual purchase."[31] Dreiser calls this, astonishingly enough, the love of "art, for art's sake,"[32] by which he means that Cowperwood has no desire to make money from the art "business." For him, the simple accumulation of the objects themselves is "distinction" enough. Art for art's sake and accumulation for the sake of accumulation thus come to the same thing.

This identification is, however, by no means a simple one. For in almost the same context that Dreiser equates art with the principle of accumulation he equates it also with what would seem its opposite, the principle of philanthropy. "Great art," he says, is the only appropriate "background" for the "great beauty" (162) of Cowperwood's mistress, Aileen. But the relation between Aileen and great art is closer than that of foreground to background, for the particular quality of Aileen as mistress, her "sacrificial, yielding, solicitous attitude" toward Cowperwood, is "related to that last word in art, that largeness of spirit which is the first characteristic of the great picture, the great building, the great sculpture, the great decoration—

[29] Ibid., 285.
[30] Ibid., 281.
[31] Ibid., 283.
[32] Ibid., 287.

namely, a giving, freely and without stint, of itself, of beauty" (173). Linking acquisition with expenditure, Dreiser defines the love of "art for art's sake" as the love of giving or receiving but never of exchanging. Another way of putting this might be to say that art, like mistresses and speculators, has no sympathy for the principles of fair trade, which animate wives, farmers, perhaps even artists. The financier loves a glut. He makes his living on the disruptions produced by excess, and he understands philanthropy and accumulation both as forms of excess. Beauty, given "freely," "without stint," "without thought of return," reinscribes excess as the principle of cornucopian generosity.[33]

Dreiser was not alone in believing that art should be free. He himself once described William Dean Howells as the "great literary philanthropist,"[34] and a few years before the interview that provoked this description, Howells had written that there was "something profane, something impious in taking money for a picture, or a poem, or a statue." But the essay in which Howells makes this claim, "The Man of Letters as a Man of Business,"[35] turns out to have a notion of philanthropy very different from Dreiser's. To begin with, Howells thinks of art's generosity as a characteristic that would ideally mark its exemption from the economic condition of a "huckstering civilization" (3). Hence, he starts by asserting a radical distinction between business and literature: "Every man ought to work for his liv-

---

[33] It is worth reiterating that Dreiser depicts this generosity as a source of great strength, particularly in sexual relations. We have already seen how even Cowperwood is a little afraid of Aileen's capacity for "self-sacrifice," and in *The Genius* (written just before the Cowperwood novels and revised just after), Angela almost loses Eugene by trying "to save herself" and Christine wins him by giving "of herself fully" (Theodore Dreiser, *The Genius* [1915; reprint, New York, 1946], 167–68, 164). By the same token, as Beth Ruby Pollock has pointed out to me, George Stener's failure to give Cowperwood the additional city money he needs to ride out the 1871 panic marks the treasurer as a "jelly-like" weakling, incapable of Aileen's passion.

[34] Theodore Dreiser, *A Selection of Uncollected Prose*, ed. Donald Pizer (Detroit, 1977), 144.

[35] William Dean Howells, "The Man of Letters as a Man of Business," in *Literature and Life* (1902; reprint, New York, 1968). Subsequent page references are cited in parentheses in the text.

ing," Howells writes, but no man "ought to live by an art" (1). Art, in other words, should never be conceived as work but only as a "privilege" for which no one should pay or be paid. Because there is "something false and vulgar" in taking money for, even setting a price on, culture, the "results" of art "should be free to all." But then, having begun by emphasizing art's independence of economic relations, Howells goes on to end the essay, surprisingly enough, by chiding artists for imagining a difference between themselves and the "working-man" (33). Artists are "the same as mechanics, farmers, day-laborers" (34); their "glory," he writes (in words that immediately evoke the agrarian hostility to finance), is that they "produce something."

These accounts of art, first as the "exercise" of a "privilege" and second as the product of "work," are obviously in some sense contradictory. But it would be a mistake to conclude from this contradiction that they are fundamentally incompatible. When Howells describes art as radically different from business, he suggests that business has no way of valuing art's "absolute" and "invariable significance" (2); "work which cannot be truly priced in money cannot be truly paid in money" (1). The strategy here is to preserve art's "absolute" value by divorcing it from all economic activity, a strategy that clearly breaks down when he goes on to conceive of the artist as a kind of day laborer. But although the strategy is altered, the end it serves remains the same. For Howells describes the artist-laborer as one of those "who live by doing or making a thing," in contrast to those who live by "marketing a thing" (33), and hence conceives of the work of art as a commodity whose value is determined by the labor invested in it and not by the fluctuations of the marketplace. Business remains "the opprobrium of Literature" (2) not because literature and work are opposed but because they are the same, both opposed to "marketing." Indeed, one might now say that the whole point of Howells's essay has been to keep "making" and "marketing" apart and to insist that value, both literary and economic, is a function always of making and never of marketing.

This attempt to save literature by understanding it as a form of labor turns out to have consequences very different from those intended. For, thinking about literature as a commodity,

Howells quickly notes its somewhat problematic relation to other commodities. The writer's product—unlike, say, "meat, raiment, and shelter" (32)—has no "objective value." Food and shelter, Howells writes, are a "positive and obvious necessity," and this necessity confers upon them their "objective" status. Literature, however, is "subjective"; "precious to one mood of the reader, and worthless to another mood of the same reader" (31), its value is "from month to month wholly uncertain" (32–33).

The cause of this instability is obvious: the value of literature depends on what Howells here calls "acceptance," and the acceptance (or lack thereof) achieved by novels can never be as stable as the acceptance of necessities. We might thus conclude that the attempt to preserve literature's "invariable significance" in an economic form has failed because the analogy between the work of art and the commodity is just not sufficiently persuasive. But the truth, in Howellsian terms, is even more disturbing—the analogy between the work of art and the commodity has turned out to be *too* persuasive. For in distinguishing between literature and the necessities, Howells has almost nonchalantly introduced as a common criterion the very determinant of value he has been concerned to deny—the market. The difference between the necessity and the work of art, he writes, is that one has a stable market value and the other does not. But the whole point of conceiving of literature as a commodity in the first place was to identify it as a form of "making" and to deny the relevance of "marketing" in the determination of its value. Admitting the market at this stage in the argument thus amounts not merely to confessing literature's instability but to proclaiming that art, which Howells wants to think of as too pure even to have a market value, has come to emblemize its own contradiction, the impossibility of ever eliminating the market. The attempt to save the absolute value of literature by thinking of art as a commodity has not only failed to save literature but has wound up jeopardizing the value of the commodity itself.

By contrast, Dreiser's conception of art as philanthropy is based neither on an attempt to contrast art with business nor on an attempt to bring them together under the rubric of a labor theory of value. If for Cowperwood "wealth and beauty and material art forms" are "indissolubly linked,"[36] what links them is the primacy of the free gift. Howells's failure is Dreiser's success: art in *The Financier* offers no refuge from the instability of the market; it embodies that instability and generalizes the principles that identify nature and the market economy. "All good things are gifts." Speculation is nature's way.

Rockefeller, as we have seen, mocked Ida Tarbell's notion of nature avenging herself on all those who sought to profit from her by spontaneously producing a market-breaking glut of oil. Refusing to think of production as ultimately a human activity, she was able first to absolve her beloved oil farmers of any responsibility for the overproduction that ruined them and then to depict all businessmen as speculating middlemen, exploiting nature as the commodity traders exploited the commodity producers. In Rockefeller's view, this sentimental naturalization of production obscured the man-made, and hence controllable, character of all economic institutions. Dreiser's economic morality, at least as I have described it, was very different from Tarbell's but surely, from the standpoint of someone like Rockefeller, no less sentimental. Nature in *The Financier* is the speculator's ally, not his enemy, but she is nevertheless as implacably uncontrollable as she was for Tarbell, and even more powerful. For Dreiser not only thinks of capitalist production as natural, he goes on to think of nature in all her manifestations as capitalistic; art and sex are as speculative as the stock exchange. Thus the "new world" (500)—Chicago and the west—toward which Cowperwood lights out at the end of *The Financier* seduces by its promise of a "vast manipulative life," sexual, aesthetic, economic. And if Tarbell's sentimentalism (like Howells's) proclaims her hatred for what the almighty dollar had wrought in America, Dreiser's proclaims his attraction to an even more powerful vision of the new world— "Earth's onely Paradise"[37] of finance capitalism.

[36] Dreiser, *The Financier*, 181.
[37] Michael Drayton, "To the Virginian Voyage," in *Poems*, ed. John Buston (Cambridge, 1953), 123.

3. ROMANCE AND REAL ESTATE

*E*xperience hath shewn, that
property best answers the purposes of civil life, especially in
commercial countries, when its
transfer and circulation are totally
free and unrestrained.

Blackstone, "Of Title by Alienation,"
Commentaries on the Laws of England

*V*isiting Salem in 1904, Henry James asked to be shown the "House of the Seven Gables" and was led by his guide to an "object" so "shapeless," so "weak" and "vague," that at first sight he could only murmur, "Dear, dear, are you very sure?" In an instant, however, James and the guide ("a dear little harsh, intelligent, sympathetic American boy") had together "thrown off" their sense that the house "wouldn't do at all" by reminding themselves that there was, in general, no necessary "relation between the accomplished thing for . . . art" and "those other quite equivocal things" that may have suggested it, and by noting in particular how Hawthorne's "admirable" novel had so "vividly" forgotten its "origin or reference."[1] Hawthorne would presumably have seen the point of James's response; his own Preface warned readers against trying to "assign an actual locality to the imaginary events" of the narrative, and for the romance as a genre he claimed an essential "latitude" with respect to reference, a latitude not allowed novelists, who aimed at a "very minute fidelity . . . [to] experience."[2] The distinction drawn here between the novel and the romance, between a fundamentally mimetic use of language and one that questions the primacy of reference, has, of course, become canonical in American literary criticism, even though (or perhaps just because) its meaning remains so uncertain. Does Hawthorne intend the romance (as some recent critics think) to pose a self-consciously fictional alternative to the social responsibilities of the novel? Or does he intend the romance (as some other even more recent critics think) to provide in its radical fictionality a revolutionary alternative to the social conservativism of the novel?[3] The last paragraph of the

[1] Henry James, *The American Scene* (Bloomington, Ind., 1968), 270–71.

[2] Nathaniel Hawthorne, *The House of the Seven Gables*, ed. Seymour L. Gross (New York, 1967), 1. Subsequent page references are cited in parentheses in the text.

[3] The texts I have in mind here are Michael Davitt Bell's *The Development of American Romance* (Chicago, 1980) and an article by Brook Thomas, "*The House of the Seven Gables*: Reading the Romance of America," *PMLA* 97 (March 1982): 195–211. Thomas contrasts the "freedom of the romance" to the "conservativism of the novel" (196) and suggests that Hawthorne "chose to

Preface suggests that neither of these formulations may be correct.

Looking for the Seven Gables in Salem, Hawthorne says, is a mistake because it "exposes the Romance to an inflexible and exceedingly dangerous species of criticism, by bringing [its] fancy pictures into positive contact with the realities of the moment" (3). The implication seems to be that the romance—unlike the novel—is too fragile to stand comparison with reality, but Hawthorne immediately goes on to suggest that the difference between the romance and the novel is perhaps less a matter of their relation to reality than of their relation to real estate. He has constructed *The House of the Seven Gables* "by laying out a street that infringes upon nobody's private rights, and ap-

---

write romances . . . because they allowed him to stay true to the American tradition of imagining an alternative to the society he inherited" (195–96). Bell sees a similar tension within the romance itself, in an opposition between the "artifice and insincerity of forms" and the "anarchic energy" of the "strange new truths" (xiv) of American life in the mid-nineteenth century.

In *House*, this opposition is embodied by the Pyncheons and Holgrave, but not, according to Bell, satisfactorily, since the "revolutionary" "alternative to the empty forms of the past" represented by Holgrave and Phoebe seems too "personal" to form "the basis of a new social system" and too transitory to "avoid recapitulating the historical cycle" that created the "repressive formalism" in the first place (182–83). Thomas reads the end in similar terms but somewhat more optimistically, arguing that Hawthorne "seems to have retained a hope for the future," imagining in Phoebe's marriage to Holgrave "a real possibility for a break with the past" (209).

But in my reading, the point of the romance is neither to renew the past nor to break with it; it is instead to domesticate the social dislocation of the 1840s and 1850s in a literary form that imagines the past and present as utterly continuous, even identical, and in so doing, attempts to repress the possibility of any change at all. For critics like Bell, *The House of the Seven Gables* fails in the end because Holgrave's "radicalism" succumbs to "conservatism" (184); democracy succumbs to aristocracy; ultimately, the "dangerous" and "subversive" fictionality of the romance succumbs to the "safe and conservative" referentiality of mimesis (14, 18). But what seemed dangerous and subversive to Hawthorne was not so much the "crisis" of reference intrinsic to the romance (Bell calls it a "crisis of belief" [149] and of "correspondence" [153]) as the violently revolutionary power of mimesis, the representing form of a market society inimical to the social stability, the individualism, and the rights to property that Hawthorne meant the romance to defend. Thus the novel actually ends triumphantly, with a transformation of "business" into inheritance and mimesis into "fairy-tale."

propriating a lot of land which had no visible owner, and building a house, of materials long in use for constructing castles in the air" (3). The romance, then, is to be imagined as a kind of property, or rather as a relation to property. Where the novel may be said to touch the real by expropriating it and so violating someone's "private rights," the romance asserts a property right that does not threaten and so should not be threatened by the property rights of others. The romance, to put it another way, is the text of clear and unobstructed title.

The Money Power

Of course, haunted-house stories (like *The House of the Seven Gables*) usually involve some form of anxiety about ownership. Frequently this anxiety concerns actual financial cost. Stephen King, the author of *The Shining*, has put this powerfully in a discussion of the movie *The Amityville Horror*. "What it's about," he says,

> is a young couple who've never owned a house before; Margot Kidder is the first person in her family actually to have owned property. And all these things start to go wrong—and the horrible part is not that they can't get out, but that they're going to *lose the house*. There was some point where things were falling, and the door banging, and rain was coming in, and goop was running down the stairs, and behind me, in the little movie house in Bridgton, this woman, she must have been 60, was in this kind of ecstasy, moaning, "Think of the bills, think of the bills." And that's where the horror of that movie is.[4]

Which is not to say that the financial implications of the haunted house are limited to the actual repair costs of the physical damage done by the ghosts. Think of the plight of the Amityville couple as investors in real estate: having risked everything to get themselves into the spectacularly inflationary market of 1975, they find themselves owning the only house on Long Island whose value is declining—the only one for a few

[4]*New York Times Magazine*, 11 May 1980, 44.

years, anyway, until rising interest rates, as intangible as ghosts but even more powerful, would begin to produce a spectral effect on housing prices everywhere. It may be worth noting that in 1850 Hawthorne was writing at the start of one of the peak periods in nineteenth-century American land speculation, a period in which, according to the agricultural historian Paul Wallace Gates, "touched by the fever of land speculation, excited people throughout the country borrowed to the extent of their credit for such investments."[5]

But the actual price of real estate may not finally be as crucial to the haunted house as the fact of ownership itself and the questions that necessarily accompany that fact: who has title? what legitimates that title? what guarantees it? Again, contemporary examples abound. Because of certain "impediments" on their house, the Lutzes in Amityville never did get clear title, although they had what their lawyer called "the best that could be fashioned for their mortgage."[6] Another movie, *Poltergeist*, centers on what is in effect a title dispute between a real estate development company and the corpses who inhabit the bulldozed cemetery the developer builds on. But title disputes have also a more intimate connection to Hawthorne and to *The House of the Seven Gables*. The most prominent and respectable witch brought to trial before Hawthorne's ancestor, the "persecuting" magistrate John Hathorne, was an old woman named Rebecca Nurse, whose family were comparative newcomers to Salem and much resented by the old and increasingly impoverished villagers. The Nurses had bought land from

[5]Paul Wallace Gates, "The Role of the Land Speculator in Western Development," in *The Public Lands*, ed. Vernon Carstensen (Madison, 1968), 352. "The peak years of speculative purchasing," Gates goes on to say, "were 1854 to 1858, when a total of 65,000,000 acres of public domain were disposed of to purchasers of holders of land warrants" (360).

[6]Jay Anson, *The Amityville Horror* (New York, 1978), 17. The main obstacle appears to have been that the only heir of the deceased former owners was the son who had murdered them, Ronald. Since Ronald, having killed his parents, was legally barred from inheriting their estate, it is unclear exactly from whom the Lutzes were buying the property. For true horror fans, however, Anson is gratifyingly explicit about who actually ended up owning their "dream house" when the demoralized Lutzes fled to California. "Just to be rid of the place, they signed their interest over to the bank that held the mortgage" (260).

James Allen (land he had inherited from the Endicotts) and were paying for it in twenty yearly installments. In 1692, when Rebecca was accused, they had only "six more years to go before the title was theirs," but the villagers still thought of them as *arrivistes* and continued to call their place "the Allen property."[7] Hathorne was fleetingly touched by Rebecca's respectability and by her claim to be "innocent and clear" of the charges against her, but he held her for trial anyway, and in the end she was one of the first witches hanged. *The House of the Seven Gables* remembers the day of Rebecca's hanging in Maule's curse on the Pyncheons, "God will give you blood to drink"—the dying words of Rebecca's fellow victim, Sarah Good. More important, Hawthorne revives the connection between witchcraft and quarrels over property by beginning his narrative with a title dispute. Owner-occupant Matthew Maule, who "with his own toil . . . had hewn out of the primal forest . . . [a] garden-ground and homestead," is dispossessed by the "prominent and powerful" Colonel Pyncheon, "who asserted plausible claims to the proprietorship of this . . . land on the strength of a grant from the legislature" (7). Maule, of course, is executed for witchcraft, with Pyncheon leading the pack of executioners.

In one sense, this reworking of the witch trials is a little misleading; as Hawthorne himself notes, one of the few redeeming qualities of the witch hunters was "the singular indiscrimination with which they persecuted, not merely the poor and aged as in former judicial massacres, but people of all ranks, their own equals, brethren, and wives" (8). But the Pyncheon persecution of the Maules does not follow this model. Indeed, it precisely inverts the pattern described in Boyer and Nissenbaum's extraordinary *Salem Possessed: The Social Origins of Witchcraft*, where the accusers are shown to have been characteristically worse off socially and economically than the accused. Hawthorne does not, however, represent the struggle between Pyncheons and Maules merely as a conflict between the more and less powerful or even in any simple way as a con-

[7] Marion L. Starkey, *The Devil in Massachusetts* (1949; reprint, New York, 1969), 77.

flict over a piece of land. He presents it instead as a conflict between two different modes of economic activity, and in this he not only anticipates recent historians' findings but begins the complicated process of articulating his own defense of property.

The devil in Massachusetts, according to Boyer and Nissenbaum, was "emergent mercantile capitalism."[8] Hawthorne understood the question in terms more appropriate to someone whose political consciousness had been formed during the years of Jacksonian democracy. Maule embodies a Lockean legitimation of property by labor, whereas the Pyncheons, with their pretensions to nobility, are something like old-world aristocrats—except that the pre-Revolutionary fear of a titled aristocracy had, during the Jackson years, been replaced by the fear of a "money aristocracy," and Judge Pyncheon is certainly more capitalist than nobleman. From this standpoint, the difference between Maule and Pyncheon is less a difference between bourgeois and aristocrat than between those whom Jackson called "the agricultural, the mechanical, and the laboring classes" and those whom he called the "money power." And yet, *The House of the Seven Gables* by no means enacts a Jacksonian confrontation between the "people" and those who sought to exercise a "despotic sway" over them. Instead, the fate of property in *House* suggests the appeal of a title based on neither labor nor wealth and hence free from the risk of appropriation.

"In this republican country," Hawthorne writes, "amid the fluctuating waves of our social life, somebody is always at the drowning-point" (38). This "tragedy," he thinks, is felt as "deeply . . . as when an hereditary noble sinks below his order." Or rather, "more deeply; since with us, rank is the grosser substance of wealth and a splendid establishment, and has no spiritual existence after the death of these but dies hopelessly along with them." The central point here, that America is a country where, as a French observer put it, "material property

[8]Paul Boyer and Stephen Nissenbaum, *Salem Possessed* (Cambridge, Mass., 1974), 209.

rapidly disappears,"[9] is, perhaps, less important than the implied comparison between the impoverished capitalist and the
dispossessed aristocrat. The capitalist who loses everything
loses everything, whereas the nobleman, losing everything material, retains his nobility, which has a "spiritual existence."
This title cannot be bought or sold; unlike the land you have
"hewn out of the forest," it cannot be stolen either. Aristocracy's claim to land is unimpaired by the inability to enforce that
claim. Indeed, it is in a certain sense strengthened, or at least
purified, since the assertion of what Blackstone calls the "mere
right of property," a right that stands independent of any right
of possession, is the assertion of a right that is truly inalienable:
it cannot be exchanged for anything else, it cannot be taken
from you, it cannot even be given away.

Such a claim to property has, from the start, its place in *The
House of the Seven Gables*. The Preface's "castles in the air"
suggest in their immateriality a parallel between romance and
the property rights of impoverished aristocrats. And in the text
itself, what Hawthorne calls the Pyncheons' "impalpable claim"
to the rich territory of Waldo County in Maine repeats this
structure. Although the "actual settlers" of this land "would
have laughed at the idea" of the Pyncheons asserting any
"right" to it, the effect of their title on the Pyncheons themselves is to cause "the poorest member of the race to feel as if
he inherited a kind of nobility" (19). This pretension is treated
somewhat nervously in Hawthorne's text as a kind of atavistic
joke, but the principle on which it is based—title so perfect that
it is immunized from expropriation—was by no means completely anachronistic in the 1850s. For example, antislavery po-
lemicists like Harriet Beecher Stowe and William Goodell admitted the comparative superiority of those slave states and
societies where, as Goodell puts it, slaves are treated as "real
estate" in the sense that they are "attached to the soil they cul-
tivate, partaking therewith all the restraints upon voluntary
alienation to which the possessor of the *land* is liable, and they

[9]Michel Chevalier, *Society, Manners, and Politics in the United States*, ed.
John William Ward (Ithaca, N.Y., 1961), 98.

cannot be seized or sold by creditors for the satisfaction of the debts of the owner."[10] Of course, it could be argued that this restraint upon alienation should itself be considered a feudal relic, reflecting primarily a nostalgia for the time when land had not yet been transformed into a commodity and, thus, Pyncheons and slaveholders alike could be seen as throwbacks. But, in fact, the notion of inalienable title was central also to one of the most radically progressive social movements of the 1840s and 1850s, the "land for the landless" agitation (opposed by southern slaveholders and northern capitalists both) that culminated in the Homestead Act of 1862.

At the heart of the homestead movement was the conviction that the land should belong to those who worked it and not to the banks and speculators. Attempting to protect themselves from speculation, the most radical reformers urged that homestead land be made inalienable, since obviously land that could not be bought or sold could not be speculated upon either. This attempt failed, but Congress did in fact require that "no land acquired under the provisions of [the Homestead Act] should in any event become liable to the satisfaction of any debt contracted prior to the issuing of the patent."[11] Thus, homestead lands, like slaves in Louisiana, represented at least a partial escape from alienability. And, indeed, the desire for such an escape was so strong that Homestead Act propagandists were sometimes willing to sacrifice their Maule-like claim to property through labor for a Pyncheon-like claim to the status of an absentee landlord. In a pamphlet entitled *Vote Yourself a Farm*, the pamphleteer reminds his readers that "if a man have a house and home of his own, though it be a thousand miles off, he is well received in other people's houses; while the homeless wretch is turned away. The *bare right* to a farm, though you should never go near it, would save you from many

---

[10]William Goodell, *The American Slave Code* (1853; reprint, New York, 1969), 65. The central state in question is Louisiana.

[11]George M. Stephenson, *The Political History of the Public Lands* (New York, 1917), 243. For a characteristically helpful discussion of the ideology of homesteading, see Henry Nash Smith, *Virgin Land* (Cambridge, Mass., 1950), 165–210.

an insult. Therefore, Vote yourself a farm."[12] In effect, the Pyncheons have voted themselves a farm, or rather, more powerfully, the bare right to one. Hawthorne himself, figuring the romance as uncontested title and inalienable right, has sought in the escape from reference the power of that bare right. His "castles in the air" of the Preface are equally Hepzibah Pyncheon's "castles in the air" (65), her "shadowy claims to princely territory." And her "fantasies" of a "gentility" beyond the reach of "commercial speculations" are his claims to a "street that infringes upon nobody's" rights and to "a lot of land" without any "visible owner." Even the map of Waldo that hangs on Hepzibah's kitchen wall images the security of romance's bare right; "grotesquely illuminated with pictures of Indians and wild beasts, among which was seen a lion" (33), the map's geography is, Hawthorne says, as "fantastically awry" as its natural history. It is itself one of those "fancy-pictures" that perish if "brought into contact" with reality, an antimimetic map, charting a way out of republican fluctuation and novelistic imitation.

For if the romance seeps out of the Preface and into the text as an impalpable claim to impalpable property, the novel, too, embodies an ongoing relation to property, in the form of certain "mistakes" provoked by the lies of mimesis. The novel's commercial world consists of "magnificent shops" with "immense panes of plate glass," with "gorgeous fixtures," with "vast and complete assortments of merchandize," above all, with "noble mirrors . . . doubling all this wealth by a brightly burnished vista of unrealities" (48). We are unable to see through these unrealities just as we are unable to see through those other "big, heavy, solid unrealities such as gold, landed estate . . . and public honors" (229). Hawthorne here conceives of mass production as a form of mimesis and of the factories that make these stores possible as novels producing the realistically unreal. At the same time, the novel is a figure for appropriation and for those men—like the aristocrat-turned-

---

[12]The quotation is in Stephenson, *Political History of the Public Lands*, 109–10.

capitalist Judge Pyncheon—who "possess vast ability in grasping, and arranging, and appropriating to themselves" those unrealities. In fact, the mirror of capitalism is itself reproduced in
such men whose own "character," "when they aim at the honors of a republic" (130), becomes only an "image . . . reflected
in the mirror of public opinion" (232). Before the Revolution,
"the great man of the town was commonly called King" (63);
now he must make himself over into a facsimile of the people.
They see themselves reflected in him, and he, "resolutely taking his idea of himself from what purports to be his image"
(232), sees himself reflected in them. Only "loss of property
and reputation," Hawthorne says, can end this riot of mimesis
and bring about "true self-knowledge."

Judge Pyncheon, who looking within himself sees only a
mirror, never seeks such self-knowledge; and the novel, aim-
ing at a "very minute fidelity" to the "ordinary course of man's
experience," never seeks it either—its goal is the department-
store doubling of unrealities. Only the romance, with its dedi-
cation to "the truth of the human heart," and, in the text itself,
only the daguerreotypist Holgrave can represent the "secret
character" behind the mirror and restore appropriated property to its rightful owner. It is, of course, extraordinary that
Holgrave, who inveighs against all property, should come to
represent its legitimation, and it is perhaps even more extraordinary that the photograph, almost universally acclaimed in the
1850s as the perfection of mimesis, should come to represent
an artistic enterprise hostile to imitation. To understand these
reversals, we need to look a little more closely at the technology of imitation and at the social conditions in which that technology and the romance itself were developed.

Holgrave's career, says Hawthorne, was like "a romance on
the plan of Gil Blas," except that Gil Blas, "adapted to American
society and manners, would cease to be a romance" (176). Although only twenty-one, Holgrave had been (among other
things) a schoolmaster, a salesman, and a dentist. His current
occupation of daguerreotypist is, he tells Phoebe, no more
"likely to be permanent than any of the preceding ones" (177).
According to Hawthorne, such mobility is typical of the "experience of many individuals among us, who think it hardly worth

the telling" (176), and certainly too ordinary to be the stuff of romance. Hawthorne exaggerates, of course, but not much. Several recent historians have noted the high degree of geographic mobility in the 1840s and 1850s, mostly among young men who, for economic reasons, frequently changed locations and jobs. This phenomenon, according to Robert Doherty, was particularly noticeable in major commercial centers like Salem, where it was associated also with increased social hierarchism. In rural agricultural areas, young men tended to stay put, and the distribution of property was comparatively even. In towns like Salem, however, "commerce and manufacturing produced great inequalities of wealth,"[13] and over one-third of Salem's population in the fifties consisted of transients. Most of these were propertyless young men whose geographic mobility came from hopes of a corresponding economic mobility. Sometimes these hopes were gratified. Many men, Doherty suggests, "spent a period of youthful wandering and then settled in at about age 30 and began to accumulate property."[14] Many more, however, "failed to gain even minimal material success." Some of these "propertyless . . . men stayed in town," Doherty writes, some "drifted from place to place, but all were apparent casualties of a social system which denied them property."[15]

The development of such an underclass had obvious social significance, and it suggests also ways in which a career like Holgrave's might not only be inappropriate for romance by virtue of its ordinariness but would even constitute a reproach to the commitment to property on which the romance is based. For a real-life Holgrave in Salem in 1851 stood a three-to-one chance of becoming what Doherty calls a "casualty," never accumulating any property and remaining stuck forever at the bottom of an increasingly stratified society. Hawthorne's Holgrave, needless to say, escapes this fate. Like only a few real-life young men, he rises from "penniless youth to great

[13] Robert Doherty, *Society and Power* (Amherst, Mass., 1977), 52–53. "Agriculture," Doherty notes, "produced greater equality, and the only communities approaching equitable distribution of property were low-level, less developed rural hinterlands" (53).

[14] Ibid., 47.

[15] Ibid., 49.

wealth," and one might perhaps interpret this rise as Hawthorne's ideological intervention on behalf of the openness of American society.

Except that, as we have seen, what made Hawthorne most nervous about American society was precisely its openness, its hospitality to fluctuation.[16] In this respect, the actual economic mobility of life in Salem, the fact that some men rose (according to Doherty, about 23 percent) and some men fell (about 13 percent), would be infinitely more disturbing to Hawthorne than the existence of a permanent class of the propertyless. If inalienable rights can be neither lost nor acquired, how then can we explain Holgrave's happy ending, his sudden rise to property? One clue is that he does not actually earn his wealth; he marries it. Which is not to say that Hawthorne is being ironic about his hero's merits—just the opposite. The whole point here is that property that has been earned is just as insecure (and, in the end, illegitimate) as property that has been appropriated by some capitalist trick. Thus, for Hawthorne the accumulation of property must be remade into an accession to property, and the social meaning of Holgrave's career turns out to be that it is not really a career at all. His period of wandering gives him instead the chance to display a stability of character that provides a kind of psychological legitimation for the fact of ownership: "Amid all his personal vicissitudes," Hawthorne writes, Holgrave had "never lost his identity . . . he had never violated the innermost man" (177). Like the romance itself, which, despite its apparent freedom from the responsibilities of the novel, "must rigidly subject itself to laws" (1), Holgrave appears "lawless" but in fact follows a "law of his own" (85). Anchoring property not in work but in character, he defuses both the threat posed by the young transients who failed to acquire property (Hawthorne simply legislates them out of existence) and the threat posed by the transients who did acquire

[16] Hawthorne apparently found the idea of a fixed income as attractive personally as it was socially. James Mellow quotes his sister Ebe: "One odd, but characteristic notion of his was that he should like a competent income that would neither increase nor diminish. I said that it might be well to have it increase, but he replied, 'No, because then it would engross too much of his attention'" (Mellow, *Nathaniel Hawthorne in his Times* [Boston, 1980]), 94.

property (since he makes that acquisition a function not of social mobility but of the fixed character of the "innermost
man"). Apparently a pure product of the "republican" world of
fluctuation, Holgrave turns out instead to embody the unchanging truth of romance.

But if Holgrave's career offers Hawthorne the opportunity
to transform the social meaning of the new class of landless
transients, Holgrave's art, the daguerreotype, hits even closer
to home and requires an even more spectacular inversion. The
terms of this inversion are quickly apparent in Holgrave's claim
that the daguerreotype, despite its apparent preoccupation
with "the merest surface," "actually brings out the secret character with a truth that no painter would ever venture upon"
(91). It was, of course, far more usual for writers of the forties
and fifties to make just the opposite point. The "unrivalled pre-
cision" of the daguerreotype and the paper photograph, painters were warned, "renders exact imitation no longer a miracle
of crayon or palette; these must now create as well as reflect
. . . bring out the soul of the individual and of the landscape,
or their achievements will be neglected in favor of the facsimiles obtainable through sunshine and chemistry."[17] For Hawthorne, however, it is the *daguerreotype* that penetrates to the
soul, seeing through republican honors to "the man himself."

The triumph of the daguerreotype in *The House of the
Seven Gables* is the portraits—Hawthorne's and Holgrave's—of
Judge Pyncheon dead. Early daguerreotype portraits were
often marred by a certain blurriness. The very oldest surviving
portrait, John Draper's picture of his sister Catherine, taken in
1840, was sent to an English photographer accompanied by
apologies for the "indistinctness" that results, Draper wrote,
from any movement, even "the inevitable motions of the
respiratory muscles." But where "inanimate objects are depicted," Draper went on to remark with satisfaction, "the most
rigid sharpness can be obtained."[18] Holgrave's job is thus made
easier by the fact that the judge has stopped breathing, but the

[17] Quoted in Robert Taft, *Photography and the American Scene* (New York,
1938), 133–34.
[18] Ibid., p. 30.

real point here is that the daguerreotype always sees through to the fixed truth behind the fluctuating movements of the "public character." It is as if the subject of a daguerreotype is in some sense already dead, the truth about him fixed by the portrait—just as the actual "fact of a man's death," Hawthorne writes in connection with Pyncheon's posthumous reputation, "often seems to give people a truer idea of his character" (310). The daguerreotype, always a representation of death, is also death's representative.

As is the romance. In a passage that anticipates by some forty years Henry James's famous remarks on "the coldness, the thinness, the blankness" of Hawthorne's America, the French journalist Michel Chevalier was struck by the absence in America of those elements that in Europe served, as he put it, to "stir" the "nerves." James would miss the sovereign, the court, little Norman churches; the effect of American life on a "French imagination," he thought, "would probably be appalling."[19] But Chevalier was thrilled, not appalled. He did miss what he called the "sensual gratifications": "wine, women, and the display of princely luxury . . . cards and dice." But, Chevalier says, the American has a way of more than making up for the absence of traditional stimulants; seeking "the strong emotions which he requires to make him feel life," the American "has recourse to business. . . . He launches with delight into the ever-moving sea of speculation. One day, the wave raises him to the clouds . . . the next day he disappears between the crests of the billows. . . . If movement and the quick succession of sensations and ideas constitute life, here one lives a hundredfold more than elsewhere."[20]

If the cold blankness of American life figured for James the difficulty of finding something to represent, that blankness was to Chevalier the setting for a business life of "violent sensations," and to Hawthorne the violent movements of business

---

[19]Henry James, *Hawthorne* (Ithaca, N.Y., 1967), 35.

[20]Chevalier, *Society, Manners, and Politics*, 298–99. Writing in August 1835, Chevalier notes, "Great fortunes, and many of them too, have sprung out of the earth since the spring; others will, perhaps, return to it before the fall. The American does not worry about that. Violent sensations are necessary to stir his vigorous nerves."

were the violence of mimetic representation itself. The world of the "money power," Andrew Jackson warned in his Farewell Address, is "liable to great and sudden fluctuations" that render "property insecure and the wages of labor unsteady and uncertain."[21] "The soil itself, or at least the houses, partake in the universal instability," Chevalier exclaimed.[22] Hawthorne required the romance to fix this instability, to render property secure. Where representations are unrealities produced by mirrors, the romance represents nothing, not in compensation for the coldness of American life but in opposition to its terrible vitality. Business makes the American "feel life," but that life is a mimetic lie, whereas "death," Hawthorne says, "is so genuine a fact that it excludes falsehood" (310). Celebrating the death—one might better call it the execution—of Judge Pyncheon, the romance joins the witch hunt, the attempt to imagine an escape from capitalism, defending the self against possession, property against appropriation, and choosing death over life.

The Slave Power

The conjunction of death and secure property has its place in another text of 1851, one intended not as a romance but, in its author's words, as a "representation . . . of real incidents, of actions really performed, of words and expressions really uttered."[23] Riding by his slave quarters late at night, Simon Legree hears the singing of a "musical tenor voice": "'When I can read my title clear/To mansions in the skies,'" Uncle Tom sings, "'I'll bid farewell to every fear/And wipe my weeping eyes.'"[24] Tom is preparing for the martyrdom toward which Le-

---

[21]Andrew Jackson, "Farewell Address," in *American Democracy: A Documentary Record*, ed. J. R. Hollingsworth and B. I. Wiley (New York, 1961), 374.

[22]Chevalier, *Society, Manners, and Politics*, 299.

[23]Harriet Beecher Stowe, *The Key to Uncle Tom's Cabin* (New York, 1969), 1. Written in 1853, this book was an extraordinarily successful attempt to defend the veracity of *Uncle Tom's Cabin* by providing massive documentation for the incidents it narrated and the characters it described.

[24]Harriet Beecher Stowe, *Uncle Tom's Cabin* (Columbus, Ohio, 1969),

gree will soon help him, and his sense of heaven as a "home" to which he has clear title is barely metaphoric. Slaves, of course, were forbidden to own property, but Stowe thought of them as, by definition, the victims of theft. Slavery, "appropriating one set of human beings to the use and improvement of another" (2:21), robbed a man of himself, and so freedom involved above all the restitution of property. Only in death did the slave's title to himself become "sure"; only in death did Uncle Tom's cabin actually become his.

It is not, in itself, surprising that freedom in the mid-nineteenth century, the period that C. B. Macpherson has called the "zenith" of "possessive market society,"[25] should be understood as essentially a property relation, but it does provide in *Uncle Tom's Cabin* some unexpected and little-noted points of emphasis. When, for example, George Shelby frees his slaves, he tells them that their lives will go on pretty much as before but with the "advantage" that, in case of his "getting in debt or dying," they cannot be "taken up and sold" (2:309). The implication here is that Shelby himself would never sell them, and in fact, voluntary sales play a comparatively minor role in Stowe's depiction of the evils of slavery. A paragraph from Goodell's *The American Slave Code* helps explain why: "This feature of liability to seizure for the master's debt," Goodell writes,

> is, in many cases, more terrific to the slave than that which subjects him to the master's voluntary sale. The slave may be satisfied that his master is not willing to sell him—that it is not for his interest or convenience to do so. He may be conscious that he is, in a manner, necessary to his master or mistress. . . . He may even confide in their Christian benevolence and moral principle, or promise that they would not sell him. . . . But all this affords him no security or ground of assurance that his master's creditor will not seize him . . . against even his master's entreaties. Such occurrences are too common to be unnoticed or out of mind.[26]

2:246. All subsequent references to this work are cited in parentheses in the text.

[25] C. B. Macpherson, *Possessive Individualism* (New York, 1964), 272.

[26] Goodell, *American Slave Code*, 65–66.

According to Goodell, then, the slave, whose condition consists in being subordinated to the absolute power of his master, may in the end be less vexed by the absoluteness of that power than by its ultimate incompleteness. It is as if the greatest danger to the slave is not his master's power but his impotence. Thus, Eliza and little Harry flee the Shelbys because, although the Shelbys were "kind," they also "were owing money" and were being forced to sell Harry—"they couldn't," she says, "help themselves" (1:128). And when Augustine St. Clare dies, his entire household is overwhelmed not so much by grief as by "terror and consternation" at being left "utterly unprotected" (2:144).

What the slaves fear, of course, is being taken from a kind master to a cruel one; this threat, Goodell thinks, makes them constantly insecure, and the mechanics of this insecurity are the plot mechanism that sells Uncle Tom down the river. But in describing the reaction of St. Clare's slaves to his death, Stowe indirectly points toward a logic of slavery that runs deeper than the difference between good and bad masters, deeper even than the master-slave relation itself. As a matter of course, she notes, the slave is "devoid of rights"; the only "acknowledgment" of his "longings and wants" as a "human and immortal creature" that he ever receives comes to him "through the sovereign and irresponsible will of his master; and when that master is stricken down, nothing remains" (2:144). The point here is not that one man in the power of another may be subjected to the most inhumane cruelties; nor is it the more subtle point that the power of even a humane master dehumanizes the slave—for Stowe, the power of the kind master and the cruel master both can be tolerated, since even a Legree, refusing Tom his every want and longing, at least acknowledges those wants by refusing them and thus acknowledges his humanity. Rather, the most terrifying spectacle slavery has to offer is the spectacle of slaves *without masters*. Since the "only possible acknowledgment" of the slave as a "human and immortal creature" is through his master's "will," when in debt or in death the master's will is extinguished, the slave's humanity is extinguished also. The slave without a master stands revealed as nothing more than "a bale of merchandise," inhuman testimony to the absolute transformation of a personal relation into a market relation.

Stowe, like most of her contemporaries, customarily understood slavery as "a relic of a barbarous age."[27] The conflict between the "aristocratic" "Slave Power" and "republican" "free labor" would prove "irrepressible," William Seward proclaimed in a tremendously influential speech,[28] and the supposed "feudalism" of the South was a northern byword. More recently, Eugene Genovese, reviving the irrepressible-conflict interpretation of the Civil War, has described the slaveholding planters as the "closest thing to feudal lords imaginable in a nineteenth-century bourgeois republic"[29] and has argued that the South was a fundamentally precapitalist society. But, as we have begun to see, Stowe was basically more horrified by the bourgeois elements of slavery than by the feudal ones. She and Goodell both were struck by the insecurity of the slave's life, and she, in particular, saw that insecurity as the inevitable fate of property in a free market. The evil of slavery lies, then, not in its reversion to a barbaric paternalism but in its uncanny way of epitomizing the market society to which she herself belongs. Rejecting the claims of southern apologists that slavery provides a social and economic refuge from capitalism, Stowe imagines it instead as a mirror of the social and economic relations coming to the fore in the bourgeois North.

Hence the slave trade, what she calls the "great Southern slave-market," dominates her picture of the South, and, despite their feudal status, the slaves in her writings share the anxious lives of Hawthorne's "republican" northerners— "somebody is always at the drowning-point." The "fluctuations of hope, and fear, and desire" (2:245) they experience appear

[27] Stowe, *Key*, 62.

[28] William H. Seward, "The Irrepressible Conflict," in Hollingsworth and Wiley, *American Democracy*, 468–69. The "experience of mankind," Seward claimed, had "conclusively established" that two such "radically different political systems" could never coexist. "They never have permanently existed together in one country," he said, "and they never can."

[29] Eugene D. Genovese, *The Political Economy of Slavery* (New York, 1967), 31.

now as transformations of their market value. Their emotions represent their status as the objects of speculation. "Nothing is more fluctuating than the value of slaves,"[30] remarks a Virginia legislator in *The Key to Uncle Tom's Cabin*. A recent Louisiana law had reduced their value: Texas's imminent admission to the Union as a slave state would increase it. The Virginians speak of their "slave-breeding" as a kind of agriculture and of their female slaves as "brood-mares," but Stowe penetrates more deeply into the nature of the commodity by imagining the product without *any* producer. What everybody knows about the "goblin-like" Topsy, that she just "grow'd," is only part of the answer to a series of questions asked her by Miss Ophelia: " 'Do you know who made you? . . . Tell me where you were born, and who your father and mother were.' " " 'Never was born,' " Topsy replies, " 'never had no father nor mother. . . . I was raised by a speculator' " (2:37). If production in *The House of the Seven Gables* is done with mirrors, production in *Uncle Tom's Cabin* is an equally demonic magic trick, substituting the speculator for the parent and utterly effacing any trace of labor, human or divine.

This replacement of the parent by the speculator assumed an even more lurid countenance when, instead of being separate, the two figures were embodied in the same man, as when a father might sell his daughter. Stowe reproduces a poem by Longfellow called "The Quadroon Girl," in which a planter and slaver bargain in the presence of a beautiful young girl:

"The soil is barren, the farm is old,"
  The thoughtful planter said;
Then looked upon the Slaver's gold,
  And then upon the maid.

His heart within him was at strife
  With such accursed gains;
For he knew whose passions gave her life,
  Whose blood ran in her veins.

---

[30] Stowe, *Key*, 289.

But the voice of nature was too weak;
  He took the glittering gold!
Then pale as death grew the maiden's cheek,
  Her hands as icy cold.

The slaver led her from the door,
  He led her by the hand,
To be his slave and paramour
  In a strange and distant land![31]

Writers like George Fitzhugh defended slavery claiming that it replaced the "false, antagonistic and competitive relations" of liberal capitalism with the more natural relations of the family. "Slavery leaves but little of the world without the family,"[32] he wrote in *Cannibals All!*; in a thoroughly paternalist society, all men, black and white, would be related to one another. Writers like Stowe and Longfellow inverted Fitzhugh's defense while preserving its terms. They, too, were concerned to defend the family against the market, but in their view slavery only weakened the "voice of nature." It might be appropriate to think of one's children as property, but to make that property alienable was to annihilate the family by dissolving nature into contract. "For the sake of a common humanity," Stowe wrote, she hoped that Longfellow's poem described "no common event."[33]

Longfellow's poem is somewhat ludicrous, and its effect, perhaps, is to make the danger it imagines seem absurdly remote—in fact, no common event. But the transformations that capitalism works upon parental and erotic relations appear elsewhere in a more penetrating (although in some respects equally lurid) form. Indeed, these transformations, intensified and above all internalized, constitute what I take to be the heart of Hawthorne's concerns in *The House of the Seven Gables*, the chief threat against which the defense of property is mounted. I would therefore like to close by returning to that

---

[31] Quoted in ibid., 295.
[32] George Fitzhugh, *Cannibals All!* in *Ante-Bellum*, ed. Harvey Wish (New York, 1960), 129.
[33] Stowe, *Key*, 294.

text and to what might be called its own representation of the quadroon girl.

"If ever there was a lady born" (201), Holgrave tells Phoebe, it was Alice Pyncheon, the daughter of a Pyncheon with aristocratic ambitions who, returning to Salem after a long stay in Europe, fervently hoped to gain "actual possession" of the Waldo territory and, having established himself as a "Lord" or "Earl," to return to England. According to tradition, the only man with access to the deed to Waldo was Matthew Maule, the grandson of the original "wizard," who was rumored still to haunt his old home "against the owner of which he pretended to hold an unsettled claim for ground-rent" (189). Summoned to the house, this young Maule (himself supposed, by the young ladies at least, to have a bewitching eye) demands to see Alice as well as her father. Ushered into his presence, the beautiful girl looks at Maule with unconcealed "admiration," but the "subtile" Maule sees only arrogant indifference in her "artistic approval" of his "comeliness, strength, and energy" (201). Her "admiration" is so open because it is so empty of desire; she looks at him, Maule thinks, as if he were "a brute beast," and he determines to wring from her the "acknowledgment that he was indeed a man." The "business" he has with her father now turns on Alice and on what Hawthorne calls the "contest" between her "unsullied purity" and the "sinister or evil potency . . . striving to pass her barriers" (203).

Alice is prepared to enter this apparently uneven struggle between "man's might" and "woman's might" because, as she tells her father, no "lady, while true to herself, can have ought to fear from whomsoever or in any circumstances" (202). She knows herself possessed of a "power" that makes "her sphere impenetrable, unless betrayed by treachery within" (203). Hence, she allows her father to stand by while Maule, gesturing in the air, puts her into a trance from which Pyncheon, suddenly alarmed, is unable to rouse her. " 'She is mine!' " Maule announces, and when Pyncheon rages against him, Maule asks quietly, " 'Is it my crime, if you have sold your daughter. . . ?' " (206).

Obviously this story repeats in some crucial respects the narrative of "The Quadroon Girl," but in pointing to this similarity I do not mean to claim that the bewitching of Alice Pyncheon is an allegory of the slave trade. Hawthorne seems to have been largely indifferent to the issue of slavery; a few years later, he would urge Charles Sumner to "let slavery alone for a little while" and focus instead on the mistreatment of sailors in the merchant marine.[34] I mean instead to see in this story some sense of how deep the notion of inalienability could run and especially of how deeply undermined it could be by conditions closer to home than the slave trade and less exotic than witchcraft. For Alice Pyncheon fancies herself immune to possession (in effect, to appropriation) simply because she feels no desire. She thinks of herself as a kind of impregnable citadel. Desires, like so many Trojan horses, would make her vulnerable; wanting no one and nothing, she is free from what Hawthorne, in McCarthyesque fashion, calls "treachery from within," and so impervious to aggression from without. That she in fact succumbs to Matthew Maule does not invalidate her analysis—it only shows that the enemy within need not take the form of felt desire. In their dreams, Hawthorne says, the Pyncheons have always been "no better than bond-servants" (26) to the Maules. Thus, Alice's Pyncheon blood makes her as much an alienable commodity as does the quadroon girl's black blood. And although *she* feels no desire, her father does, "an inordinate desire," Hawthorne calls it, "for measuring his land by miles instead of acres" (208). The bewitching of Alice is here imagined as a business transaction; witches, it turns out, are capitalists by night, and, having appropriated her spirit as the Pyncheons did his land, Matthew Maule makes Alice live out her life in unconscious mimicry of the original Salem girls: breaking out, wherever she might be, into "wild laughter" or hysterical tears, suddenly dancing a "jig" or "rigadoon," obeying the every command of "her unseen despot" (209).[35]

---

[34] Quoted in Mellow, *Nathaniel Hawthorne*, 435.

[35] In this connection, it may be worth remembering not only Hawthorne's lifelong fear and dislike of mesmerism but also Stowe's remark that "negroes are singularly susceptible to all that class of influences which produce catalepsy, mesmeric sleep, and partial clairvoyant phenomena" (*Key*, 46). Mesmer-

Despot is a crucial word here; Andrew Jackson described the National Bank as exerting a "despotic sway"[36] over the financial life of the country; Harriet Beecher Stowe called slavery "a system which makes every individual owner an irresponsible despot";[37] Hawthorne calls Maule, the capitalist wizard, an "unseen despot." The force of the term is in all three cases to represent (internal) conflict as (external) oppression. For example, the point of characterizing the Bank as despotic was to associate it with old-world aristocracy and literally to represent it as un-American. Readers of Jackson's veto message cannot help but be struck by his obsessive concern with "foreign stockholders" in the Bank and with the anonymous threat they pose to "our country." By the same token, Stowe, fearing slavery (if I am right) as an emblem of the market economy, nevertheless thought for many years that the slave problem could be solved by repatriation to Africa, as if exorcising the slaves would rid the South of feudalism and the North of capitalism. Hawthorne, too, imagines a Maule become a Holgrave, renouncing "mastery" over Phoebe and leaving her "free" out of "reverence for another's individuality" (212). Indeed, the very idea of the romance asserts the possibility of immunity to appropriation in an Alice Pyncheon-like fantasy of strength through purity.

For what does the notion of inalienability entail if not a property right so impenetrable that nothing on the outside can buy it or take it away from you and so pure that nothing on the inside will conspire to sell it or give it away? That no actual possession of land could meet these criteria we have already seen. What slavery proved to Stowe was that even the possession of one's own body could not be guaranteed against capitalist appropriation. "The slaves often say [she quotes an "acquaintance"] when cut in the hand or foot, 'Plague on the old

---

ism, as a threat to property, works most easily on those whose title to themselves is least secure, but no one in Hawthorne's world can be entirely safe from the threat of expropriation.

[36] Andrew Jackson, "Farewell Address," 374. See also his "Veto of the Bank Bill," in Hollingsworth and Wiley, *American Democracy*, 309–21.

[37] Stowe, *Key*, 204.

foot. . . . It is master's, let him take care of it; nigger don't care if he never get well.' "[38] Even the slave's soul, she thought, could not be kept pure when the "nobler traits of mind and heart" had their own "market value": "Is the slave intelligent?—Good! that raises his price two hundred dollars. Is he conscientious and faithful? Good . . . two hundred dollars more. Is he religious? Does that Holy Spirit of God . . . make that despised form His temple?—Let that also be put down in the estimate of his market value, and the gift of the Holy Ghost shall be sold for money."[39] Only death offered an escape from this "dreadful commerce." Legree says to George Shelby, who has made him an offer on Uncle Tom's corpse, "I don't sell dead niggers" (2:282).

In Hawthorne's republican world, however, everything is for sale. If not exactly dead niggers, then at least some version of them, like the Jim Crow gingerbread men Hepzibah Pyncheon sells to her first customer. And if not exactly the Holy Spirit, then at least the "spirit" of Alice Pyncheon, held for debt by her father's "ghostly creditors," the Maules. In fact, the whole project of the romance, with its bizarrely utopian and apparently anachronistic criteria for legitimate ownership, had already played a significant, if ironic, role in opening the American land market. The irony, of course, is that Hawthorne and others like him were uncompromisingly opposed to speculation in land. Jackson, for example, reacted against his own early career as a land speculator by defending, in Michael Rogin's words, "original title against actual residents whose long-standing possession was contaminated at the core."[40] But if the goal was purity, the effect on the western frontier was chaos; criteria like Jackson's were so rigorous that they left no man's title secure. Hence, the separation of title from possession, the very condition of romance's attempt to defend against specu-

[38] Ibid., 22.

[39] Ibid., 280.

[40] Michael Paul Rogin, *Fathers and Children: Andrew Jackson and the Subjugation of the American Indian* (New York, 1976), 96. Although he does not explicitly point to the intrinsically self-defeating character of the demand for pure title, Rogin does go on to note that occupancy laws were opposed by "aspiring speculators" as well as by "purists over contractual rights" (97).

lation, turned out to be the condition that enabled speculators to flourish. Apparently imagining the terms of a text that would escape republican fluctuation, Hawthorne imagined in fact the terms of the technology that made those fluctuations possible.

The problematic at the heart of this reversal becomes even sharper if we turn from commerce in land to commerce in people. Stowe opposed slavery, but she did so, as we have seen, in defense of property. Slaves, she thought, were the victims of theft; their property rights in their own persons had been violated. Attacking southern feudalism, she spoke for free labor and against slave labor. But insofar as her critique of slavery came to be a critique of the "Southern market," it had inevitably to constitute a repudiation of free labor as well. What Stowe most feared was the notion of a market in human attributes, and of course, free labor is just shorthand for a free market in labor. Hence, her conception of freedom was itself a product of the economy epitomized for her in the slave trade—free market, free trade, in Blackstone's words, "free and unconstrained" "circulation" of "property."

Hawthorne valued freedom too; it was essential to the "individuality" he cherished and to the "reverence" for individuality he held highest among the virtues. Matthew Maule leaves Alice Pyncheon's spirit "bowed" down before him; Holgrave demonstrates his own "integrity" by leaving Phoebe hers. But the specter of "treachery within" cannot be so easily laid to rest. For the real question raised by Alice's story is whether "reverence" for "individuality" is not ultimately an oxymoron. How should we read what Hawthorne calls Alice's loss of "self-control"? We may read it as a conflict between two forces—the individual self and the market—opposed in principle to one another.[41] In this instance, the market wins—but it need not,

---

[41] Such a reading is adopted in effect by Michael T. Gilmore, who argues that Hawthorne, writing *The House of the Seven Gables*, "was unable to suppress his misgivings that in bowing to the marketplace he was compromising his artistic independence and integrity" ("The Artist and the Marketplace in *The House of the Seven Gables*," *ELH* 48 [Spring 1981]: 172–73). Gilmore's valuable essay seems to me typical of much recent work on the artist in the market in that it calls attention to the importance of the market only to draw ever more firmly the line between the values of that market and the values of art. The

and indeed, when Holgrave liberates Phoebe, it does not. Or we may read it as a conflict in which the individual is set against a market that has already gained a foothold within—the McCarthyesque imagination of conspiracy. Here the enemy is still regarded as fundamentally other but is seen successfully to have infiltrated the sphere of the self—it must be exorcised.

But if we remember that Alice, as a Pyncheon, is already in bondage to the Maules, and if we remember that this fact of her birth seems to her the guarantee of her "self-control," we may be led to a third reading. Here Alice is ultimately betrayed not only by her father's desire but by the very claim to individual identity that made her imagine herself immune to betrayal. Individuality, in this reading, is its own betrayal—the enemy cannot be repulsed by the self or exorcised from the self, since the enemy of the self is the self. "Property in the bourgeois sense," C. B. Macpherson has written, "is not only a right to enjoy or use; it is a right to dispose of, to exchange, to alienate."[42] Property, to be property, must be alienable. We have seen the fate of Hawthorne's attempt to imagine an inalienable right in land; now we can see the fate of his attempt to imagine an inalienable right in the self. The slave cannot resist her master because the slave is her master. If, from one perspective, this looks like freedom, from another perspective it looks like just another one of what Stowe called "the vicissitudes of property."

---

point I am urging in this essay is the rather different one that for Hawthorne qualities like independence and integrity (artistic or otherwise) do not exist in opposition to the marketplace but are produced by and contained within it.

[42] Macpherson, *Possessive Individualism*, 92.

4. *THE PHENOMENOLOGY OF CONTRACT*

"*E*ven in my early childhood I loved to revel in ideas about the absolute mastery of one man over others. The thought of slavery had something exciting in it for me, alike whether from the standpoint of master or servant. That one man could possess, sell or whip another, caused me intense excitement; and in reading *Uncle Tom's Cabin* (which I read at about the beginning of puberty) I had erections."[1] This reading of *Uncle Tom's Cabin* marks the sexual awakening of Case 57 in Richard von Krafft-Ebing's *Psychopathia Sexualis*, an example, according to Krafft-Ebing, of "typical masochism in which the whole circle of ideas peculiar to this perversion appears completely developed" (144). The literary origins of Case 57's masochism are in keeping with its literary genealogy (Krafft-Ebing named it, of course, after the novelist Sacher-Masoch); more important, they help to mark what was for Krafft-Ebing the essence of sexual perversity, its "purely psychical" character. Case 57 never attempts to act out his masochistic impulses, to "connect them with the world," because, he thinks, neither a hired woman nor a real-life Messalina could ever "take the place of my imagination of a 'cruel mistress'" (146). Thus he contents himself with masturbating, or rather—anticipating Freud's remark some forty years later that for the masochist "the real situations are in fact only a kind of make-believe performance of the phantasies"[2]—he delights in masturbating, disdaining the inferior reality of the real, preferring the reality of the imagination, his own or Harriet Beecher Stowe's.

Today, Krafft-Ebing is something of a forgotten figure in studies of sexuality or even in the history of sexuality, and those few writers who do discuss him at any length do so mainly to abuse both him and his emphasis on the dangers of masturbation. In his book *The Sex Researchers*, for example, Edward

---

[1] Richard von Krafft-Ebing, *Psychopathia Sexualis* (1902; translation, New York, 1943), 144. Subsequent page references are cited in parentheses in the text.

[2] Sigmund Freud, "The Economic Problem in Masochism" (1924), in Freud, *General Psychological Theory*, with an Introduction by Phillip Rieff (New York, 1963), 192.

Brecher describes the *Psychopathia Sexualis* as "deeply damaging nonsense," accomplishing "the most harm" with its "insistence on masturbation as a factor in the development of all sexual deviations."[3] Indeed, after quoting a few of what he regards as the more retrograde case histories (with their accounts of the disastrous consequences of youthful masturbation), Brecher finds himself too disgusted with Krafft-Ebing to continue. "No useful purpose would be served by prolonging this discussion," he writes, and moves on with obvious relief to "the saner attitudes toward sexual variations developed by subsequent researchers."[4]

But such a reading simultaneously misses and makes Krafft-Ebing's point. Finding the *Psychopathia* "fascinating" while condemning it as a central document in "the suppression of human sexuality," Brecher ends by claiming that his chapter on Krafft-Ebing would itself "have been omitted altogether" were it not for the "distressing circumstance" that the *Psychopathia* "is still amazingly popular," advertised by mail-order houses with slogans like "Monstrous, strange, almost unbelievable sex acts! For mature adults only!"[5] For Brecher, then, the *Psychopathia*, despite its supposed horror of masturbation, has somehow replaced *Uncle Tom's Cabin* as an incitement to masturbatory fantasies, tempting readers into Case 57's perverse preference for the represented whips of the pornographic text over the real whips that sexual life might offer. Brecher's fascinated fear of the *Psychopathia* simply expresses his own sense that, as Case 57 puts it, in sexual perversion "the ideas . . . are the end and the aim" (147).

Krafft-Ebing's career as an expert in legal psychiatry was built on this insight. Sexual perversion, he thought, was easy enough to define; it consisted of any "expression" of the "sexual instinct" that did not "correspond with the purpose of nature—i.e., propagation" (79). But easy definition did not necessarily make for easy diagnosis. "The *nature of the act*," he

[3] Edward M. Brecher, *The Sex Researchers* (Boston, 1969), 60, 51.
[4] Ibid., 60.
[5] Ibid.

wrote, "can never, in itself, determine a decision as to whether it lies within the limits of mental pathology. . . . *The perverse act does not per se indicate perversion of instinct. . . . The perversion of feeling must be shown to be pathological*" (501). This requirement obviously creates an opportunity for the legal psychiatrist. If acts as such cannot be either healthy (hence subject to moral and legal judgment) or diseased (and thus outside the purview of the law), then judges, who characteristically consider "only the crime and not its perpetrator," are never in possession of all the "facts necessary to allow a decision." Krafft-Ebing's greatest contribution, as he saw it, was thus the invention of the "medico-legal examination . . . made according to the rules of science" and making possible for the first time a clear distinction between criminal "immorality" and medical "abnormality" (502).

But, while locating the perversity in the feeling instead of the act clearly produces a professionally useful refinement, it also provides something of a psychological problem. What exactly does it mean for a *feeling* to be perverse? Later writers would tend to describe perversion as the abnormal expression of a normal feeling, as when, for example, Helene Deutsch calls female masochism "the strongest of all forms of love."[6] The masochist wants, Deutsch thinks, what everyone else wants—love; what makes her perverse is the way she goes about trying to get it. But for Krafft-Ebing the perversity must lie not in the action but in the feeling—and it obviously won't do to characterize a feeling as perverse just because it involves the fantasy of a perverse act, since, if perverse acts aren't in themselves perverse, fantasizing about them can't in itself be perverse either. What, then, is a perverse feeling? What does Krafft-Ebing think that perverts want?

The clearest answer to this question is provided in Krafft-Ebing's own discussion of female masochism, an illness that, from the standpoint of the indeterminacy of the act, is paradigmatic, and this despite the fact that he can cite only two recorded cases of it up to the year 1900. The reason so few in-

[6]Helene Deutsch, *The Psychology of Women* (New York, 1944), 269.

stances are recorded, he thinks, is that "intrinsic and extraneous restraints—modesty and custom—naturally constitute in women insurmountable obstacles to the expression of perverse sexual instinct" (197). But in his actual analysis of female masochism, the difficulty seems to be not that the behavior of women doesn't express perverse sexuality but that it expresses nothing else. "Owing to her passive role in procreation and long-existent social conditions, ideas of subjection are, in woman, normally connected with the idea of sexual relations" (195); hence, the behavior of so many women always looks so masochistic that the psychiatrist can't possibly figure out from it which ones are the real perverts. Indeed, even the masochists themselves are uncertain as to what could constitute perverse sexual behavior and so experience some difficulty in conjuring up sexually exciting fantasies. One of the cases on record, Case 84, says that she sometimes fancies herself the slave of the man she loves, but then notes bitterly that "this does not suffice, for after all every woman can be the slave of her husband" (199).

The plausibility of such complaints prompted Krafft-Ebing to develop a distinction between masochism and what he called "sexual bondage." Bondage and masochism, he wrote, "both consist of the unconditioned subjection of the person affected . . . to a person of the opposite sex" (200). But where the woman in bondage is motivated to submit by the normal, albeit excessive, "fear of losing the companion and the desire to keep him always content, amiable, and inclined to sexual intercourse" (203), the masochist is motivated only by the love of submission. The woman in bondage puts up with the "tyranny" of her lover in order to "obtain or retain possession of him," or perhaps even because she regards his mistreatment of her as an expression of his love. The masochist, however, has no such "independent purpose." Her only motive is the "charm of the tyranny"; hence, the "acts in which masochism is expressed are, for the individual in subjection, not means to an end, as in bondage, but the end in themselves" (206).

Thus, a case like 84, while it points to the extraordinary similarity (not to say, identity) between normal and perverse behavior, actually demonstrates what Krafft-Ebing understands as the radical otherness of perversion. Many women are virtual slaves to their lovers; many women like being virtual slaves to their lovers; but only the masochist likes it for the sake of the subjection itself. The difficulty Case 84 experiences in conjuring up an erotic fantasy that will express her otherness thus illustrates the purity of her masochism while at the same time underlining its literal inexplicability by reference to more normal motives. The woman in bondage can give reasons for enduring (and even enjoying) the tyranny of her lover; the masochist cannot—in fact, that is just what makes her a masochist. Instead of explaining her behavior by appealing to some "independent purpose," all the masochist can say is that she likes being tyrannized.

Something like this invisible but definitive distinction between the submissiveness of normal women and that of masochistic women makes its way also into what is probably the first representation of masochism in American literature, Frank Norris's *McTeague* (1899). In being frequently beaten, and finally murdered, by her dentist husband, Trina McTeague pursues a career identical to that of her friend Maria Macapa, but where Maria only tolerates her husband's brutality, Trina takes an explicitly erotic pleasure in it. He particularly likes to bite her fingers, "crunching and grinding them with his immense teeth."[7] Sometimes he does it to extort money from her, sometimes for "his own satisfaction," but his motives are in any case irrelevant to Trina, who derives from this torture "a strange unnatural pleasure" that makes her "all the more affectionate" to him by arousing in her "a morbid unwholesome love of submission" (174). She "loved her husband," Norris says elsewhere, "because she had given herself to him" (104)—not she gave herself to him because she loved him. Insisting on this inversion, Norris repeats the autotelic logic of Krafft-Ebing's masochists. Whether McTeague actually possessed any of the "qualities that inspire affection" was irrelevant: "The dentist

---

[7] Frank Norris, *McTeague*, ed. Donald Pizer (New York, 1977), 174. Subsequent page references are cited in parentheses in the text.

might or might not possess them, it was all one with Trina." She doesn't love the tyrant; like Case 84, she loves the tyranny.

Interestingly enough, however, Trina's masochism is by no means the dominant expression of autotelic desire in *McTeague*, or the most erotic. Perhaps no scene from the novel is better known than the one depicting Trina in bed with her gold coins, "taking a strange and ecstatic pleasure in the touch of the smooth flat pieces the length of her body" (202). It is customary to read this scene as a particularly spectacular instance of the way in which, "under the pressure of events," as one reader puts it, Trina's "love of money and her sexual nature begin to merge,"[8] and there is clearly some truth in this interpretation. But since the only thing that eroticizes sex for Trina is her love of submission, we can't explain her love of money as displaced sexuality entirely, even when Norris seems to tempt us with this reading. At one point, fairly early in their relations, Trina decides to give McTeague some of the money he's been asking for and counts ten silver dollars "into her palm" from the bag where she keeps her coins. "But what a difference it made in the appearance and weight of the little chamois bag!" Norris writes, "The bag was shrunken and withered, long wrinkles appeared running downward from the drawstring. It was a lamentable sight. Trina looked longingly at the ten broad pieces in her hand. Then suddenly all her intuitive desire of saving, her instinct of hoarding, her love of money for the money's sake, rose strong within her" (119). And she puts the money back.

Whoever genitalia we ultimately imagine these to be, the example of Krafft-Ebing allows us to see that their erotic charge for Trina derives not from the resemblance between the sack of money and the scrotal sac but from the fact that the money, like submission, is loved for its own sake. We have no reason, after all, to believe that Trina finds any of the "qualities" that usually "inspire affection" exciting, including the male genitalia. The bag can only become exciting because it contains money that

[8]Donald Pizer, *The Novels of Frank Norris* (Bloomington, Ind., 1966), 69–70.

hasn't been, and won't be, spent, and the genitalia themselves can only become exciting insofar as they become symbolic, of saving for the sake of saving or submitting for the sake of submitting. The miser and the masochist both take their pleasure in mistaking means for ends.

How does this mistake get made? According to the associationist psychology of the mid-nineteenth century, misers came to love money for its own sake through frequent experience of the pleasure induced by the things money bought. Eventually, Herbert Spencer wrote, "the act of appropriating comes to be one constantly involving agreeable associations, and one which is therefore pleasurable, irrespective of the end subserved."[9] A similar explanation of masochism was available to Krafft-Ebing, several of whose cases reported experiencing their first sexual excitement when spanked or whipped as children. Since, Krafft-Ebing wrote, "passive flagellation . . . has a tendency to induce erection reflexly by irritation of the nerves of the buttocks" (141), it might plausibly be argued that masochism was learned through the early association of reflex pleasure with the humiliation of punishment. In theory, then, the miser and the masochist might both be thought to have *acquired* their perversions—one by the constant but accidental association of pleasure with money, the other by the rarer but equally accidental association of pleasure with punishment.

In practice, however, sexual perversion is almost never learned, Krafft-Ebing thought. The "majority" of masochists never undergo flagellation at all; their "perverse impulse [is] directed to purely symbolic acts expressing subjection" (209). Hence, no experience of any kind can be a factor in producing "genuine, complete, deep-rooted masochism," which, "with its feverish longing for subjection from the time of earliest youth, is congenital" (207). By the same token, Spencer's explanation of the desire to own as a kind of mnemonic for the pleasures produced by the things owned had begun to give way to William James's account of the desire "to appropriate" as a

---

[9]Quoted in William James, *The Principles of Psychology* (1890; reprint, Cambridge, Mass., 1983), 1271.

"blind primitive instinct." As such, it was inexplicable in instrumental terms. People commonly talk about the "purpose[s]" that instincts may be supposed to "subserve," James wrote in *The Principles of Psychology*; in fact, these supposed purposes are irrelevant. An instinctive act "is done for its own sake exclusively": "Why do men always lie down, when they can, on soft beds rather than on hard floors? . . . Why do they sit round the stove on a cold day? . . . Why does the maiden interest the youth so that everything about her seems more important and significant than anything else in the world? Nothing more can be said than that these are human ways, and that every creature *likes* its own ways."[10]

From James's perspective, then, the autotelic logic—loving money for its own sake—that seems to make the miser's instincts perverse is, instead, just what makes them instinctive. And the inexplicability of masochistic behavior—loving submission for its own sake—becomes a token for the ultimate inexplicability of normal behavior. With "her passion for her money and her perverted love for her husband when he was brutal," Norris writes, Trina McTeague was a "strange woman" (179). He might just as well have said that Trina, like every creature, liked her own ways; for the logic that makes Trina strange is precisely the logic of liking one's ways, and the logic that makes her like her ways is, of course, the logic that makes her like everyone else—normal.

But even if there is a sense in which Trina's masochism and her hoarding are nothing more than her ways and so unremarkable examples of the workings of instinct, hoarding and masochism nonetheless have, in Norris's representation of them, an interesting and slightly complicated relation to one another. The complication is this—they seem to be contradictory. Trina's passion for McTeague consists, as we have already seen, in her deep conviction, that *"she was his"* (104). But her passion for her money involves the equally deep conviction that, whatever might happen, the money is *hers*. Thus, forced to give up dentistry, McTeague takes temporary consolation in the notion that

[10] James, *Principles of Psychology*, 1007.

Trina's $5,000 will give them enough to live decently until they can get a "fresh start," but he is soon disabused. When Trina objects to his claim that "*we've* got the money," McTeague responds, " 'Well, it's all in the family. What's yours is mine, and what's mine is yours, ain't it?' " " 'No, it's not; no, it's not; no, it's not,' " Trina cries, " 'It's all mine, mine. There's not a penny of it belongs to anyone else' " (153). The contradiction, then, is that Trina belongs to McTeague but her money doesn't. And this contradiction is by no means incidental to the story of *McTeague*; rather, it is the necessary condition of that story. The plot's two main events are Trina's marrying Mac and then being murdered by him; if she had just loved money she would never have married him, and if she had just loved pain she would have given him the money and so never been murdered by him. The "brusque access of passion" that seizes Trina in the presence of "McTeague's enormous body" (143) thus shadows and is shadowed by the "brusque access of cupidity" (200) that comes upon her at the thought of her money and at the touch of the "smooth flat pieces" of gold against her body. The simultaneous desires to own and to be owned constitute the emotional paradox Norris sets himself to elaborate in *McTeague*.

This paradox, the opposition between owning and being owned, is vividly dramatized in the perverse reading of *Uncle Tom's Cabin* with which this essay began. Case 57 finds pleasure in scenes meant to dramatize the horrors of slavery, finds pleasure, that is, in being owned where Stowe meant only to represent the pleasure of *owning*. The "sudden light of joy" that shines in Tom's face when Augustine St. Clare declares his intention to set him free testifies to this pleasure, and the ensuing conversation between them makes the connection between freedom and ownership explicit. St. Clare wonders a little at Tom's eagerness to leave, asking him if he hasn't been "better off" a slave than he would have been "free." " 'Why, Tom,' " he points out, " 'you couldn't possibly have earned, by your work, such clothes and such living as I have given you.' " Tom acknowledges the force of this classic apology for slavery but insists, in response, on the purer pleasures of ownership:

" 'Knows all that, Mas'r St. Clare; Mas'r's been too good; but, Mas'r, I'd rather have poor clothes, poor house, poor everything, and have 'em *mine*, than have the best, and have 'em any man's else,—I had *so*, Mas'r: I think it's natur Mas'r.' "[11] The desire to own—one's clothes, one's labor, one's self, one's everything—this constitutes the natural desire for freedom; the masochist, wanting not to own but to *be* owned, sets himself against nature.

But if the masochist's desire to be owned is perverse, it is nevertheless a perversion made possible only by the bourgeois identification of the self as property. Without that, no truly modern slavery is possible, since only if you identify freedom with self-ownership can being owned by someone else seem an intrinsic abridgment of that freedom. Hence, an increased investment in the values of autonomy will naturally be accompanied by an increased insecurity about the status of that autonomy; a self that can be owned can also be sold or stolen or gambled away. In "Romance and Real Estate," I argued that texts like *Uncle Tom's Cabin* and Hawthorne's *The House of the Seven Gables* exemplify this insecurity by imagining barriers between what they value (the owning self) and what they fear (the owned self) while at the same time enacting the collapse of those barriers. The masochistic reading of *Uncle Tom's Cabin* provides in itself a reminder of the inevitable intimacy between these two modes of selfhood, but the founding text of masochism, Sacher-Masoch's *Venus in Furs* (1870) marks even more clearly the erotic potential of the self in a market economy.

"The ancient world's freedom of pleasure," observes Wanda, the cruel mistress of *Venus in Furs*, "would have been unthinkable without slavery,"[12] and she grows "melancholy" contemplating the apparent impossibility of ever really making Severin, Sacher-Masoch's hero, her slave. Even more eager to be enslaved than Wanda is to enslave him, Severin immediately

---

[11] Harriet Beecher Stowe, *Uncle Tom's Cabin* (Columbus, Ohio, 1969), 126.
[12] Leopold von Sacher-Masoch, *Venus im Pelz* (Leipzig, n.d.), 82. This and the following translations are by Frances Ferguson and me.

proposes that they travel to Turkey where slavery is still legal, but Wanda soon has a better idea. After all, anyone can have a slave in Constantinople, she says; she wants her slave here, in the "civilized, reasonable and philistine" world of Europe. And she proposes to Severin that they draw up a contract, making him "completely her property," giving her the right to "mistreat" him and even kill him if she pleases, and requiring her, in consideration, to "appear as often as possible in furs, particularly when she is being cruel to her slave."[13]

The erotic advantages of such a contract are considerable. For one thing, it is, with its narrative of promised duties and punishments, itself something of a pornographic text. Indeed, Sacher-Masoch was so enamored of the genre that, in addition to the contract in *Venus in Furs*, he drafted two real-life contracts,[14] one committing him to six months of servitude with Fanny von Pistor and one for life with Aurore Rumelin, who called herself Wanda and whom he married in 1873. But more important than the contract's pornographic possibilities is its recasting of slavery and of the "ancient world's freedom of pleasure."

Slavery in the West had ended, at least nominally, with the American Civil War, but Progressives like Richard T. Ely worried that it had really only changed its form and was now reappearing in the guise of the "peonage contract" employed in the South and increasingly in the world at large. In his massive *Property and Contract in Their Relations to the Distribution of Wealth*, Ely offers the example of a contract that came before a South Carolina judge in 1901 in which, having acknowledged the "right" of his employer "to use such force as . . . he may

---

[13] Ibid., 122.

[14] These contracts are reprinted in Gilles Deleuze, *Présentation de Sacher-Masoch* (Paris, 1967). Deleuze brilliantly insists "qu'il n'y a pas de masochisme sans contrat" (67) but then, bypassing the relation between contracts and markets, identifies contract with the "law" and thus reads the masochistic contract as a parodic attack upon the law and hence upon contract itself, "une sorte de dénonciation du contrat par excès de zèle" (80). This seems to me a misreading both of *Venus in Furs* and, more important for my argument, of the nature of contract in the second half of the nineteenth century.

deem necessary to compel me to . . . perform good and necessary services," the contracting laborer goes on to specify that his employer "shall have the right to lock me up for safekeeping, work me under the rules and regulations of his farm, and if I should leave his farm or run away he shall have the right to offer and pay a reward of not exceeding $25 for my capture and return together with the expenses of same, which amount so advanced, together with any other indebtedness, I may owe . . . I agree to work out under all rules and regulations of this contract."[15] The only thing missing is the right to murder the laborer, but, as Ely points out, "in some cases they have been shot for attempting to escape." Citing the one-sided contracts laborers sign in Angola, Ely quotes Henry Nevinson's *Modern Slavery*: "In what sense does such a man enter into a free contract for his labour? In what sense, except according to law, does his position differ from a slave? . . . The difference between the 'contract labour' of Angola and the old-fashioned slavery of our grandfather's time is only a difference of legal terms. In life there is no difference at all" (583). Such contracts epitomized to Progressives like Ely the unfortunate tendency of contract "to preserve advantages once secured," "to keep the existing condition of things" (579). Thus the elimination of "old-fashioned" slavery in the West had not really brought an end to slavery after all. And Wanda is right to think that she needn't go to Constantinople to obtain the freedom of pleasure that slavery makes possible; the contract makes pleasure possible even in "philistine" Europe.

But at the same time, it is impossible to understand the masochistic contract as a straightforward transformation of "old-fashioned" or "feudal" slavery. Apologists for American slavery had praised its familial and paternalist character, contrasting the security of a society modeled on the natural order of the family to the insecurity of an industrial society indifferent to natural modes of organization, and preferring the sentimen-

[15] Richard T. Ely, *Property and Contract in Their Relations to the Distribution of Wealth* (New York, 1914), 716–17. Subsequent page references are cited in parentheses in the text.

tal relations of the South to the market relations of the North. Sacher-Masoch, however, repudiates these feudal attractions. The offer of contract made him by Wanda stipulates that he be "neither a son, nor a brother, nor a friend" to her,[16] and the contract with Fanny von Pistor explicitly deprives him of any "pretention to her love, or right to be her lover."[17] If slavery in the "ancient world" invoked, however disingenuously, the ties of family and affection, modern slavery, as depicted in the masochistic contract, prohibits any noncontractual relation between owner and owned and seems to derive part of its erotic power from the very absence of any such relation.

Furthermore, at the same time that the contract proclaims its hostility to traditional social forms, it declares its indifference to the values that accompany those forms. For a long time, Ely notes, there was no idea of contract, no idea, that is, of "binding agreements to be enforced by public authority"; "our English ancestors had no notion of the state's duty to enforce private agreements" (557). Sometimes the Church might exert a certain moral pressure on the parties to an agreement, but not until the eighteenth century did the "secular courts" begin to play a role. And even then, "the theory under which a creditor could collect debts due him was . . . that he was getting back his due and it was not looked upon as the result of contract" (559); parties to an agreement might thus be held accountable, but the source of this accountability was a certain religious morality or a social sense of what was fair. In the modern understanding of contract, however, the source of accountability is the contract itself, and what Ely calls the "police power" of the state serves only to guarantee the contract, not to enforce some external morality. The state appears here in collaboration with the individual, recognizing and enforcing the desires of its subjects, holding them accountable neither to religious nor to civic morality but only to the wants they have themselves expressed.

The character of these wants and their value relative to one

[16] Cited in Deleuze, *Sacher-Masoch*, 256.
[17] Ibid., 255.

another are thus imagined as a purely private matter. Ely points out that, although in contract "there must be some consideration," there is "no inquiry into the adequacy of the consideration. . . . We can have a consideration which is merely nominal" (573). A radical inequality of exchange—Severin's "body" and "soul," say, for Wanda's appearance in furs—will thus be permitted and enforced by contract with no attention to the moral or social equity of the exchange. Or perhaps one should say, with no attention to the equity of the exchange as perceived by anyone other than the contracting parties—for the institution of the contract assumes that any voluntary exchange is equitable, that the match between what the contracting parties want supersedes any external judgment about the relative worth of what they exchange. In this respect, the contract may be said to legitimate every desire, if only by enacting a legal form in which to imagine its satisfaction. And, in the same gesture, the contract provides a mechanism for determining the value of those goods or services offered in exchange. How else, in what Ely calls "the struggle between buyers and sellers," could Wanda's occasional appearance in furs be thought a suitable compensation for Severin's enslavement? It is suitable because it is what he wants, and so, although even the contract laborer in South Carolina is, in some sense, better paid than Severin, Severin, whose very subjectivity bears the inscription of the free market, has struck a better bargain.

For what does the contract laborer want, and what must he give up to get it? According to Ely, the laborer is unlike the "seller of goods" insofar as in the "labour contract he binds himself and must render his service with his person" (713). He thus gives himself over to his employer for eight, ten, or twelve hours a day, performing the required service and receiving in payment the wherewithal to sustain himself on his own for the remaining hours of the day. He gives up his labor, and hence something of his "person," in order to retain something of his "person." The masochist, by contrast, is on the job twenty-four hours a day, receiving in payment only an occasional beating or a glimpse of Wanda in furs. But it would be wrong to think of this as an unequal exchange of services; in fact, it would be wrong to think of it as primarily an exchange of services at all.

Severin values Wanda's appearing in furs not as payment for his enslavement but as the mark of that enslavement. He offers her the opportunity to have a slave; she repays him with the opportunity to be a slave: his work is, literally, its own reward— not merely labor but the very commodity labor is designed to buy. Where the contract laborer enslaves himself, as it were, temporarily, in order to buy a little freedom, the masochist enslaves himself permanently and buys his own enslavement.

To put this more strictly in Ely's terms, we might say that the contract laborer sells his labor and only incidentally his person, whereas the masochist sells his person and only incidentally his labor. The masochistic contract thus bespeaks the indifference of both parties to the conveniences or inconveniences of ownership, to the services a slave's labor might provide or the attentions that might be provided him. The masochist is, in this sense, more truly a slave than the wage slave of South Carolina. But, imagining the slave as a buyer and seller, the contract at the same time defeudalizes slavery, replacing a social fact that exists independent of the desires of master or slave with a market agreement that insists on and enacts the priority of those desires. Stowe's and Hawthorne's fear of slavery as a modern invention rather than a feudal relic is thus ecstatically borne out in the masochistic contract, where all things are made alienable and the thrill is in the act of alienation itself. Here the ancient world's freedom of pleasure made possible only by slavery has been transmogrified into a pleasure available to no one in that ancient world, the pleasure of buying and selling in a free market.

Hence, the "new feudalism" that Progressives like Ely feared and that Wanda briefly flirts with when she contemplates taking Severin off to Constantinople can never quite come into being, not because conditions as bad as and even worse than those obtaining under "old-fashioned" slavery cease to exist but because the intervention of the market, even when it leaves these conditions intact, alters their meaning. In other words, the apologists for "modern slavery" defended it not by appealing to the usual paternalist ideals but by appealing to freedom, in particular freedom of contract.

"The Supreme Court of Illinois has declared unconstitutional the factory and sweat shop act limiting the working day for women to eight hours," wrote Ely's Wisconsin colleague John Commons in 1895. "The grounds . . . seem to be that the Constitution guarantees freedom of contract . . . that women are receiving higher legal rights in other directions; and to deprive them of the right to freely sell their labor power under any conditions whatever is to remand them back again to a lower legal position" (652). Would the court "permit the sweaters' victims to sell themselves by contract into absolute slavery"? Commons knew, of course, that it wouldn't, but the question has, nevertheless, its force. At what point and by what theory would the court deem itself justified in interfering in what Supreme Court Justice Peckham had, in the famous "Bakers' Case" in 1905, characterized as "the general right of an individual to be free in his person and in his power to contract in relation to his own labor" (664)?

There are in Ely's text two strains of argument against unlimited freedom of contract, not very clearly distinguished from one another but nonetheless different in some important respects. One involves an appeal to the authority of the state on behalf of the "natural rights" of the individual. Ely cites the case of *American Base Ball and Athletic Exhibition Co. v. Harper* (1902), in which a St. Louis court ruled that the "natural rights of free men" to what Ely characterizes as "life, liberty, and the enjoyment of the gains of their own industry" are "rights which cannot be bartered away by either contract or consent" (743). The strength of this argument lies in its appeal to the widely honored notion of natural rights; but that, obviously, is its weakness too, for, conservatives could (and did) argue, the right to contract is itself a natural one, an aspect of the right to liberty, and it is absurd to invoke the natural right to liberty against it. But if it makes no sense to invoke the police power of the state against freedom on behalf of freedom, it does make sense to invoke that power against freedom on behalf of something else. And this is, in fact, Ely's major argument—that freedom is not the ultimate goal, that "liberty can be allowed only as it is not an impediment to social good" (750).

In this context Ely quotes Mazzini on the dangers of conceiving freedom as valuable in itself: "If you enthrone it alone, as at once means and end, it will lead society first to anarchy, afterward to the despotism which you fear" (613). "The French Revolution," Ely adds, "affords a good illustration of this,—of putting up freedom as an end itself. . . . In that case, we did have first a condition of anarchy and then of despotism." The autotelic logic that marked the perversity of the masochist for Krafft-Ebing and the perversity of the miser for Norris thus marks for Ely the perversion of political economy. From his perspective, the sweatshop workers are like Krafft-Ebing's women in bondage, putting up with freedom as their sisters put up with tyranny, not for the "charm" of the freedom itself but for the "independent purposes" they hope that freedom will serve—food and shelter. Only from the perverse perspective of the masochist or the Illinois Supreme Court will these women be imagined to love freedom itself.

Speaking in the tones of Krafft-Ebing, Ely thus insists that "freedom of contract is only valuable as a means to an end" (613); mistaking that means for an end will produce only the despotic libertinism of the owner or the servile libertinism of the owned. But the point here is not simply that, by means of a certain logic, the love of freedom may come to seem as perverse as the love of tyranny; it is instead that from the standpoint of the market, from the standpoint, that is, of the phenomenology of contract, the love of freedom and the love of tyranny are the same thing. Ely himself exemplifies this point, even though he nowhere means to assert it and even though his account of the need to protect the weak from the strong everywhere denies it. "The strong," he writes, "want unregulated contract" and so reject all regulations as infringements upon their freedom. But theirs is a primitive, merely "negative idea of freedom." They don't understand that

> freedom is something positive, and is a social product, a social acquisition. . . . The freedom of savagery is not true freedom. It gives not strength but weakness. The powers of the noblest savage are not equal to those of the humblest citizen of a law-abiding state. We have in this freedom of savagery a slavery to nature,

which can only be removed by submission to social restraint through which true freedom is acquired. (612–13)

The strategy of this passage is to make freedom "true" by making it in itself unlovable. Ely here follows T. H. Green, who characterizes freedom as "a positive power or capacity of doing or enjoying something worth doing or enjoying . . . in common with others" (612). Freedom is thus made instrumental, and restraints upon it are justified in the name of the "social good." These restraints, in the form of "regulation of contract," enable those whom Ely calls the "reform forces" to protect the weak against the strong, who, loving liberty for itself, "want unregulated contract." The sweaters must be prevented from enslaving their workers; regulation protects the freedom of the "humblest citizen."

But in justifying the restraints that will keep the strong from enslaving the weak, Ely has also suggested that the strong, insisting on their natural right to unregulated freedom of contract, are already slaves themselves. Transforming "freedom of contract" into "freedom of savagery" and "natural right" into "slavery to nature," Ely imagines the strong as already enslaved. In this, he extends—by inverting—the argument the Illinois court used to strike down the sweatshop laws. The court had outrageously interpreted regulation in that case not as an effort to protect the weak against the strong but as an attempt to limit the rights of the weak. Now, imagining the strong as slaves to their own conception of natural right, Ely invokes the restraints of "true freedom" in an unwitting but inevitable attempt to protect the strong against themselves. What the Illinois court had refused to do for the sweatshop workers, Ely rushes to do for the sweatshop owners—they all need to be protected against their perverse love of freedom.

What makes that love perverse is that it's indistinguishable from the masochistic love of slavery. Loving freedom of contract for its own sake, Ely thinks, you will end by destroying what you love and will find yourself enslaved. But the masochist cannot love a freedom that does not lead to slavery; indeed, what the masochist loves is only the freedom to be a slave, a freedom, in other words, that is confirmed, not betrayed, by enslavement. To put this another way, the masochist loves what the capitalist loves: the freedom to buy and sell, the inalienable right to alienate.

In this respect, the masochist embodies the purest of commitments to laissez-faire while at the same time somewhat altering our usual sense of what those commitments were. "The strong want unregulated contract" (590), Ely writes; the "economic conservatives" want their freedom. They want it, he tries to think, because they know that without regulation there will be no limit to their accumulation of property; eventually, they will own everything and everyone. But what the masochist understands (and what Ely's own text begins to show) is that the desire to own cannot be separated from the desire to be owned. The masochist wants to be owned—which is to say really that he wants to be sold, to sell himself, to own the right to sell himself. The masochist wants, in other words, to own. If, according to Ely, "voluntary contract must . . . sometimes be forbidden in order to avoid slavery" (582), then according to the masochist, slavery must be allowed in order to guarantee freedom. The right of the individual to own himself must not be infringed, and so the right of the individual to sell himself and to be owned by someone else must not be denied. Insisting on these rights—loving property, loving freedom—the capitalist and the masochist are one and the same.

At the end of *Venus in Furs*, having returned to his father's estate and, on his father's death, taken his place as proprietor of that estate, Severin receives a letter from Wanda. She describes her life during the three years since she abandoned him in Florence, and more important, explains her reasons for leaving. From the moment he wanted to be her slave, she writes, she knew he could never be her husband. She had agreed to act out his "ideal" partly to amuse herself and partly in the hope that her cruelty might "cure" him—as indeed, Severin notes, it has. When Wanda ran off with her Greek, the "strong man" she "needed," Severin himself began to turn into a version of that strong man. With women, he says, you can be either a "slave" or a "tyrant"; now he beats his serving girls (they love it), and when asked for the "moral" of his story, he replies, in the accents of a certain social Darwinism, "anyone who lets himself be whipped, deserves to be whipped."[18]

This ending enacts a double effort of normalization. Most obviously, the sexes are returned to their appropriate roles: Wanda finds a real man and Severin becomes one. More important, however, than the reordering of the sexes is the simple fact of reordering itself. With women, you can be only a tyrant or a slave; this makes it seem as if Severin, having made the wrong choice before, now makes the right one. But the either/or logic of this choice means more than the particular role you might choose. It definitively separates the tyrant from the slave, the strong from the weak, and it leaves the individual free to find his place according to his preference, ability, or nature. "Anyone who lets himself be whipped, deserves to be whipped." *Venus in Furs* ends with a gesture toward the free market as meritocracy and with a vision of the masochistic contract as an instrument of social and natural selection.

But the text itself, the actual masochistic contract, does not allow such a separation and does not authorize the appeal to a natural law, a set of natural distinctions between strong and weak, owner and owned. Indeed, the whole point of contract, as I have described it, is to exhibit these distinctions as aspects of identity rather than identity itself. In contract no one is simply a tyrant or a slave; everyone is a buyer *and* a seller. This is why the contract, in making slavery modern, makes it, in a certain sense, no longer slavery at all, or at least no longer the feudalism that writers like Stowe and Ely imagined they feared. What Ely really feared was contract, and what he really wanted was the feudalism he thought he feared, a feudalism in which the restraints on alienation that once derived from "custom" would derive instead from the state. Ultimately, then, for Ely and Severin both, the strong are the strong and the weak are the weak; the difference is just that Ely wants to regulate the tyrant whereas Severin wants to be one.

Curiously enough, the text that comes closest to maintain-

[18]Sacher-Masoch, *Venus im Pelz*, 203, 204.

ing the conditions of contract and to eschewing the climb to what Ely called "something higher" is the text that never mentions contract, Norris's *McTeague*. For if the plot of *Venus in Furs* works toward rereading the masochistic contract as an agreement between two entirely separate parties, two opposing sets of desires, the plot of *McTeague* sacrifices everything to the intimacy of slavery and freedom. In particular, it sacrifices Trina herself who, oddly living up to the conditions of Severin's contract with Wanda, dies for the rights of property.[19] McTeague's final words to Trina are "For the last time, will you give me that money?" And her final words to him are "No, no" (210). By this refusal she insists on her absolute right to own and simultaneously provokes McTeague into producing the sign of her absolute right to be owned. In Trina's death the contradiction between owning and being owned is resolved; the capitalist's freedom of contract and the masochist's freedom of pleasure are finally made indistinguishable.

Conceiving the self as property and freedom as a man's "right" to "a character of his own," Harriet Beecher Stowe saw in slavery an expropriation of that right, a betrayal of ownership unhappily made possible by the very idea of owning. Sacher-Masoch's contract, however, represents a less discriminating enthusiasm for the institutions of property. In its pornographic rehearsal of the mutual rights and obligations of owner and owned, the contract dissolves opposition into complementarity, a dissolution that Trina McTeague, even less fastidious than Sacher-Masoch, takes as far as it can go. Where Stowe is torn between the desire to own and the fear of being owned, Trina experiences no such conflict—owning and being owned seem to her equally desirable. And where Sacher-Masoch ultimately reconciles the simultaneous desires to own and be owned by distributing them in different people, Trina's "economical little body" contains them both. Once the self is imagined as its own

[19]The relevant clause reads: "She even has the right to kill him if she pleases; in short, he belongs entirely to her" (122). And Krafft-Ebing declares that "in its extreme consequences, masochism must lead to the desire to be killed" (158).

proprietor, after all, it must also be imagined as its own property. It may finally be that the best way to understand Trina's husband is as an allegory of the self when it is owning, and that the best way to understand her gold is as an allegory of the self when it is being owned. Thus, for all her perversity and unnaturalness, Trina embodies in an extraordinarily literal way the normal workings of the self in contract; her perversions are, in fact, characteristic functions in the instinctual life of property.[20] Owning and owned, fondling her money and yielding her fingers to the dentist's bite, Trina welcomes all the possibilities of the market economy.

[20] It should nonetheless be noted that the market's freedom of pleasure was at the turn of the century already on its way to becoming an anachronism. If the history of freedom in the West had, as Sir Henry Maine put it, moved "from status to contract," Ely's version of a statist, modernized feudalism was only one of many texts and practices beginning to establish the logic by which freedom of contract would indeed come to seem perverse. Hence, insofar as the "invention" of masochism can be seen as an extension into sexuality of the law of contract, its status as a perversion can be seen as a reminder that the law of contract was already being displaced; the point is not that freedom extended becomes perverse but that the love of freedom in itself was coming to seem a perversion. Perhaps Trina should be understood as a harbinger of twentieth-century sexual freedom, at least to the extent that the eroticization of freedom should itself be understood as a nostalgic phenomenon, a dabbling in laissez-faire sexuality made available by the passing of laissez-faire economy. Although to put the point in this way is to do Trina an injustice—Trina is no dabbler.

5. THE GOLD STANDARD AND THE LOGIC OF NATURALISM

*D*emocracy is threatened not only by armies but by debt and austerity. We must liberalize the trade of the world and give the world again a money it can rely on, a dollar "as good as gold."

Rep. Jack Kemp (New York), in a speech before the Republican National Convention, 1984

*W*hy does the miser save? Trina McTeague, writes Frank Norris, saved "without knowing why"—"without any thought, without idea of consequence—saving for the sake of saving."[1] But to say that Trina saved for the sake of saving doesn't so much explain her behavior as identify the behavior in need of explanation: why would anyone save just for the sake of saving? Psychology in the late nineteenth century had begun to question whether anyone actually did. The "common lot of misers," according to William James, "value their gold, not for its own sake, but for its powers. Demonetize it, and see how quickly they will get rid of it."[2] In fact, as the economist Otto-mar Haupt wrote in January 1897, "a certain tendency of hoarding had been developing" in the United States, "brought about by the fear of free coinage of silver, and coupled with the hope that later on a substantial premium might be obtained for gold."[3] These hoarders were clearly not saving for the sake of saving, and after Bryan's defeat in 1896, when, as Haupt puts it, "the cause for the alarm had been removed, everybody was glad to get rid of his gold coin."[4] Trina, however, is never glad to get rid of her gold. She does, on one occasion, speak of herself as saving up "some money against a rainy day" (187), but it is perfectly clear that not even the election of William Jennings Bryan could make the day rainy enough for her to start thinking of her hoard as an investment or a speculation, much less provide an occasion for her to spend it. Why, then, does Trina save?

The power that James thinks misers love is, of course, the power to buy, and in arguing against the associationist notion that misers had developed an attachment to "gold in se," he

[1]Frank Norris, *McTeague*, ed. Donald Pizer (New York, 1977), 72. Subsequent page references are cited in parentheses in the text.

[2]William James, *The Principles of Psychology* (1890; reprint, Cambridge, Mass., 1983), 1041. Subsequent page references are cited in parentheses in the text.

[3]Ottomar Haupt, "Is Gold Scarce?" in *The Gold Standard: A Selection from the Papers Issued by the Gold Standard Defense Association in 1895–1898* (London, 1898), 56.

[4]Ibid.

was insisting that the miser's real interest was in money. But this, if true, only underlines the puzzle of the miser's behavior, since if he just loved saving gold we could think of him as a collector who loved gold the way some people love stamps, whereas what he seems to love instead is the power to buy, although at the same time he refuses ever to exercise that power. In extreme cases, James thought, this could only be described as "insanity." The "common" miser, however, the "excessively niggardly man," "simply exhibits the psychological law that the potential has often a far greater influence over our mind than the actual. A man will not marry now, because to do so puts an end to his indefinite potentialities of choice of a partner. He prefers the latter" (1041). And this analysis was extended by Georg Simmel, who, in *The Philosophy of Money* (1900), denies that the miser has any interest at all in the "possible uses of money." Rather, the miser experiences "the power that money-stored-up represents . . . as the final and absolutely satisfying value."[5] This power would be "lost" if "it were to be transposed into the enjoyment of specific things." "Old people," Simmel remarks, become avaricious because, "subjectively," "the sensual enjoyment of life has lost its charm" and the "ideals" have lost their "agitating power." With nothing to buy and nothing to look forward to buying, they take pleasure in the "abstract power" of money itself, the "absolute means" of buying.

As a description of Trina, however, this clearly won't do— not only because Trina isn't old and because her life notoriously retains a good deal of its "sensual charm," but also because Trina's miserliness, as Norris describes it, doesn't exactly consist in a refusal to spend. It is true, of course, that she won't buy clothes, and that she spends as little as possible on rent, and that she "grudged even the food that she and McTeague ate," preferring to steal scraps from a "coffee-joint" and "enjoying the meal with the greater relish because it cost her nothing" (166–67). But the moment in which Trina's "avarice had grown to be her one dominant passion" (198) is depicted by

[5]Georg Simmel, *The Philosophy of Money*, trans. Tom Bottomore and David Frisby (Boston, 1978), 245.

Norris not as an absolute refusal to spend any money but as an absolute unwillingness to forgo the pleasure of having "her money in hand," even if that means paying for it. Thus she gradually withdraws her capital from Uncle Oelbermann's store, "reducing her monthly income" (200) but obtaining for herself "an ecstasy of delight." Norris here represents her saving as a kind of spending, not only because she pays for her gold with her monthly income but also because, refusing to use her gold to pay for food, she is in essence spending it instead on the gold itself.

Simmel gives an example that shows why this must be so. Noting that the "wampum of the North American Indians consisted of mussel shells, which served as money but could also be worn as a decorative belt," he pointed out that the "role of the shells as jewelry" acquires "an air of distinction by virtue of the fact that it requires abstention from using them directly as money."[6] What he seems to imagine here is something like the associationists' collection of gold. But why should we say that using the shells as jewelry involves abstaining from using them as money? Shouldn't we say instead that the shells as jewelry have been paid for by the shells as money, and that the "air of distinction" Simmel acutely ascribes to the belt derives precisely from the fact that it is at every moment of its existence as a belt being paid for by its existence as money? The only difference between Trina and the Indian is that Trina places no value on her gold as decoration, as what Simmel calls an "object." In this account, the attraction of gold is indeed its power to buy, but the miser exercises this power neither (like the Indian) by buying objects nor (like avaricious old people) by refraining from buying objects, but instead (like Trina) by buying money. According to Norris, then, what Marx called the miser's "asceticism" is in fact a "debauch": her hoard is a perpetual buying machine, and she herself is a spendthrift.

But if the miser is a spendthrift, what is the spendthrift? Why does the spendthrift spend? This question seems at first sight less puzzling than the question about why the miser saves, no doubt because spending money, even foolishly, finds

[6]Ibid., 155.

its place more easily than does saving in what Simmel characterizes as the normal transaction in a money economy—the
movement from "possession of money" to "expenditure of
money upon the object" to "enjoyment through the ownership
of the object."[7] When, for example, Vandover, Norris's spendthrift, begins "flinging away money with both hands," he does
it by chartering "a yacht for a ten-days cruise about the bay,"
buying "a fresh suit of clothes each month," and recklessly giving "suppers" to "actresses."[8] And while it is easy to imagine
circumstances in which such expenditures might be unwise
(Vandover's, for instance), the objects and activities Vandover
buys don't seem in themselves implausible sources of enjoyment. But, according to Simmel, the recklessness of expenditure is not in itself the mark of the spendthrift: "The pleasure
associated with squandering is attached to the moment of
spending money upon any object whatsoever, and has to be
distinguished from the pleasure provided by the fleeting enjoyment of objects; . . . rather it relates to the pure function of
squandering without regard to its substantial content and at-
tendant circumstances."[9] The spendthrift buys objects, then,
not because he likes the objects but because he likes buying;
he likes, Simmel says, "the moment of transposition of money
into other forms of value."[10]

Put with Simmel's clarity, this is not a difficult point to
grasp, but the difficulty of distinguishing in practice between
spending for objects and spending, as we might put it, for the
sake of spending may be considerable. Since even spending
for the sake of spending involves buying something, how can
we know that the spendthrift's "nonsensical purchases" don't

[7] Ibid., 248.

[8] Frank Norris, *Vandover and the Brute*, with an introduction by Warren
French (1914; reprint, Lincoln, Neb., 1978), 290. Subsequent page references
are cited in parentheses in the text. Although *Vandover* was not published until
after Norris's death, James D. Hart argues convincingly that it was "pretty well
finished" in 1895, the year that also saw most of *McTeague* completed (Frank
Norris, *A Novelist in the Making*, ed. James D. Hart [Cambridge, Mass., 1970],
27).

[9] Simmel, *Philosophy of Money*, 248.

[10] Ibid.

appear to him as plausible objects of desire, worth buying for the pleasure they will bring? When Norris describes Vandover's pleasure in spending as a "hysterical delight," he certainly alerts us to its unusual character, but his narration of Vandover's "degeneration" betrays a certain confusion about what kind of spending really is degenerate. Having made $15,000 from the sale of his "old home," Vandover "gambled or flung" the money "away in a little less than a year": "He never invested it, but ate into it day after day, sometimes to pay his gambling debts, sometimes to indulge an absurd and extravagant whim, sometimes to pay his bill at the Lick House, and sometimes for no reason at all, moved simply by a reckless desire for spending" (290). The difficulty here is that some of these expenditures seem perfectly reasonable (he has to pay his hotel bill), some of them seem at least imaginably reasonable (the gambling debts), and some of them seem to go beyond even "nonsensical purchases" ("for no reason at all"). Only the "absurd and extravagant whim" presents a clear-cut case of spending for the sake of spending, no doubt because, although these whims clearly involve buying something, by not telling us what Vandover buys Norris focuses all our attention on the act of buying itself.

But taxonomizing Vandover's expenses in this way may do more than simply indicate Norris's confusion; it may lead to a different way of understanding the spendthrift's efforts. Paying his hotel bill, Vandover buys an "object," or, at least, the use of one. Paying his gambling debts, Vandover buys "excitement": "It was not with any hope of winning that he gambled . . . it was only the love of the excitement of the moment" (289). But the excitement of Vandover's gambling is not just any kind of excitement. It is not, for instance, the excitement of the football game that he passes up for another game of cards. It is not even the excitement of perhaps winning a great deal of money—the "desire of money was never strong" in Vandover. It is instead the excitement of losing money. What you buy when you pay your gambling debts, Norris seems to suggest, is the excitement of paying your gambling debts, a purchase that seems nonsensical only because it doesn't seem like a purchase at all. The excitement bought by the ordinary gambler is nonsensical because, although he hopes to win, he knows he is likely to lose. He pays for the excitement of seeing what will happen to his money. But Vandover doesn't so much pay for excitement; rather he is excited by paying. Spending his money on spending his money, he comes as close as Norris can get to spending his money "for no reason at all," to the pleasure not exactly of buying but rather of spending without buying.

Simmel's spendthrift loves buying; he loves the "transposition of money into other forms of value." But Norris's spendthrift loves buying *nothing*; into what then is his money transposed? From the standpoint, at least, of the spendthrift himself, into nothing—his money simply disappears. And this indeed seems to be Norris's point. It is as if, from the spendthrift's point of view, the miser's refusal to spend money represents a failed attempt to withdraw from the money economy, failed because in a money economy, the power of money to buy can never be denied. It will always at least buy itself. Going the miser one better, the spendthrift tries to buy his way out of the money economy. If the miser is always exchanging his money for itself, the spendthrift tries to exchange his for nothing and so, by staging the disappearance of money's purchasing power, to stage the disappearance of money itself. The spendthrift thus embodies a return to what Ignatius Donnelly in *The American People's Money* called "barbarism," the condition of having "no money at all."[11]

For Donnelly, the threat of a society without money seemed a direct consequence of adherence to the gold standard. Having demonetized silver in the "crime of '73" and thus cut the money supply in half, the "Wall Street Misers" now wanted "to drive gold out of circulation" and to bring about a return to the "Dark Ages," which, in Donnelly's view, had originally been caused by the gradual exhaustion of the gold and silver mines of Spain. Without any new sources of money, "the supply diminished; the usurer plied his arts and the capitalist grasped the real estate; all wealth was concentrated in a few hands, just as it is becoming today; and the multitude were re-

[11] Ignatius Donnelly, *The American People's Money* (1895; reprint, Westport, Conn., 1976), 34.

duced to the lowest limit of degradation and wretchedness."[12] Only the free coinage of silver could keep money in circulation and save the American people from a similar fate.

But if the imagination of a society without money held obvious terrors for free-silverites, who feared that the world's supply of gold was disappearing from circulation, it also played a central role in the economic imagination of goldbugs, who were convinced that there was more than enough money to go around. For them, the moneyless society—"but one remove from barbarism," as David Wells put it—was the inevitable starting point for an evolutionary history of finance that culminated in what numerous writers, Wells among them, called the "natural selection" of gold as money.[13] In his own *Robinson Crusoe's Money* (first published in the 1870s as an anti-Greenback tract and reprinted in 1896 as an attack on free silver), Wells imagines Crusoe's wreck as a Donnelly-like return to economic savagery, where nothing has any "purchasing power," but he goes on to narrate the islanders' natural development through barter to the exchange of cowries and finally to the discovery of gold, which, stumbled upon accidentally, soon became "an object of universal desire," "acquired spontaneously a universal purchasing power, and from that moment on, became *Money*" (40). Only when, under the stress of financing their war with the cannibals, the islanders begin to print paper money and then mistake that paper (the "representative of a thing") for gold (the "thing itself") do they run into trouble.

For Wells and the other goldbugs, the moral of such stories was that economic disaster could be brought on not, as Donnelly thought, by the disappearance of gold but rather by any attempt to tamper with its "natural purchasing power." At the same time, however, imagining money as a "thing itself," the

[12]Ibid., 45.

[13]David A. Wells was a civil servant (chairman of the Special Revenue Commission from 1865 to 1870) and journalist who wrote widely on the money question. Readers interested in the oedipal question in American history may wish to consult Wells, *The Silver Question: The Dollar of the Fathers Versus the Dollar of the Sons* (New York, 1877). My own reference here is to *Robinson Crusoe's Money*, with illustrations by Thomas Nast (1896; reprint, New York, 1969), 5. Subsequent page references are cited in parentheses in the text.

sort of thing, for example, that the world might run out of, the gold conservatives and the silver radicals held in common a view of money that was in certain respects more powerful than their differences. As against the Greenbackers or fiat-money men like Tom Nugent, who advocated the use of "inconvertible paper,"[14] gold and silver men both stood for a currency backed by metal. "Nothing," Wells wrote, "can be reliable and good money under all circumstances which does not of itself possess the full amount of the value which it professes on its face to possess" (26). The value of money was thus, in Coin Harvey's word, "intrinsic,"[15] the value of the thing, gold or silver, money was made of.

This conception of money is striking, of course, in that it identifies money as a kind of natural resource, like coal or cows. Thus, by identifying money with its physical form, one can come to think that the supply of money in the world is identical to the supply of gold (and/or silver) in the world. To think (as the fiat-money men did) that "paper money" could supplement or replace precious metals was to succumb to what Wells called a "mere fiction of speech and bad use of language," for paper could only represent money; it could no more be money than "a shadow could be the substance, or the picture of a horse a horse, or the smell of a good dinner the same as the dinner itself" (57). Hence Trina, dissatisfied with the "paper" that "represented five thousand dollars" given her by Uncle Oelbermann, demands what she thinks of as "the money itself" (199). And hence one of the climactic moments of *Coin's*

[14]Thomas L. Nugent, in a speech delivered in the state meeting of the Farmers' Alliance at Campasas, Texas, in August 1895, reprinted in part in *The Populist Mind*, ed. Norman Pollack (New York, 1967), 326. Nugent argues that there must be no silver "compromise" between the populists and the gold men: "Populists favor the free and unlimited coinage of gold and silver at the present rate, and the emission of inconvertible paper to supply any lack of circulation. . . . We cannot compromise on the perilous plan proposed by silver democrats."

[15]William H. Harvey, *Coin's Financial School*, ed. Richard Hofstadter (1895; reprint, Cambridge, Mass., 1963), 164. Coin is actually quoting Webster: "It has been said that silver and gold have no intrinsic value; this is not true. They are the only things used by Webster in the copy of his dictionary which I have to illustrate the meaning of the word 'intrinsic.'"

Financial School (the most popular of the free-silver tracts) takes place when Coin, the "little bimetallist," demonstrates to a shocked audience that all the gold in the world would fit inside the Chicago wheat pit. Richard Hofstadter cites this episode as an example of Harvey's "staggering gift for irrelevancy,"[16] and, in a certain sense, he is obviously right: "No one was disposed to deny that gold was a scarce commodity."[17] But, given just this fact and given also the general identification of money with precious metals, Coin has made a telling point.

If money is a commodity like horses or wheat, then what he and the other bimetallists feared was a scarcity of gold precisely in the same way that people might fear a scarcity of wheat. Thus the radical polemics of the nineties are filled with detailed accounts of exactly how much gold and silver there were in the world, accounts motivated by the fear that if one day there should be no more gold or silver, then on that day there would be no more money. And conservative polemics as late as 1900 are similarly dominated by the distinction between "*Real Money*," which is "always a *commodity* of some kind," and "*Representative Money*," which is "nothing but a *promise*,"[18] distinctions mobilized to warn against the folly of trying to print or coin more money than the world naturally contained.

"In civilized nations," wrote Wells, "natural selection has determined the use of gold as a standard." But this attempt, common to gold and silver men both, to see the precious metals as nature's money embodied a rather complicated sense of the place of a money economy in nature. For in insisting that "good money" must "of itself possess the full amount of the value which it professes on its face to possess" (26), writers like Wells were insisting that the value of money as money be determined by (and indeed identical to) the value of money as the commodity it would be if it weren't money. Gold thus occupies a strange position in the movement from a barter economy, exchanging commodities for each other, to a money economy,

[16] Ibid., 34.
[17] Ibid.
[18] David Jayne Hill, *An Honest Dollar the Basis of Prosperity* (Chicago, 1900), 3.

exchanging commodities for money. As money, of course, it replaces barter, but since its value as money is only a function of its value as a commodity, the exchange of any commodity for gold as money is identical to the exchange of that commodity for gold as a commodity. All money exchanges, in other words, are also simultaneously barter exchanges, and the "intrinsic" value that fits the precious metals to be money guarantees at the same time that nothing ever really need be money. The assertion that money exists in nature is thus identical to the assertion that money doesn't exist at all. Defending gold or silver, the money writers end up articulating an economic theory that, in its most outlandish and fetishized claims on behalf of "real" or "primary" money, actually stages for itself, like Vandover giving in to the brute, the escape from a money economy.

This fantasy, in which the circulation of currency becomes a natural phenomenon and in which money itself is always either threatening or promising to return to nature, would seem to find its most powerful figure in the miser, whose savings deplete the supply of circulating money and whose perfectly fetishized love of money is already a love of the material money is made of, gold. Identifying money with its physical form, the commodity gold, the miser makes the existence of money in one sense precarious and in another sense superfluous—precarious because to take away the commodity is to take away everything, superfluous because to add anything to the commodity is to add nothing. Hence, the threat is that money will disappear and the world will lapse into "barbarism," while the promise is that only a money that might disappear could possess the "natural purchasing power" required by "civilized nations." But we have already seen how Trina's saving fails to deter her money from being money, and, as *McTeague*'s plot develops, she can't even keep her gold out of general circulation. McTeague, with his "old-time miner's idea of wealth easily gained and quickly spent" (75), steals it, causing Trina "unspeakable anguish" as she correctly imagines him "spending her savings by handfuls; squandering her beautiful gold pieces that she had been at such pains to polish with soap and ashes" (198).

It would be a mistake, however, to conclude from Trina's

failure that the miser's theory of money goes unenforced in *McTeague*. Instead, it is McTeague himself, despite his temperamental (and, as a former miner, professional) inclination to circulate gold, who bears the responsibility for staging its disappearance and so confirming its natural value. For one thing, he is a dentist—in the iconography of the 1890s, a kind of anti-miner. "There is good reason to believe," worried a speaker at the Bryan Silver Club of Berkeley, "that the annual additions to our stock of the precious metals have been insufficient to counteract their increased use in the arts. For instance, dentists now use large quantities of gold for filling teeth; considerable amounts are used for signs and like purposes, none of which is recovered."[19] McTeague, with his "tapes" of dentist's gold and especially with his "big gilded tooth" (47), the "immense" "golden molar" he uses as a sign, is a nightmare embodiment of the Bryanites' fears, draining gold out of the economy more quickly than the miners can bring it in. In fact, even when, forced to give up dentistry and in flight from the law, McTeague returns to mining in Placer County, he remains economically an antiminer. Having stolen Trina's entire hoard this time, he carries it up into the mountains—as if the point were not to put the money back into circulation but instead to put it back into the ground. The "miner's idea of money quickly gained and lavishly squandered" (172) is irrelevant here, partly because, although Norris claims it "persisted" in McTeague's mind, he seems, in fact, to have forgotten all about it, and partly because whatever is in his mind doesn't seem to matter much to Norris, who is himself determined to take the gold out of circulation, to put it in people's teeth, or under their beds, or back in the mines, or finally in the middle of Death Valley, where no one will ever be able to get at it.

This notorious ending—McTeague and Marcus Schouler destroying their water, fighting over a treasure that neither of them can live to spend—restages as melodrama the "lesson in political economy" taught by *Robinson Crusoe's Money*, where, wrecked on an island almost as "desolate" as Death Val-

---

[19]General Theo. Wagner, in a speech delivered to the Bryan Silver Club of Berkeley (untitled pamphlet [Berkeley, 1896], 6).

ley, Crusoe begins by noting that all the gold and silver he takes off his ship is not worth as much as a single one of the knives. The point of his story, as Wells characterizes it, is to show how gold can "acquire value" (13), how something "useless" can become "good and true money" (118); but, as we have already seen, this characterization is, in certain crucial respects, misleading. Since the value of gold as money is determined, in Wells's view, by its value as a useful commodity, Crusoe's bags of money never really *acquire* value, they just lie there waiting for the value they already have to be discovered. The real point of *Robinson Crusoe's Money* is to show that nothing ever acquires value, that no money can become good and true unless it already is good and true, and therefore that nature's money, like Robinson Crusoe's, must be made of gold.

What then is the real point of McTeague's dying in the desert with his five thousand gold dollars? In what might be called the Erich von Stroheim interpretation, the point is that greed kills. But it isn't exactly greed that gets McTeague into Death Valley, and besides, Norris is careful to postpone the fight between him and Marcus until after they have lost their water— neither of them is fighting to be rich. Perhaps, instead, reading Death Valley as the last stage in gold's disappearance from circulation, we should understand it as a kind of ironic alternative to the coffers of the Wall Street Misers. On this view, *McTeague* invokes the free-silver specter of a contracting currency, but rather than putting all the money into eastern banks, Norris abandons it on a western desert, thus staging the great fear of the silver men as a fatal triumph for them. Greed doesn't kill; the gold standard does.

But to read *McTeague* as a silver tract would be finally to miss the point of gold and silver's shared fantasy, as "real" or "primary" money. Stressing the importance of this fantasy, I don't mean to slight the difference between the gold and silver interests: socially, politically, even economically, they were substantial. Rather, it is just these differences that make the shared commitment to precious metals so striking. Neither the goldbug fear of inflation nor the free-silver desire for it can quite explain the nearly unanimous hostility to fiat money, since, of course, the essence of legal tender is that its supply can be controlled by the government that issues it to produce either of these effects. Indeed, it is just this fact that excited the most hostility. Nast's famous illustration for *Robinson Crusoe's Money* (Fig. 1),[20] juxtaposing a piece of paper made into milk by an "act of Congress" with a piece of paper made into money in the same way, brilliantly captures Wells's sense that fiat money was nothing but dangerous "hocus pocus" (84). And the government's ability to enforce its hocus pocus is, of course, precisely what starts McTeague on his journey into the desert. The "authorities" at "City Hall" forbid him to practice dentistry because he hasn't got a diploma, a "kind of paper," as Trina describes it to the bewildered dentist, without which "you can't practice, or call yourself doctor." "Ain't I a dentist? Ain't I a doctor?" (147), McTeague protests, appealing finally to the gold tooth she herself gave him as proof of his identity and insisting that he "ain't going to quit for just a piece of paper" (149). But, in the event, McTeague can't practice dentistry, he can't *be* a dentist, unless he has the diploma, the piece of paper on his wall that says, "This is a dentist," like the piece of paper drawn by Nast that says, "This is money." Paper here is more powerful than gold; dentists can only be made by precisely the kind of governmental alchemy that Wells imagined in the making of milk.

It is more accurate, then, to say that McTeague dies *for* the gold standard than *from* it. He and Trina are united in their distaste for "representative" paper. At the same time, however, as Norris's plot works to remove all gold from circulation and so authenticate it as nature's money, his language pulls in the opposite direction. Few critics have failed to bemoan the unrelenting accumulation of gold imagery in *McTeague*: "The gold tooth, the $5,000, Trina's twenty-dollar gold pieces, the imaginary gold plate of Maria Macapa, the absurd canary in the gilt cage. . . . The wonder," wrote Vernon Parrington, "is that he

---

[20] This illustration is also reproduced in Marc Shell, *Money, Language, and Thought* (Berkeley and Los Angeles, 1982), in the context of an interesting and informative discussion of Poe's "The Gold Bug."

MILK-TICKETS FOR BABIES, IN PLACE OF MILK.

Figure 1. Thomas Nast, *Milk Tickets*. From David A. Wells, *Robinson Crusoe's Money* (1896; reprint: New York, 1969).

didn't give Trina gold hair instead of black."[21] In some respects, of course, this proliferation of gold is compensatory. Having lost her money, Trina takes a temporary pleasure in the sunlight that falls "in round golden spots" on the floor of her room, "like gold pieces" (197), she says to herself. Nature, which provided the gold in the first place, now offers to replace it with sunlight. But what exactly is the "like"-ness between "golden spots" of light and gold coins? In affirming this likeness, is Trina (like a prospector) discovering a mine of nature's money? Or is she (like Congress) making money by fiat? Does *McTeague's* language of gold compensate for gold's narrative disappearance, or does it, like bad money driving out good, actually help to produce that disappearance?

Norris's most serious attempt to address, if not precisely to answer, this question involves his depiction not of Trina but of his other miser, the red-headed Polish Jew, Zerkow. Zerkow is a junk dealer, a trade that seems somewhat odd for a miser, since the junk dealer tries to wring every last bit of exchange value out of nearly worthless commodities, whereas the miser seeks to deny the exchange value of the most precious commodity. But Zerkow, it turns out, doesn't really deal junk; he collects it. Described by Norris as "a man who accumulates, but never disburses," he buys junk without ever selling it, and so his "shop" is not a shop at all but rather "the last abiding-place, the almshouse, of such articles as had outlived their usefulness" (25). His real "passion," of course, is for gold, but instead of trying to turn his junk into gold by selling it, he keeps it around him as if it already were gold. Neither a means to an end nor an end itself, Zerkow's junk serves instead as a representation of the end. It represents gold by substituting for it, but in that act of substitution it also suggests something about the nature of gold and of the miser's peculiar passion for it. For, if junk becomes junk by outliving its "usefulness," then in the hands of the miser, gold becomes junk, outliving its value in use by being deprived of its value in exchange. Junk can rep-

[21]Vernon Louis Parrington, *The Beginnings of Critical Realism in America: 1860–1920* (1930; reprint, New York, 1958), 331.

resent gold, in other words, because the miser's passion for gold is itself a passion for junk.

Demonetize gold, James thought, and the miser will lose interest. In one sense, he was obviously wrong. The miser is not, as James imagined everyone was, interested in gold simply as money. Indeed, in one sense, as we have seen, no one was really interested in gold as money; the miser's attempt to escape the money economy was simply emblematic of everyone else's attempt to deny that there was any such thing. Gold as "money itself" was gold as no money at all. But there is an important sense also in which James was right, for the miser isn't exactly indifferent to gold as money either. Trina doesn't just like to collect things; she likes to collect money. And Zerkow likes junk, but only because he sees in it a representation of gold, or rather because in its relation to gold he sees something like the possibility of representation itself. If gold, to be money itself, need never be money at all and so, as I have argued, *can* never be money at all, then what Zerkow likes is a way of seeing gold that, identifying it as junk instead of money, allows it for the first time actually to become money. Here the figure of the miser is turned inside out; instead of marking the continuity between nature and the economy, between a natural money and no money, he marks the sudden emergence both of money out of junk and of a puzzling question: If there is no value in nature, how can there be value at all?

It is just this question that the commitment to precious metals is designed to answer or, better, to forestall—forestall it by insisting that there is value in nature and answer it by suggesting that should the value in nature run out, then there would indeed be no value left anywhere. Thus stories about the origin of money tend to be stories about the remarkable physical properties of gold and about the natural "instinct" that leads men to appreciate them. Henry Poor, for example, begins his *Money and Its Laws* by imagining the discovery of precious metals not only as the discovery of money but as the discovery of exchange itself: "The first lump of gold or silver dug from the earth, as soon as its beauty and uses were displayed, became the object of universal admiration; each beholder sought to become its owner by exchanging therefor such articles of merchandise or property as he possessed, not necessary to his immediate wants. This preference expressed nothing less than an instinct or sentiment common to mankind."[22] Furthermore, as if to emphasize the primitive status of our desire for money, Poor and Wells both insisted on the priority of gold's aesthetic attraction over its metallurgical utility. "Of all objects those are most prized that minister in the highest degree to our sense of beauty,"[23] Poor declares, and Wells describes his islander discovering a metal of "remarkable brightness and color" and bringing it home to his wife, who immediately hangs it "by a string about her neck as an ornament" (38). Grounding the economic in the aesthetic, both writers imagine that our response to money is virtually physiological, on the order of our natural response to beauty. The existence of value in nature is thus nothing more than an instance of the existence of beauty in nature, and our love of gold is as instinctive as our love of a beautiful sunset.

James himself, arguing in the *Principles of Psychology* for the possibility of an instinctive "desire" to "appropriate," insisted on the primacy of the "aesthetic sense." Everyone, he wrote, could feel the attraction of "glittery, hard, metallic, odd pretty things." "The source of their fascination lies in their appeal to our aesthetic sense, and we wish thereupon simply to *own* them" (1271). Despite his earlier skepticism about misers, James asserts here that we can have some desires "quite disconnected with the ulterior uses of the things" desired, and he insists, against Herbert Spencer and the associationists, that these miserly desires are "entirely primitive." Spencer agreed that the "act of appropriating" could be "pleasurable irrespective of the end subserved," but only because the act of acquisition would itself evoke "agreeable associations"[24] with useful objects previously acquired. Thus, saving money could produce a pleasure of its own, but a pleasure that was ultimately compounded out of pleasant associations with all the things

---

[22] Henry V. Poor, *Money and Its Laws* (1877; reprint, New York, 1969), 1.
[23] Ibid., 2.
[24] Herbert Spencer, "Review of Bain," quoted in James, *Principles of Psychology*, 1271.

money had previously bought, and so logically and chronolog-ically dependent on a more common and less miserly concep-tion of the instrumental value of money. James, however, in-sisting on the "primitive" status of our desire for the useless, denies that it is dependent on our memories of having ac-quired useful things and, insisting on its "aesthetic" status, lo-cates, like Wells and Poor, the attraction of these objects in their materiality. The aesthetic offers him a way out of the in-strumental and the economic both; we like the glittery objects for what they are, not for what they will buy or what they rep-resent.

But while it is clear that Norris's misers don't follow the Spencerian model (loving their gold as a kind of mnemonic for the pleasures it has brought them), it is equally clear that Zer-kow, at least, doesn't love gold because it is pretty either. As James goes on to give a more detailed account of the objects of our primitive desires, he begins to provide some sense of what it is that Zerkow loves. For, as much as or even more than we love "pretty things," James says, we love

> curious things . . . natural objects that look as if they were artifi-cial, or that mimic other objects—these form a class of things which human beings snatch at as magpies snatch rags. They sim-ply fascinate us. What house does not contain some drawer or cupboard full of senseless odds and ends of this sort, with which nobody knows what to do, but which a blind instinct saves from the ash-barrel? (1271)

At the simplest level, James is distinguishing here between what it means to love a sunset and what it means to love the representation of a sunset. But the difference is not simply be-tween beauty and represented beauty; it is instead the differ-ence between "pretty things" and things that "mimic other ob-jects," between beauty and mimesis. When we love glittery objects, we love beauty; when we love objects that look like other objects, we love representation. Furthermore, the sug-gested paradigm of objects that "mimic other objects" is "nat-ural objects that look as if they were artificial." Thus the representation that originally fascinates us is the natural reproduction of a man-made artifact, not the man-made reproduction of a natural one. It is as if we can love the sunset either as a sunset or as the representation of a painting. In this analysis of our love of representation, the mark of human agency is simultaneously produced, effaced, and reproduced: produced because we see in the sunset a representation, effaced because it turns out to be nature that is doing the representing, and reproduced because nature is representing something that was itself made by man.

From the standpoint of the money controversies, this account of the "primitive" desire to "appropriate" is doing some fairly complicated ideological work. For if the difference between loving "glittery" things and loving things that look like something else is the difference between loving beauty and loving representation, then, for the miser, this is the difference between loving gold because it *is* money and loving gold because it looks like money, because, in other words, it is a natural object (metal) that looks like an artificial one (money). To think of gold simply as being money is, as we have already seen, at the same time to deny the existence of money, to turn all the money exchanges into barter exchanges by deriving the value of gold as money exclusively from its "intrinsic" value as a commodity; whereas to think of gold as looking like money is to distinguish between what it is and what it represents and so, admitting the discrepancy between material and value, to admit the possibility of money and a money economy. Hence, the fact that gold isn't in itself money but only looks like money would be what allows it finally to become money. But while James's logic repudiates the hard-money fantasy of nature as a kind of mint, it by no means denies nature a role in the production of money. For although, according to James, we are not originally attracted by nature, we are not originally attracted by artifice either. What attracts is the natural representation of the artificial. Such representation must by definition be accidental—James goes on to call it a *lusus naturae*—but without this accident, it seems, there would be no "primitive form of desire." We don't want things in themselves, but we can't begin by wanting representations of things in themselves either; we want things in themselves that look like representations. We begin, in other words, with the illusion that representation itself is natural, and without this illusion we would never develop any interest either in representation or in nature. To the question as to how there can be value at all if there is no value in nature, James thus responds by locating the genesis of value in an accident, a moment when nature seems unnatural. Imitating something made by man, nature sets man the example of imitation and produces in him the primitive desire for mimesis.

It is thus, perhaps, a sign of Zerkow's "atavism" that his passion for gold finds its most powerful expression in his love of Maria's story about her lost set of gold service. "The story," Norris says, "ravished him with delight" (28). Indeed, as Zerkow's passion progresses, it focuses more and more on "Maria's recital," which becomes "a veritable mania with him" (73). He compels her to tell the story over and over again, each repetition enabling him to "see that wonderful plate before him, there on the table, under his eyes, under his hand," sharpening both his desire and his disappointment when Maria finally refuses to tell it another time. "What a torment! what agony! to be so near—so near, to see it in one's distorted fancy as plain as in a mirror." Indeed, it is the eventual withholding of the story that provokes the crisis in Zerkow's relations with Maria and leads to her murder. "Sweating with desire," Zerkow himself begins to tell the story of the gold—"It was he who could now describe it in a language almost eloquent" (137)—while at the same time escalating his violent efforts to "make" Maria "speak." The distinction between his desire for the gold and his desire for the description gets lost here, a confusion anticipated in Maria's own early accounts of the gold service, when she describes it both as a source of light and as a reflector: it was "a yellow blaze like a fire, like a sunset"; it was "like a mirror . . . just like a little pool when the sun shines into it" (27). It is as if the gold reflects itself and so really is its own reflection, an object that becomes what it is by representing itself. Thus, it isn't so much that the distinction between the gold and its representation is lost as that the representation is here understood to be an essential part of the gold itself. If Zerkow's fancy is a mirror that reflects the gold, and if Maria's language is a mirror that reproduces it in simile, then the gold itself is also a mirror, so that in taking the representation for the thing itself, Zerkow is not making some quixotic mistake about fictions and the real but is instead rightly recognizing the representation as an ontological piece of the thing. Zerkow is a miser of mimesis, and when he dies clutching "a sack full of old and rusty pans—fully a hundred of them—tin cans, and iron knives and forks" (180), he dies happy. He seems, like Wells's islanders, to have mistaken the worthless artifacts of men for nature's gold; but that mistake is, in reality, only a kind of tribute to the mistake embodied in gold itself, to the necessary resemblance of material object to representation. Junk, like language, can represent gold only because, for Norris, gold, like language, is already a representation. Loving language and loving gold, Zerkow also loves the junk that is the material condition of their representability and hence of their identity.

At work in *McTeague*, then, are two very different conceptions of the miser and his love of gold. In one, the miser loves gold because he thinks of it as "money itself"; like the gold Republicans and the silver Bryanites, he identifies the value of money with the value of the material it is made of. In the other, the miser loves gold because it emblemizes the impossibility of anything being "money itself." Seeing gold in junk, he transforms the claim that nothing can be money into the imperial possibility that anything can be money, and he does this by insisting with James on the potential discrepancy not only between material and value but also between what a thing is made of and what it is. For what excites the Jamesian miser's "primitive" desire "to own" is the very separation between materiality and identity that must be possible if one thing is ever to be able to count as an imitation of another. This is why, as James recognizes, it isn't enough simply to say that we like objects that "mimic other objects." How do we come to think of one as mimicking the other? Physical resemblance is obviously an inadequate criterion; we don't think of one sunset or one tree as an imitation of another sunset or another tree. Two natural objects that look just like one another are simply two examples of the same thing—two sunsets, two trees. But James's natural objects that look artificial cannot be understood on the model of two trees that look just like each other, because the trees are, in a certain sense, the same. Rather, the distinction between natural and artificial itself constitutes an immaterial but ineradicable and defining difference. This difference in origin makes it possible to imagine a sunset that not only looks like but also imitates another sunset—a sunset, in other words, that, looking just like another sunset, isn't really a sunset at all, but a representation of one. Imagining our fascination with natural objects that look like artificial ones, James is thus imagining the moment in which we discover a resemblance that cannot be an identity and so discover the possibility of representation. And it is, of course, this discovery in nature of accidental representation that first makes available to us the possibility of intentional representation.

Gold, at once a precious metal and, to Zerkow, a reflecting one, embodies both the natural value of the hard-money men and the accidental appearance in nature of value as representation. But if, from Zerkow's standpoint, the accident of mirrors in nature constitutes the possibility of representation and so of money, from the standpoint of the hard-money men it constituted the possibility of deception and so of counterfeit. Thus Nast's cartoon juxtaposes the picture of a cow bearing the legend "This is cow by the act of the artist" with the picture of a dollar bill bearing the legend "This is money by the act of Congress," suggesting that paper money should be understood as an illusionistic painting of real money, an attempt to fool people into mistaking the "representative for the real" (94). And Wells's text describes how, in the wake of adopting paper money, the islanders extended the domain of exploitative mimesis:

> They employed a competent artist, with a full supply of paints and brushes, and when any destitute person applied for clothing, they painted upon his person every thing he desired in way of clothing of the finest and most fashionable patterns, from top-boots to collars, and from blue swallow-tailed coats to embroidered neckties, with jewelry and fancy buttons to match. (93–94)

Just as the counterfeiting Congress can make worthless paper look like valuable money, so the competent artist can conjure up a costly suit of clothes "without the waste of any raw material more expensive than paint." Accepting the derivation of value from raw material, the illusionistic goal of both these representations is to disguise themselves and by looking "so exactly like the real articles" to "make the shadow of wealth supply the place of its substance" (114).

There are, on this view, two kinds of objects that a painting can be: by some artistic "hocus pocus," the object that it represents, or, in the demystifying vision of the goldbug, the paint and paper it is made of. Money theorists sought to prevent the ontological transformation of paper into currency, but, as the vogue for *trompe l'oeil* during this period indicates, American artists were eager to exploit the illusionistic potential defined by the money theorists' terms. The *trompe l'oeil* goal, of course, was to conceal itself as representation; *trompe l'oeil* painters like William Harnett and John Haberle measured their success in the numerous stories of viewers mistaking, as Wells might have put it, the "representative for the real." Wherever they were exhibited, as Alfred Frankenstein has noted, Harnett's paintings were protected with "guards and rails . . . to keep people from pulling off their 'real' envelopes and newspaper clippings."[25] *Trompe l'oeil* paintings of paper money were especially successful in this regard. Frankenstein records, for example, a story in which Haberle is supposed to have been persuaded by "intimates of Grover Cleveland, in the spirit of practical joking . . . to paint a five-dollar bill on a library table at the White House. When the President happened to pass, he, of course, tried to pick it up."[26] This particular joke may have

---

[25] Alfred Frankenstein, *After the Hunt*, rev. ed. (Berkeley and Los Angeles, 1969), 81.

[26] Ibid., 120. There are numerous stories of this kind, most involving beholders who fail to realize that the money is fake, that it is just a painting, but some involving critics who set out to expose the *painting* as fake by showing that it is just money. An art critic for the *Chicago Inter-Ocean*, for example, described Haberle's "alleged still life," *U.S.A.*, "supposed by some to be a painting of money," as a "fraud": "A $1 bill and the fragments of a $10 note have been pasted on canvas, covered by a thin scumble of paint, and further manipulated to give it a painty appearance" (quoted in ibid., 117). The career of Emanuel Ninger (alias Jim the Penman), the most famous American counter-

derived some of its force from the fact that Cleveland was a notorious hard-money man and so already committed to seeing paper money as a kind of illusion, but Frankenstein is no doubt correct in attributing the general popularity of money as a *trompe l'oeil* subject more to its physical qualities than to its status as a symbol of "the American love of filthy lucre in the Gilded Age."[27] The "representation of flat or very shallow objects is of the very essence of *trompe l'oeil*," according to Frankenstein, since the reduction of depth in the subject reduces "the discrepancy between the muscular experience required for the perception of nature and that which is required for the perception of painting" and so heightens the "pictorial illusion of reality."[28] The choice of flat subjects is a device for reproducing in the perception of representations the physiology of perceiving the objects they represent.

But it would be a mistake to think that this technical, even physical, explanation of money's popularity with *trompe l'oeil* painters empties it of its economic significance. Rather, it is just this insistence on the physical that marks the economic character of *trompe l'oeil* money and of the other usual *trompe l'oeil* subjects: envelopes, photographs, newspaper clippings, even paintings. Focusing on objects so flat that they are physically similar to the support on which they will be represented, the *trompe l'oeil* painter repeats the goldbug demand for a material equivalence between the representation and the objects represented, an equivalence that guarantees the representation's authority by minimizing the degree to which it is a representation. Flatness, not money, carries the weight of *trompe l'oeil*'s economic commitments. And nowhere is this more evident, even if somewhat paradoxically so, than in the hostility to

---

feiter of the late nineteenth century, is exemplary in both these regards, since after his arrest the hand-drawn hundred-dollar bills that he had been passing as money were worth more as works of art, thus raising the possibility that real hundred-dollar bills might be put into circulation as forgeries of the forged bills that Ninger had been circulating. For an entertaining account of Ninger and other counterfeiters, see Murray Teigh Bloom, *Money of Their Own* (New York, 1957).

[27] Frankenstein, *After the Hunt*, 43.
[28] Ibid., 54.

trompe l'oeil and to illusionism in general that would become (was indeed already becoming) a central preoccupation of modernist painting.

The history of this painting, as Clement Greenberg characterized it in a series of brilliant and influential essays of the 1950s and 1960s, is a history of the gradual abandonment of "three-dimensional illusion" (1954)[29] in favor of "the relatively limited illusion of shallow depth" (1958),[30] until finally (1962),

> It has been established . . . that the irreducible essence of pictorial art consists in but two constitutive conventions or norms: flatness and the delimitation of flatness; and that the observance of merely these two norms is enough to create an object which can be experienced as a picture: thus a stretched or tacked-up canvas already exists as a picture—though not necessarily as a *successful* one.[31]

Flatness here signifies modernism's break with illusion, its insistence that before we see what is "in" a picture, we see the picture "as a picture." Grover Cleveland reaching for the painted five-dollar bill provides a limit case, perhaps, of seeing what is *in* the picture first, while Greenberg's own example of the tacked-up canvas provides the limit case of seeing the picture

[29] Clement Greenberg, *Art and Culture* (Boston, 1961), 137.

[30] Ibid., 211.

[31] Clement Greenberg, "After Abstract Expressionism," *Art International* 6 (October 1962): 30. My attention was first drawn to this example by a footnote in Michael Fried's seminal essay "Art and Objecthood" (in *Minimal Art*, ed. Gregory Battcock [New York, 1968], 116–47). My use of the term *surface* in the following paragraphs—my sense in particular of "surface" as a plausible alternative to "flatness"—derives largely from a certain tension in Fried's wonderful description of Jules Olitski's sculpture *Bunga*: "The use of tubes, each of which one sees, incredibly, as *flat*—that is, flat but *rolled*—makes *Bunga*'s surface more like that of a painting than like that of an object; like painting, and unlike both ordinary objects and other sculpture, *Bunga* is *all* surface" ("Art and Objecthood," 139). My own experience of recent paintings by Olitski and of the photographs of James Welling convinces me that surface remains crucial, and I note that Fried has recently remarked that while "the concept 'flatness' . . . has lost much of its urgency," the "pressure" to "come to terms with issues of *surface* . . . is more intense than before" ("How Modernism Works," in *The Politics of Interpretation*, ed. W. J. T. Mitchell [Chicago, 1983], 232n.16).

Figure 2. John Haberle, *Reproduction*, ca. 1889. From Alfred Franken-stein, *After the Hunt*, rev. ed. (Berkeley, 1969).

as a picture. In fact, Greenberg explicitly opposed the possibil-ity of such a picture to the work of Jasper Johns, which he com-pared to Harnett's and Peto's in its use of flatness only to pro-duce the "vivid possibility of deep space."[32]

But if *trompe l'oeil* flatness operates primarily to produce the illusion of three-dimensionality, it does so only by suggest-ing how little space is required for space to become deep. In Haberle's *Reproduction* (Fig. 2), for example, the edges of the ten-dollar bill are folded toward the beholder, establishing on a plane that is flat and contains a representation of flatness at least three different levels of deep space. The photo overlap-ping a newspaper clipping, which in turn overlaps another, makes four, and two layered stamps sticking out from under the ten-dollar bill raise the number to five. The point of this vir-

[32] Greenberg, "After Abstract Expressionism," 26.

tuoso display is precisely to demonstrate what everyone, of course, already knows, that even the flattest objects are irreducibly three-dimensional. Insisting on the impossibility of an image that can escape three-dimensionality, *trompe l'oeil* produces a flatness that can never be conceived as just a surface. Indeed, *trompe l'oeil* paintings of money and photographs work precisely by staging the triumphant failure of even those objects that are nearest to being nothing but surface ever actually to be nothing but surface.

Greenberg's blank canvas, despite (or, rather, because of) its repudiation of all illusion, participates directly in the *trompe l'oeil* production of three-dimensionality.[33] By virtue of its blankness, it has no surface; or rather—since everything has a surface just as everything has depth—one might say that it has a surface that it won't allow to be a surface. What makes it so flat is that there is nothing on it, but the fact that there is nothing on it is what makes it at the same time nothing more than a (very flat) three-dimensional object, like any other object. Thus, while the blank canvas provides, in a certain sense, a rather spectacular alternative to the *trompe l'oeil* ideal, it is an alternative with a well-established place in the *trompe l'oeil* economy, the place, quite literally, of the "raw material" that Wells opposed to the representation. Replacing the illusion of three-dimensionality with the physical fact of three-dimensionality, the blank canvas identifies value with material, picture with support. The painting that can represent nothing and still remain a painting is "money itself," and the modernist (or, perhaps, literalist) aesthetic of freedom from representation is a goldbug aesthetic.

This by no means contradictory progression from painting as illusion by way of flatness to painting as object, whatever relevance it may have for twentieth-century art history, clearly finds an antecedent in what Norris depicts in *Vandover and the*

[33] In discussing Greenberg here, I should make it clear that I am concerned only with the consequences of this particular example. My quarrel, in other words, is not with his attack on minimalism's commitment to "the third dimension" ("Recentness of Sculpture," in Battcock, *Minimal Art*, 182) but only with his failure to recognize the congruence between the values of minimalism and the values of flatness as embodied in the unpainted canvas.

Brute as Vandover's regression from man to beast. Vandover, like Norris himself in his youth, is a painter who begins by sketching out of books, but whose "style improved immensely the moment he abandoned flat studies and began to work directly from Nature" (25).[34] Convinced, after a long period of neglecting his "art," that it alone can "stay the inexorable law of nature" that is turning him into "a blind, unreasoning . . . animal" (309), he sets to work on his "masterpiece," only to find that his "technical skill" has mysteriously vanished; the "forms he made on the canvas were no adequate reflection of those in his brain" (224). And this inability to reproduce on canvas the figures he sees in his imagination becomes almost immediately an inability to imagine the scene he wants to represent; a "strange numbness" grows "in his head": "All the objects in the range of his eyes seemed to move back and stand on the same plane" (226). The failure of Vandover's imagination is a failure of perspective, and the brute appears as a flatness that turns what should have been the depiction of a dying soldier and his (also dying) horse into a "tracing" of "empty lines."

The fact that not even Norris regarded Vandover's failure to complete *The Last Enemy* as a loss to art should not distract us from the interest of the process. For even though Vandover at his best is no master of illusion, the disappearance of his art is exclusively identified with his loss of painting's chief illusionistic device, perspective, and the appearance of the brute is, by the same token, identified with the flattening transformation of living figures into charcoal lines: "The very thing that would have made them intelligible, interpretive, that would have made them art, was absent" (224–25). As a painter, then, the brute is a minimalist; where Vandover excels at painting nature, the brute replaces the painting with nature itself. But this, as I have suggested, is ultimately a distinction without a difference. Vandover the artist can so easily devolve into Vandover

---

[34] For a good discussion of *Vandover* in the context of early-nineties aestheticism, see Don Graham, *The Fiction of Frank Norris* (Columbia, Mo., 1978), 16–42. Graham's sense of the "subversion of art by economic power" (29) in *Vandover*, however, is about on a par with the "filthy lucre" interpretation of *trompe l'oeil* money paintings.

the brute precisely because both artist and brute are already committed to a naturalist ontology—in money, to precious metals; in art, to three-dimensionality. The moral of Vandover's regression, from this standpoint, is that it can only take place because, like the invention of money on Robinson Crusoe's island, it has already taken place. Discovering that man is a brute, Norris repeats the discovery that paper money is just paper and that a painting of paper money is just paint.

In the course of reproducing Wells's and Nast's aesthetic economy, however, Norris also introduces a crucial variation on their *trompe l'oeil* materialism. Vandover's most cherished possessions are the furnishings he acquired for his fashionable rooms on Sutter Street: a tile stove, a window seat, casts of three Assyrian bas-reliefs "representing scenes from the life of the king" and a "wounded lioness," "photogravures" of Rembrandt's *Night Watch* and a Velázquez portrait, an "admirable reproduction of the 'Mona Lisa'" (178). Contemplating his reproductions, he has replaced what Wells thought of as *trompe l'oeil* pictures of money with *trompe l'oeil* pictures of other pictures.[35] But as the brute gains the upper hand, Vandover is forced to sacrifice his things and to move from his apartment to a hotel room where the "walls were whitewashed and bare of pictures or ornaments" (270). Only months before, the sight of "the heavy cream-white twill" of his "blank" and "untouched" "stretcher" (223) had inspired him to try to save himself by painting again; now the empty walls of his room produce a similar response: "His imagination was forever covering the white walls with rough stone-blue paper, and placing screens, di-

---

[35] Discussing Haberle's *Torn in Transit* (the picture of a painting wrapped for shipping from which most of the wrapping has been torn to reveal the painted landscape underneath), Frankenstein notes suggestively that the remaining paper, string, and shipping labels are all "illusionistic" but "occupy a minimum of space": "When one arrives at the point at which the nonillusionistic elements in a work of *trompe l'oeil* occupy nearly all the space, one can go no further; this is the end of the line" (*After the Hunt*, 121). But following the *trompe l'oeil* logic that I have been tracing here, we can see that the end of the line consists not in reducing the *trompe l'oeil* elements to the minimum but instead in eliminating them altogether—painting nothing but painting or (as with the blank canvas) painting nothing at all.

vans, and window seats in different parts of the cold bare room" (280). But this time, when it comes to producing on those walls an "adequate reflection" (224) of the forms he has imagined, he pins up "little placards which he had painted with a twisted roll of the hotel letter-paper dipped into the ink stand. 'Pipe-rack Here.' 'Mona Lisa Here.' 'Stove Here.' 'Window-seat Here'" (280). Instead of drawing the forms "in his brain," he writes them.

This substitution of writing for illusion is also a substitution of writing for paint or charcoal. Unlike Nast's posters, the painted words on Vandover's walls are neither *trompe l'oeil* nor raw material. They can't be *trompe l'oeil* because they don't, of course, look like what they name, and they can't be raw material because they do name something other than what they are. Writing here becomes, in other words, a model for representation without illusion and for a flatness that isn't simply a shallow three-dimensionality. As opposed to both the *trompe l'oeil* reproduction of the Mona Lisa and to the minimalist wall left bare by that reproduction's absence, " 'Mona Lisa' Here" is all surface, the art not only of a brute but of a brute that can write. Thus, if in one of his manifestations the brute represents the possibility of reducing everything to nature, here he represents the impossibility of reducing everything to nature. Norris's tendency to define the change in Vandover's art as a replacement of the "true" illusionistic "children of his imagination" by unintelligible "empty lines" gives way to an image of the children become "changelings," transformed but by no means unrecognizable: "It was as if the brute in him, like some malicious witch, had stolen away the true offspring of his mind, putting in their place these deformed dwarfs, its own hideous spawn" (229). The problem is not that these children don't represent you but that they do. Where the naturalist brute reduces the illusion of the man to the material of the beast, the malicious witch, producing unnatural offspring, gives birth neither to beasts nor to illusions. No longer the demystification of representation, the brute appears here as representation itself.

Of course, there are at least two ways in which those painted words could be reclaimed for *trompe l'oeil*: instead of painting *as* writing, they could be thought of as painting *of* writing, and so could be construed as an extension of the physical flatness involved in paintings of money and of other paintings; or they could, following the lead of Vandover's first teacher, who, "besides drawing," "taught ornamental writing" (13), be emptied of their meaning as words and so understood solely as ornament. But there is one other example of the conjunction of writing and visual representation in *Vandover and the Brute* that makes it clear that this is not what Norris intended. Reading through the morning paper, Vandover sees a report of the suit being brought against him by the father of Ida Wade (who killed herself after discovering she was pregnant) and sees "his name staring back at him from out the gray blur of type, like some reflection of himself seen in a mirror" (233). Imagining print as a reflecting surface, Norris gestures here toward a presentation of the self that would involve neither the illusion of the artist nor any mark of his physical presence. Vandover finds himself represented in the newspaper not by a self-portrait (which would look like him) or by a signature (which would, as an extension of him, in a certain sense, be him) but by a set of mechanically produced marks that, having no illusionistic likeness to him and no material identity with him, nevertheless mirror him vividly to himself. Painting must be transformed into script and script into type to produce this image of the brute.

One thing these transformations suggest is that the brute, like Frank Norris, has ceased to be a painter and has become instead a writer. But they suggest also a last set of variations on the question and answers with which this essay began. Why does the miser save? He saves to escape the money economy; he saves to reenact for himself the origin of that economy. How can metal become money? How can paint become a picture? One set of answers to these questions repeats the escape from money: metals never do become money; they always were; hence they never are; a picture is just paper and paint pretending to be something else. The logic of these answers is the logic of goldbugs and Bryanites, *trompe l'oeil*, and a certain strain of modernism. The attraction of writing is that it escapes this logic. Neither a formal entity in itself nor an illusionistic image of something else, it marks the potential discrepancy between

material and identity, the discrepancy that makes money, painting, and, ultimately, persons possible. But how are persons
possible? Or, to put the question in its most general form, how
is representation possible?

Norris's favorite teacher at Berkeley, the geologist Joseph
Le Conte, had raised this question in these terms in the second
edition of his *Evolution* (1892): how were "physical phenomena" like the "vibrations of brain molecules" related to "psychical phenomena" like "thoughts"? "There are, as it were, two
sheets of blotting paper pasted together. The one is the brain,
the other the mind. Certain ink-scratches or blotches, *utterly
meaningless* on the one, soak through and appear on the other
as *intelligible writing*, but how we know not and can never
hope to guess."[36] Le Conte's is the tone of those who, as William James mockingly put it, "find relief . . . in celebrating the
mystery of the Unknowable" (179), but James himself had no
more convincing account of the relation between mind and
brain, and he ends his own discussion of the subject by imagining impatient readers muttering, "Why on earth doesn't the
poor man say *the soul* and have done with it?" (181). The difficulty with just saying "the soul" and having done with it is, of
course, the confusion this would cause for a psychology that
was seeking "to avoid unsafe hypotheses," to "remain positivistic and non-metaphysical." Thus James resolves, at least until
"some day" when things have been "more thoroughly thought
out," "in this book" to "take no account of the soul" (182). But,
simply in acknowledging the distinction between brain and
mind, James has already admitted the existence of something
very like the soul, and, in fact, we have already begun to see in
his discussion of our "primitive" love of objects that "mimic
other objects" how little he was able to honor the resolution to
remain "non-metaphysical." The point of that discussion was
to explain the "acquisitiveness" of such people as misers, and,
in keeping with his positivist commitment, James emphasized
the "entirely primitive" status of the miser's desire, describing

[36] Joseph Le Conte, *Evolution* (New York, 1892), 310. The best general discussion of Le Conte's influence on Norris is by Donald Pizer, *The Novels of
Frank Norris* (Bloomington, Ind., 1966), 12–22.

it as a "blind instinct," a "blind propensity," and comparing the way human beings collect "curious things" to the way "magpies snatch rags" (1272). Magpies snatch rags, however, because they think they look nice or because they can use them for something, whereas beachcombers save "curious things" not for their beauty or utility but for their mimicking likeness to other things. Hence the conclusion we drew from James was that the miser loves gold neither for its beauty as a metal (cf. Wells) nor for its buying power as money (cf. Spencer) but for its resemblance as a natural object (metal) to an artificial one (money). Misers love gold because they love representation, and when we, like misers, bring curious things home from the beach, we are testifying with our own instinctive behavior to the primitive possibility of representation and the equally primitive possibility of a money economy.

The presence of the magpie in this example marks James's ambition to keep the instincts as "non-metaphysical" as he can, but just as no magpie can love something that is neither beautiful nor useful, so, by James's own account, no human being, loving representation, can ever remain as nonmetaphysical as a magpie. In nature—which is to say, from the positivistic and material standpoint of the brain—objects may look like one another but never represent one another. Only the unnatural makes representation possible, and it makes it possible by imagining the natural as artificial. In a certain sense, of course, this proves to be a mistake; the objects we find on the beach aren't really mimicking other objects. But in imagining that they are, we imagine for the first time the possibility not just of other brains but of other minds. Indeed, we imagine for the first time the possibility of our own minds. The mistaken love of representation that makes representation possible must first appear as a mistake about itself, as when we take the magpie's love of beauty for the human love of mimesis. In this respect, the love of natural things that resemble artificial ones is itself an instance of that resemblance, epitomizing the immaterial distinction between what we are made of and what we are. Thus, our primitive love of natural things that look artificial turns out to be nature's way of revealing to our brains the existence of our minds. And when the brute in Vandover paints "writing on the wall" (220), it horrifies him by reflecting not his body but his beastly soul. Or, to put it another way, seeing himself reflected in writing, he sees in the failure of his own materiality the inevitability of paper money.

The interchangeability of these terms—*soul* and *money*—is itself mirrored on the goldbug side by a somewhat more elaborate set of transformational possibilities. The love of precious metals is just the fear that men will regress into beasts, which is, in turn, the fear that money will disappear, which, transposed and inverted, is the love of *trompe l'oeil* painting. It would be possible, in my view, to extend these transformations—in the case of painting (as I have already suggested), forward into minimalism; more typically, as in the case of anarchist labor agitation, laterally: "The human *law*-maker," wrote Albert R. Parsons in 1886, is (like the human moneymaker) "a human humbug," because "laws" (like gold and silver) "are discovered, *not* made."[37] Parsons, convicted for murder in the Haymarket trial, is even farther from Grover Cleveland than John Haberle is from minimalism, but they are all equally committed to hard money—which is not to say that they were all aware of this commitment or even that they would necessarily have recognized or acknowledged it if it had been pointed out to them. Such speculations are somewhat beside the point. What I mean to say is that, having taken up a position (on the similarity of men to animals, say) or having adopted a practice (for example, illusionist painting), they had involved themselves in a logic that, regardless of their own views, entailed a whole series of other commitments, and it is this logic and these commitments that locate them in the discourse of naturalism.

There are at least two such logics running through this discourse, or rather, two such logics that constitute it. One could, perhaps, best describe naturalism as the working-out of a set of

[37] Albert Parsons, "Autobiography," in *The Autobiographies of the Haymarket Martyrs*, ed. Philip Foner (New York, 1969), 44. Parsons goes on to imagine a society in which "natural leaders" replace government and "self-preservation becomes the actuating motive as now, minus the . . . domination of man by man" (45).

conflicts between pretty things and curious ones, material and representation, hard money and soft, beast and soul. But this doesn't mean that the naturalist writer is someone who has chosen the beastly side of these dichotomies (the side literary history ordinarily associates with naturalism)[38] or even that he is someone who has chosen with any consistency either side. The consistency—indeed, the identity—of naturalism resides in the logics and in their antithetical relation to one another, not necessarily in any individual, any text, or even any single sentence. Le Conte, for example, describes the relation of animals to men in terms that repeat the goldbug description of the relation between paper and precious metals: "The resemblance is great, but the difference is immense. . . . It is the shadow and substance, promise and fulfillment"; but he goes on to finish the comparison, "Still better, it is like embryo and child."[39] The weirdness of this set of similes is that while it begins by imagining animals as *trompe l'oeil* representations of men (understanding the words uttered by a trained magpie, to use a Jamesian example, as *trompe l'oeil* representations of language), it ends by imagining the reflecting shadow turned into

[38] In his chapter on Norris in *The American Novel and Its Tradition* (New York, 1957), for example, Richard Chase describes McTeague as an "animal like man" and the "naturalistic novel" as one in which "the beast shows through the human exterior" (188), while he describes Norris himself as a sort of literary McTeague, who succeeds because "he is able to write instinctively out of his natural genius" (191). And Donald Pizer, determined to rescue naturalism from Chase's witty determinism and to secure for it "an affirmative ethical conception of life," nevertheless follows Chase in asserting Norris's primary commitment to "the strength of man's animality" (Pizer, *Realism and Naturalism in Nineteenth-Century American Literature* [Carbondale, Ill., 1984], 14, 19). My own point is not so much to quarrel with these characterizations as to suggest an understanding of naturalism in which their negations would also have a place.

[39] Le Conte, *Evolution*, 324. In addition to Wells, see, for example, Edward Atkinson, who (against the term "fiat money") urges that money be defined "in such a way that the substance cannot therefore be confounded with the shadow—the thing for the promise of the thing carrying no obligation for the performance of the promise" (Atkinson, *The Distribution of Products* [New York, 1885], 5–6). I owe this reference to Howard Horwitz. For directing my attention to several other documentary texts, I would also like to thank Gillian Brown.

an anticipating embryo (as if the talking magpie were not imitating human speech but originating it). In the first instance,
animals are deceptive representations of humans; in the second, they have already become humans precisely because of
their capacity to represent. And this opposition is repeated
more penetratingly in *Vandover and the Brute*. Vandover,
prowling about his room on all fours, utters "a sound, half
word, half cry, 'Wolf—wolf!'" (310). In the mouth, or rather the
"throat," of the brute, the name of a thing is revealed to be
really the sound the thing makes. Norris presses home the denial of representation by way of onomatopoeia; words are reduced to the sounds they are made of, and instead of the magpie imitating language, language imitates the magpie. But at the
same time, Vandover's gambling companion, a deaf-mute
known as "the Dummy," is made so drunk that, as Vandover
does his "dog act," the Dummy begins to "talk," "pouring out
a stream" of "birdlike twitterings" among which one could
"now and then . . . catch a word or two" (298). Never having
spoken any words, never even having heard any, the Dummy
(like the magpie) nevertheless produces sounds that inexplicably turn out to be language.

    Vandover and the Brute does not resolve these contradic-
tions, and, more important, it does not thematize them
either—it isn't *about* the conflict between material and representation, it is an *example of* that conflict. And it doesn't exemplify the conflict because literary language (at a sufficiently
high level of sophistication) characteristically enacts some such
conflict. To think this is only to imagine a thematics in which
authors have been replaced by language, the characteristic gesture not of literature but of a certain literary formalism so eager
to preserve the ontological privilege of the text that it becomes
in its most desperate moments indistinguishable from goldbug
materialism. But my point here is not to criticize that literary
materialism per se any more than it is to attack the notion that
democracy needs a dollar "as good as gold." I want only to locate both these positions and their negations in the logic, or
rather the double logic, of naturalism and, in so doing, to suggest one way of shifting the focus of literary history from the

individual text or author to structures whose coherence, interest, and effect may be greater than that of either author or text.

If, then, *Vandover and the Brute* does not resolve its contradictions—does not choose between Vandover and the brute—and if, from the standpoint of literary history, my own effort has been to locate *Vandover* and some other texts in a network of related contradictions and controversies (over the nature of money, art, professionalization, and persons), I have not myself tried to demonstrate which side of these controversies the texts take or, perhaps more important, which political and economic interests they express. Wells's *Robinson Crusoe's Money* was clearly written in support of the bankers' view of money, but Wells thought of it, of course, as arguing for the truth, not for the bankers, a view that the virtually unanimous commitment to hard money would have made plausible. Norris's case is more complicated, if only because his own economic commitments seem less obvious; neither *Vandover* nor *McTeague*, for example, contains any but the most trivial and inconclusive reference to the money controversies: Vandover's father's ironic description of twenty-dollar gold pieces as "Good for the masses" (6) and McTeague's prospecting companion's claim that he had been "fitchered" when "the skunks at Washington lowered the price of silver" (222) by demonetizing it in the "crime of '73." My strategy has not been to ascribe a new importance to these passages but rather to show how the fact that neither text directly addresses the "battle of the standards" seems comparatively insignificant once it is recognized how involved both texts are with the fantasy of money's disappearance, a fantasy that was central not just to the money controversies but to the very idea of money. Thus, the social involvement of these texts depends not on their direct representation of the money controversies but on their indirect representation of the conditions that the money controversies themselves articulated. But this indirect representation—depicting McTeague as a dentist, for example, rather than as a banker—is in its own way as explicit as the direct alternative. Indeed, it is in a certain sense more explicit; the dentist who puts gold in teeth, the miner who puts it back in the ground,

the thief who leaves it in Death Valley, all speak more powerfully to the fear that money will disappear than does the banker
who merely deposits it in his vaults. I don't want to be misread,
then, as arguing for the recovery of a social allegorical dimension of Norris's writing. I am arguing instead for the recovery of
something like its literal meaning—not a meaning that has
been obscured, but a meaning that has been, one might say,
read through, as if it were transparent.

But even on their economic surface, Norris's texts remain
contradictory and their commitments uncertain. Perhaps one
could argue, accepting the most radical Populist endorsement
of fiat money, that these contradictions involve the periodic irruption of the truth about money against the economic mystification of the goldbugs, and hence one could identify Zerkow's equation of gold with language and junk as a moment of
Populist demystification. The only problem with this reading is
that it is hard to see exactly how Populist (as opposed to goldbug) interests were served by knowing the truth about money.
The chief consequence of accepting fiat money is to make possible a certain flexibility in the supply of money, and the ability
to manipulate the money supply has scarcely proven to be an
effective weapon in the fight against finance capitalism. And if
we cannot say precisely whose interests were served by the
commitment to paper money or precious metals, how can we
say whose interests were served by the conviction that men had
or did not have souls, or by the claim that the irreducible element of painting was flatness? Seeking to go beyond the usual
generalizations about Norris's interest in gold (that it symbol-
izes animal greed or capitalist fetishism, for example), we have
located it in the context of the particular economic and ideological issues of the 1890s only to remain as uncertain as we
were before about the real ideological interest and hence the
real ideological function of his texts. Insofar as the love of gold
in Norris is seen to express the fear of money, it serves only to
neutralize the opposition between gold and silver; and insofar
as it is seen to express the love of money and a money economy, it serves to neutralize not just the difference between silver and gold but the difference between fear and love—once
the possibility of money has been identified with the possibility

of persons, the money economy comes to seem inevitable. Thus the process of locating *McTeague* in a specific economic debate serves not only to empty *McTeague* of its ideological significance but to empty the economic debate of its ideological significance as well.

My point here is not that complicated literary texts resist ideology. It is instead that when we look closely at the structure of beliefs that constitute the logic of naturalism, we see no consistent connection between them and the political and economic interests of the people or groups of people (e.g., classes) who held them. Which is not to say that the interests of some people and some groups were not in fact served by the logic of naturalist representation, but only that their interests did not *produce* the beliefs that constitute that logic. This is something like what I take Foucault to be saying when, in the course of his well-known critique of the concept of ideology, he remarks that such a concept "refers . . . necessarily to something of the order of a subject";[40] it assumes, that is, the existence of subjects complete with interests and then imagines those subjects in more or less complicated (and more or less conscious) ways selecting their beliefs about the world in order to legitimate their interests. The subject of naturalism, however—at least as I have depicted him here—is typically unable to keep his beliefs lined up with his interests for more than two or three pages at a time, a failure that stems not from inadequate powers of concentration but from the fact that his identity as a subject consists only in the beliefs and desires made available by the naturalist logic—which is not produced by the naturalist subject but rather is the condition of his existence.

All the same, given an account of representation that ultimately identifies the possibility of money with the possibility of being a person, it would be foolish to imagine that the effect of such an account with respect to legitimating the money economy would be neutral. I would suggest instead that *trompe l'oeil* paintings, soulless brutes, and hard money were all con-

---

[40] Michel Foucault, *Power/Knowledge*, ed. Colin Gordon (New York, 1980), 118.

servative attempts to assert the ontological impossibility of what was already an historical fact, and that by identifying the possibility of a moneyless economy with what seemed to be the impossibility of soulless persons, this conservative reaction served only to legitimate what it reacted against. Identifying persons with money made money as irrevocable and unquestionable as persons. From this perspective, then, the logic of naturalism served the interests not of any individual or any group of individuals but of the money economy itself.

From the standpoint of Foucault's critique of ideology, however, this description remains problematic. The point of that critique (indeed, the point of Foucault's whole project) was "to dispense with the constituent subject, to get rid of the subject itself . . . to arrive at an analysis which [could] account for the constitution of the subject within an historical framework."[41] But to speak of the interest of the money economy is hardly to get rid of the subject; it is instead to relocate it, to inscribe it at the level not of the individual or the class but of the economy. And rather than accounting for the constitution of the subject, such a procedure continues to insist that it is the subject that does the constituting. Thus the effect of insisting on the primacy of interests is to save the constituent subject. One might even say that the subject of naturalism becomes the money economy so that the economy can become a subject.

But can economies be subjects? Can they have intentions, desires, beliefs? Can they have interests? Individuals obviously can, classes can, but insofar as an economy is neither an individual nor a class, it is hard to see how it can be said to have interests. Indeed, from a certain standpoint, the whole point of the analysis I have attempted here has been, by subverting the primacy of the subject in literary history, to subvert also the primacy of interest. From this standpoint, the ascription of interests to a money economy (or, for that matter, to a disciplinary society) is only a figure of speech or a mistake, personification or pathetic fallacy. At the same time, however, as literary critics—and as critics in particular of naturalism—we can hardly

41 Ibid., 117.

dismiss this mistake, this particular figure, as merely one among others. For according to the logic of naturalism it is only because we are fascinated by such mistakes—by natural objects that look as if they were made by humans—that we have any economy at all. The foundation of our economy, the primitive desire to own, is nothing but our response to these mistakes, our desire to own the mistakes themselves.

If, however, the personification of nature constitutes the possibility of bourgeois economy, the personification of that economy provides another turn of the screw. For, unlike the "curious" things we find on the beach, the economy really is man-made, and yet it is still not a person. "People know what they do," Foucault once remarked; "they frequently know why they do what they do; but what they don't know is what what they do does."[42] An economy is made up of what people do, and what people do is a function of, among other things, what they want; but what the economy does may not represent either what people do or what they want. It is, one might say, made up of people, and it acts like a person; but the person it acts like is not the people it is made up of. From this perspective, the desire to personify the economy is the desire to bridge the gap between our actions and the consequences of our actions by imagining a person who does not do what we do but who does do what what we do does. As it happens, there is no such person. But precisely because there is no such person, because the economy cannot, on the one hand, be reduced to the material it is made of (desires, actions) or, on the other hand, be turned into some other person and reduced to the

[42]Quoted in Hubert L. Dreyfus and Paul Rabinow, *Michel Foucault: Beyond Structuralism and Hermeneutics* (Chicago, 1983), 187. Dreyfus and Rabinow themselves raise this issue, pointedly asking "how to talk about intentionality without a subject, a strategy without a strategist?" But instead of answering that you can't, they go on to perform their own act of personification, attributing intentionality to the "technologies and innumerable separate localizations which literally embody what the analyst is seeking to understand" (187). For discussion of these questions, I would like to thank the members of my realism seminar at Berkeley (Fall 1984), and for their contributions to this essay as a whole I want especially to thank Frances Ferguson and Steven Knapp.

material that person is made of (consequences), it provides a singularly compelling image of the naturalist distinction between material and identity. Failing to be a person, it images by the way it isn't a person the condition in naturalism of the possibility of persons.

6. CORPORATE FICTION

*T*oward the end of *The Octopus*—after the shoot-out between the railroad and the ranchers, and after the railroad has put its "dummy buyers" in possession of the ranchers' property—Norris contrives a dramatic way of illustrating some of the consequences of this event. He cuts back and forth between scenes of the immigrant rancher's widow Mrs. Hooven and her daughter starving in the streets of San Francisco and scenes of a fashionable dinner party at the home of the railroad magnate Gerard. The contrast is crude but powerful. The "wrecked body" of Mrs. Hooven "clamor[s] for nourishment; anything to numb those gnawing teeth—an abandoned loaf . . . a half-eaten fruit."[1] Mrs. Gerard describes how her asparagus is brought in fresh every day by a "special train": " 'Fancy eating ordinary market asparagus,' said Mrs. Gerard, 'that has been fingered by heaven knows how many hands' " (430). By the time the dinner party ends, Mrs. Hooven is dead.

But stark as this contrast is, it is compromised by Norris's depiction of what Mrs. Hooven actually experiences in the moment of starving to death. The "numbness" she had yearned for now begins to "creep over her" and the "torture" of "famine" begins to fade. "She no longer felt the pain and cramps of her stomach"; the moment when starving becomes starving to death is here depicted as a curious form of satiation: "Even the hunger was ceasing to bite" (430). It is almost as if starving to death represents somehow a failure to be hungry enough and hence as if Mrs. Hooven's final experience of her body is in some sense comparable to the satisfaction experienced by the Gerards and their guests. " 'We aindt gowun to be hungry enymore,' " Mrs. Hooven has promised her daughter, " 'we gowun to die' " (429). Norris seems to imagine satiation not as a pleasurable sensation but as the beginning of the end of sensation, "a pleasing semi-insensibility" (430). The moment in which one ceases to feel hunger becomes the moment in which one ceases to feel anything at all, and the body, becoming insensible, becomes "inert"; a good meal is a harbinger of mortality.

[1]Frank Norris, *The Octopus* (New York, 1964), 427. Subsequent page references are cited in parentheses in the text.

Lest this account of death (even death by starvation) as a form of satiation seem implausible, it is worth noting that Dreiser in *Sister Carrie* associates Hurstwood's death with the failure of desire[2] (Norris had read *Sister Carrie* in manuscript for Doubleday, Page). Perhaps more to the point, it is worth noting that satisfaction in *The Octopus* also is a sure sign of mortality. The "picture of feasting" (428) at the Gerards' party is anticipated by the self-consciously Homeric barbecue on Annixter's ranch, "a feeding of the people, elemental, gross, a great appeasing of appetite, an enormous quenching of thirst" (355). "Everyone had his fill," Norris writes, and while the people feast, the railroad takes possession of their ranches and within hours the ranchers have been killed. "Dabney dead, Hooven dead, Harran dead, Annixter dead, Broderson dead, Osterman dying" (378), writes the poet Presley. More striking still, the "immense satisfaction" (434) of S. Behrman, the railroad agent who takes possession of the Rancho de los Muertos, turns out to be only a foretaste of his own extinction. Examining the wheat—once the ranchers', now his—being shipped to the "starving bellies" of Asia, Behrman falls into the hold and, "deafened with the roar of the grain, blinded and made dumb with its chaff" (454), is, like Mrs. Hooven, exhausted and rendered insensible. "The wheat leaping continuously from the chute, poured around him. It filled the pockets of the coat; it crept up the sleeves and trousers legs; it covered the great protuberant stomach; it ran at last in rivulets into the distended, gaping mouth." The cause of Behrman's death is, no doubt, suffocation, but Norris manages to make it sound like he has eaten too much, or rather, like he has been unable to eat enough. Even the gluttonous Behrman isn't hungry enough to eat his way out of the wheat, and his death, too, is imagined as a moment in which appetite fails.

Despite its place as the first novel in Norris's projected trilogy dealing with "(1) the production, (2) the distribution, (3) the consumption of American wheat," *The Octopus* is much less concerned with its presumed subject (production) or even

---

[2]For further discussion, see "*Sister Carrie's* Popular Economy" (chapter 1 in this volume).

with its titular subject (the railroad, hence distribution) than with the final stage in Norris's economic cycle—consumption, the imagination of an appetite for American wheat. "The great word of this nineteenth century has been production. The great word of the twentieth century will be . . . markets" (216). Set in the early 1880s, the novel, in traditional agrarian terms, imagines the railroad as an obstacle between producers and their markets; "between the fecund San Joaquin, reeking with fruitfulness, and the millions of Asia crowding toward the verge of starvation, lay the iron-hearted monster of steel and steam, implacable, insatiable, huge . . . its ever hungry maw glutted with the harvests that should have fed the famished bellies of the whole world of the Orient" (228).

But, written in 1900, in the wake of Populism's spectacular rise and fall, the novel begins to imagine not only production but also the opposition between producers and distributors as something of an anachronism. The Populist dream of "the farmer and manufacturer" is to do away with the "middleman" (216–17), to "free" themselves from the "speculator" and the "trust" (226), and, "acting for themselves," to sell their own wheat in the "markets" of the Orient. The title of *The Octopus* marks the failure of this dream but not, by the same token, the triumph of the middleman. For instead of describing the railroad as controlling the flow of wheat from producer to consumer, Norris describes it as if it were itself the consumer, competing with rather than profiting from the hungry Asians, replacing their "starving bellies" with its own "ever hungry maw." Rather than dramatizing the customary agrarian fear of the middleman, the novel here transforms distribution into consumption, and indeed, throughout *The Octopus*, the final stage in Norris's cycle seems on the verge of swallowing up the first two. The railroad that distributes the wheat turns out to be imagined as consuming it; even the machine that harvests the wheat is a "monster, insatiable, with iron teeth . . . devouring" (433) it.

Finally, the "insatiable ambition to write verse" of the poet Presley, who (like Norris) will seek to produce an "Epic of the Wheat," is identified with the fact that he is "threatened with consumption" (13). He comes to California in search of his

health and a "subject" and leaves having found the subject—
he has written "The Toilers"—but not his health. For what is
truly insatiable in Presley is the hunger that drives his body to
consume itself, his "vast desire" for "some terrifying martyrdom, some awe-inspiring immolation, consummate, incisive,
conclusive" (397–98). Presley's poem of production, his own
productivity, is depicted as an epiphenomenon of his consuming desire to be consumed. Putting him, at the end of the
novel, on a ship loaded with wheat for "the hungry Hindoo"
(the wheat belongs to Behrman, and the ship carries him too,
dead, in its hold), Presley's friend Cedarquist urges him to "get
fat yourself" (455). But all the wheat in the San Joaquin couldn't
make Presley fat. Indeed, in shipping both the wheat and Presley to the Orient, it isn't clear whether Cedarquist is exporting
food or hunger; given Norris's account of production as a by-
product of the desire to consume, it isn't even clear whether
the difference between them survives. What is clear is that in
the market of the twentieth century, as Norris foresees it, there
will be no place for the too-easily-satisfied appetites of the
wheat farmers. Only "insatiable" poets like Presley and "ever
hungry" corporations like the Southern Pacific Railroad will
survive.

The Octopus thus displaces what Tom Watson characterized as labor's fundamental question to capital—"Why is it you
have so much and do so little work, while I have so little and do
so much?"[3]—with a question that was in some respects more
puzzling: why, having so much, do you want still more? "A man
cannot wear more than one suit of clothes at a time," as Ignatius Donnelly put it; the spectacle of "the Goulds and the Van-
derbilts and the Rockefellers" spending "nights and days of
ceaseless labor"[4] in pursuit of fortunes they could never live to
spend was more perplexing and ultimately more terrifying than
Watson's imagination of the idle capitalist. What did these men

[3]Tom Watson, "A Labor Day Message" (1891), in *The Populist Mind*, ed.
Norman Pollack (Indianapolis, 1967), 424.
[4]Ignatius Donnelly, *The American People's Money* (1895; reprint, Westport, Conn., 1976), 100.

want? Or, to put the question in terms more appropriate to *The Octopus*, how, having everything they wanted, did they manage to keep on wanting? Donnelly's answer to this question took the form of a parable about "the hog in human nature." A farmer out to raise prize-winning pigs would feed them all they could eat, but "at a certain point they stopped laying on fat. Nature had got all it wanted and would go no farther."[5] Then, to get his best pig eating again, the farmer would put "a poor, half-starved, hungry shoat" into the pen, arousing in "the porcine bosom" all the "instincts of the millionaire." "It turns and gorges the food for which before it had no appetite."[6] In this analysis, the natural limits on desire can be transcended by supplementing the desire to eat with the desire to keep someone else from eating. But why anyone should want *that* remains a mystery: "It is a thing no man can understand."[7]

But its ultimate failure to explain was not the only unsatisfactory aspect of Donnelly's explanation. Eventually even the prize-winning pig, like Norris's S. Behrman, can eat no more; it runs up against nature in the form of its own body and of that body's inability to consume all the food around it. For Behrman, in the ship's hold, this food comes to constitute his entire environment, as if the world contained nothing but men and food and as if the identity of a man—the difference between him and his food—depended on the moment in which he was unable to make his food a part of himself, unable to incorporate the world into himself. The mere fact that Behrman has a body seems, from this standpoint, a mark of what must be a principled satiability, since the fact of his body being his body (as opposed, say, to just being the world) requires a world outside his body, a world, in the ship's hold, of food that he has failed to consume. To imagine insatiability seems then to involve imagining not an insatiable body but something that is not a body at all, something that really is as "intangible" as S. Behrman ("there ain't nothing can touch me") mistakenly

[5]Ibid., 99.
[6]Ibid., 100.
[7]Ibid., 101.

imagines himself to be. And of course, in *The Octopus* itself, as in the polemical literature of Populism, it is the corporation, "a mere ideal being, an artificial creation of imaginary workmanship, set up as a person . . . to move among natural persons,"[8] that embodies, if that's still the right word, the possibility of such an "intangible" person and hence of a truly "exhaustless greed for lucre."

To writers like James "Cyclone" Davis and Henry D. Lloyd, it was this combination of personhood and intangibility that conferred upon corporations "unprecedented" powers— above all, the "power to act as persons, as in the commission of crimes, with exemption from punishment as persons."[9] As persons, corporations, like natural persons, could cheat or steal; but as intangible persons, corporations, unlike natural persons, could not be sent to jail. To writers like Josiah Royce, the great philosopher of American corporate life, however, the perfection in commercial life of the intangible person seemed a practical fulfillment of the promise of Absolute Idealism. Thus in his last book, *War and Insurance*, Royce took the insurance company, consisting, in its most stripped-down form, "of what is usually called a *principal*, of an *agent*, and of a *client . . . to whom the agent represents the principal*" as a model for the *"Community of Interpretation"*[10] whose epistemological importance he had discovered in reading the early essays of C. S. Peirce. An "international corporation" constructed along the lines of a "community of insurance" would constitute, Royce thought, "a distinctively new entity which would be neither a nation, nor a court of arbitration, nor an international congress, nor a federation of states, nor any such body as at present exists."[11] As a corporation designed to insure against risk, this international body, in order to be free itself from the risks besetting comparatively more material corporate bodies (such

---

[8] Judge A. W. Terrell (of Texas), quoted in James H. Davis, *A Political Revelation* (Dallas, 1894), 240.
[9] Henry D. Lloyd, *Wealth Against Commonwealth* (New York, 1894), 519.
[10] Josiah Royce, *War and Insurance* (New York, 1914), 47.
[11] Ibid., xix–xx.

as nations), would itself be finally separate from any body at all: "it would possess no territory which could be seized, it would lay claim to no neutrality which could be violated. . . . Its individual trustees might be made prisoners or executed; but such efforts might well kill its body without touching its essentially intangible soul."[12]

From Royce's standpoint, the ultimate immateriality of the international insurance corporation was the necessary condition of its success in preventing war. Writing in August 1914, he was only too aware of the failure of international courts to maintain peace and of the susceptibility of such institutions to political pressures and military threats. Even the neutrality of a nation can be violated, since even a neutral nation, like a body, has borders, and those borders can be crossed. His solution was to imagine an utterly disembodied entity, to think of the relation of the corporation to its employees, its board of directors, and its shareholders as the relation of soul to body. Whereas in a partnership, the death of a partner dissolves the partnership, in Royce's model of the corporation, no physical event can jeopardize the existence of the corporate entity—its soul is immortal. If it is the fact that persons have bodies that makes insurance desirable, it is the possibility of a person without a body that makes the absolute insurance of Absolute Idealism possible.

Both the promise and the threat of corporate personality are thus linked to idealism, an idealism that must itself be defined in opposition to the organic materialism of the body and, eventually, to the mechanical materialism of the automaton. And despite its materialist subject (or rather, by way of it), this idealism finds its way into the "Epic of the Wheat." Imagining "the very first little quiver of life that the grain must feel after it is sown," the shepherd Vanamee insists that this "premonition of life" must take place "long, long before any physical change has occurred—long before the microscope could discover the slightest change" (155). The novel's central image of materiality is here converted into an emblem of the immaterial, a conver-

---

[12] Ibid., xxvii–xxviii.

sion authorized by the Pauline sermon of Father Sarria: "Your grain of wheat is your symbol of immortality; It is sown a natural body; it is raised a spiritual body" (106). The corporate enemy of producers in *The Octopus* thus turns out to be present from the start in the object that is produced, present in fact in the utterly idealized possibility of production. For in identifying the germination of the wheat with the emergence of a spiritual out of a natural body, Norris describes production itself as the transcendence of the material. The moral of this description according to Vanamee is that "evil dies" but "the good never dies" (447). We might say that in moralizing the process of production, Vanamee removes it altogether from the sphere of economy, that he speaks in Royce's voice—a voice that Norris also attempts to make his own when, distinguishing between the "individual" who "suffers" and the "race" that "goes on," he ends by asserting that the "larger view . . . through all shams, all wickednesses, discovers the truth that will, in the end, prevail, and all things surely, inevitably, resistlessly work together for good" (458). The cheerless optimism of this passage seeks to override the troublesome character of its distinction between the individual and the race. Is the individual's relation to the race that of part to whole? Body to soul? Natural person to corporate person? A race would seem to be made up of individuals, but a soul could never be described as made up of a body. Was a corporate person, like a race, composed of natural individuals? Or did it, like the soul, have an independent, intangible existence?

Royce's commitment to the priority of the social, to the "community of interpretation" as a "corporate entity" "more concrete" than "any individual,"[13] was virtually lifelong, finding expression not only in minor pieces like *War and Insurance* but also in his major philosophical works, *The World and the Individual* and *The Problem of Christianity*. Even the early history *California* taught "the sacredness of a true public spirit."[14] But the particular place of the corporation in this ontological

[13] Josiah Royce, *The Problem of Christianity* (1918; reprint, Chicago, 1968), 93 and passim.
[14] Josiah Royce, *California* (1886; reprint, Santa Barbara, 1970), 366.

hierarchy was not always as unequivocal as it came to be in the later writings. And, interestingly enough, what unease Royce felt about the ontology of the corporation surfaces most explicitly in his only novel, *The Feud at Oakfield Creek*, written in 1886 (just after the history of California) and based, like *The Octopus*, on the land dispute at Mussel Slough.

But there are important differences. *The Octopus* is set, like the original dispute, in the San Joaquin valley; Royce's *Feud* takes place almost entirely in San Francisco and the hills of the East Bay. Although Norris converts the dirt-poor farmers of Tulare county into facsimiles of the wealthy ranchers of Santa Cruz, he at least recreates the economic struggle between the farmers and the railroad. Royce leaves the railroad out and turns the whole affair into the aftereffect of a soap opera quarrel between two old California pioneers, the rich landowner, Alonzo Eldon, and the poor poet-professor, Alf Escott. Indeed, early on in the novel Royce makes a point of the unbusinesslike and economically trivial nature of the feud. "Men are so strange," remarks Alonzo's daughter-in-law, Margaret:

> You call us women mere creatures of feeling. But dear me, the thing seems easy enough to me. Perhaps it's all my womanly stupidity, but if the poor people have their rights, and you know it, why do you want to turn them out of house and home, just for a mere matter of pride? I think men are the least rational beings on earth. Women wouldn't have such troubles with settlers, I know.[15]

The moral tone of this passage suggests an opposition between justice (the settlers' rights) and business (Alonzo's attempt to claim the land for himself and his "Land Improvement Company"); its real target, however, is not business but the irrationality and sentimentality of businessmen. From the standpoint of what Royce elsewhere calls "pure business," the Oakfield Creek (unlike the Mussel Slough) affair is not a difficult one—the differences between the settlers (who claim squatters' rights to the property) and Eldon (who claims legal title)

---

[15] Josiah Royce, *The Feud at Oakfield Creek* (1887; reprint, Upper Saddle River, N.J., 1970), 28–29. Subsequent page references are cited in parentheses in the text.

might easily be adjudicated. But the settlers are now led by Escott, who, having bought up some of their claims out of "enmity" to Eldon, sees the "business" as one of "eternal justice" (31). Escott is a "confirmed romancer"—by which Royce turns out to mean that, unlike the settlers, he has no real interest in the land: "Escott has lived on one of the tracts twice or thrice since he purchased the claim, though always for short periods. Part of the land he has lent, without rent, to poor families. At other times, he has employed two men to take care of some of it for him" (41). Escott is thus an absentee squatter. The structure of his commitment to the settlers' claims undermines the basis for those claims, and the intensity of his commitment to justice makes an equitable adjudication impossible. This is not to say that Eldon has any interest in the land either or even, finally, in the money that might be made from selling it. "In the course of the controversy," he has become "so much wrought up" that he has declared he will "never settle with the old claimants at any price" (39). "For the money he doesn't care now" (40). Like Escott, he is motivated by something beyond self-interest. Indeed, he is willing to take a loss to get rid of the settlers: "He would eject them, if it cost him half a million."

Alonzo's son Tom dismisses such threats as "the words of passion" and asserts what the novel continuously seeks to demonstrate—"Father is not so bad as that." But neither the contrast between Escott's noble purposes and Eldon's ignoble ones nor Royce's and his family's attempts to rehabilitate Alonzo should be allowed to obscure the essential "irrationality" of their positions: the champion of squatters' rights is a kind of absentee landlord; the land-grabbing capitalist is willing to lose money to assert his rights. "A woman simply can't understand such passions," says Margaret. She is speaking of Alonzo's vindictiveness, but in effect she characterizes what is most puzzling about the Oakfield Creek situation and especially about Royce's representation of it. The "whole question of California land titles," Royce had written in 1885, was "a critical one" for "the new community," involving the "universal question of the conflict between abstract ideas and social authority, at a moment when the order of a new society, and the eternal conflict between the private and the universal Selves had to be settled."[16] Yet in *Feud*, the struggle over land titles is represented as a struggle between two men with absolutely no interest in the land or in the "abstract question" of legitimate title. And despite Royce's claim that the history of California teaches only one "lesson"—"We are all but dust, save as this social order gives us life"[17]—*The Feud at Oakfield Creek*, by its very mode of narration, resolves the eternal conflict of private and universal in favor of the private, thus transforming public events, at every opportunity, into private ones. It is as if the genre of the novel seemed to Royce to require a valorization of the individual that as a historian and philosopher he would have found intolerable. Converting the struggle between the settlers and the railroad into a quarrel between two old men caused by the son of one having jilted the daughter of the other, Royce turns a political and economic dispute over "abstract principle" and "social authority" into "a personal and private fight" (470) over a girl.

One way to account for this anomaly might be to note, with R. Jackson Wilson, that Royce's "critique of individualism was psychological and metaphysical, not economic or political." "Royce's political and economic ideas always remained essentially those of the Berkeley and San Francisco businessmen who had financed his year in Germany. . . . In the main, he was simply frightened by turn-of-the-century America, and fright provoked the usual conservative response, a reassertion of what he thought were the traditional concepts of property and obligation."[18] Transposing this account of Royce's politics to *The Feud at Oakfield Creek*, we might argue that the requirements of the sentimental novel as Royce understood them —"two bloody fights, three heroes, two heroines, several villains, and almost no morals"[19]—provided him with an opportunity to defuse the threat to the self: the threat, that is, to "traditional concepts of property and obligation" posed not only

[16] Josiah Royce, "An Episode of Early California Life: The Squatter Riot of 1850 in Sacramento" (1885), in *The Basic Writings of Josiah Royce*, 2 vols., ed. John J. McDermott (Chicago, 1969), 1:126, 122.

[17] Royce, *California*, 394.

[18] R. Jackson Wilson, *In Quest of Community* (New York, 1963), 163.

[19] Josiah Royce, *Letters*, ed. John Clendenning (Chicago, 1970), 202.

by developments in American political and economic life but by the tendencies of his own philosophical work. Eventually, Royce would come to regard the individual as "essentially defective" and to equate "the very form of his being as a morally detached individual" with "original sin."[20] From the radically Pauline perspective of *The Problem of Christianity*, only the "destruction" of the "natural self" could make "salvation" possible. But the Royce of the mid-1880s was as yet unable to seek the solution to social problems in the miraculous subsumption of the individual by the "corporate entity" embodied in "the Christian community" and as yet unwilling to identify the business corporation with that Christian corporate entity. The "personal and private" life of the novel might well have seemed the saving grace of the business life of California. We might say that the political and economic had first to be reduced to the personal so that later they might be transformed into the religious.

But the novel itself, concerned though it is to represent the public history of California as an epiphenomenon of the private lives of some of the state's more prominent citizens, nevertheless experiences some difficulty in separating the private and personal from the public and political. To some extent, this is probably due to Royce's incompetence as a novelist. Virtually all the action of the novel consists of secret intrigues designed to avoid a violent confrontation between settlers and landowners at Oakfield Creek; and the people engaged in these intrigues are so clever, so dedicated and noble, that it begins to seem (about three-quarters of the way through) that their plans must succeed. But they can't succeed if the novel is to end in the required tragic manner. So Royce causes an evil newspaperman miraculously to hear of some private interviews between the unmarried hero and the married heroine; the newspaperman publicizes this information in the appropriate places and attributes the publicity to the boasting of the hero. Since the interviews were secret, who else could be the source? Having thus managed, in the most arbitrary manner, to revive old

[20] Royce, *Problem of Christianity*, 194.

enmities, Royce pushes the story on to the violent climax demanded by the Mussel Slough affair.

Something more than incompetence, however, is involved in this arbitrary authorial intervention. For Royce has managed things so that the narrative insists on the sanctity of emotions so personal that they never can be and never are revealed ("Their secret was safe, their mutual understanding perfect" [398]), while at the same time it inexplicably reveals them. And this inexplicability is, in a certain sense, necessary, since any plausible account of how the secret and ultimately innocent love of hero and heroine was made public would compromise both the integrity of the secret and the innocence of the love. By means of this hole in his plot, then, Royce asserts simultaneously the absolute primacy of the private and the absolute impossibility of keeping anything private. There is a gap between the world of persons and the world of politics, a gap that must be left unbridged if persons are to be saved from politics but that must at the same time be constantly crossed if politics are to be causally accounted for by reference to persons. Thus the formal incoherence of Royce's plot corresponds to an incoherence in his conception of the relation between public and private, an incoherence the novel serves above all to defend.

These uneasy relations between public and private emerge as thematically central to the novel in Royce's even more uneasy introduction of what was, after all, the central character in the Mussel Slough affair, the Southern Pacific Railroad. The railroad turns into a "Land and Improvement Company," and instead of being, as Norris would describe it, "huge," a "colossus" (42), it is only, as Margaret Eldon puts it to her father-in-law, its chief stockholder, "something about as big as your own thumb" (264). Nevertheless, it presents a serious obstacle to resolving the feud, since while Alonzo Eldon professes himself willing "in my private capacity as his old friend" (259) to settle things with Alf Escott, he reminds his daughter-in-law that as president of the company he "can't act alone" but must bear in mind the "capital of innocent shareholders" (258). Not Eldon but the Land and Improvement Company owns the Oakfield Creek property. To his listeners this "explanation" seems "to have a certain hollow sound," but Eldon insists on the distinction between himself and the company: "A man isn't a corporation."

Margaret Eldon responds to this argument by urging him to take the corporation private. She tells him to buy back the rights he ought "never" to have sold so that "all will be in [his] hands again" (264). Having thrown this sop to the "miserable little monster" of the corporation (since what he claims to "fear is *its* bitterness of feeling towards Escott"), Eldon can then go ahead and deal fairly with the settlers. And with Eldon holding all its shares, the corporate "monster" will be reduced to the man (Eldon himself) that Margaret already understands it to be. The "hollow sound" of a corporate body will be replaced by the sound of flesh and blood.

The only difficulty here is that what Margaret has proposed, as a "woman of business," is too businesslike for the corporation—"the passions that had been aroused couldn't be allayed today or tomorrow" (267). The shareholders don't want their money; they want to know that the settlers have been "beaten in the courts" (266). The corporation is here identified with the irrationality and sentimentality of the original quarrel between Eldon and Escott, and the difference between a man and a corporation begins to blur. "A woman simply can't understand such passions." Men and corporations both are too passionate for "pure business"; the "miserable little monster" of a corporation is doubled by Margaret's "powerful, capricious monster of a father-in-law" (270). Where the novel's plot requires miracles, its cast of characters requires monsters, and what is most monstrous is finally the difficulty of saying exactly why and in what way a man isn't a corporation.

In effect, Alonzo Eldon asserts what most writers of the period were coming to recognize as "the theory of the existence of the corporation as an entity distinct and separate from its shareholders,"[21] when he distinguishes between a man and a corporation. What he means, of course, is that, even as the

[21] I. Maurice Wormser, *Disregard of the Corporate Fiction and Allied Corporation Problems* (New York, 1927), 43. The essay from which this remark is drawn, "Piercing the Veil of Corporate Entity," was first published in 1912.

chief shareholder in the Land and Improvement Company, he can't be held personally responsible for that company's actions. His daughter-in-law expresses a skepticism about this difference that goes hand in hand with the developing doctrine of corporate entity. If the chief officer or the chief stockholder isn't responsible for the corporation's actions, who is? It is sometimes necessary, as one writer put it, to "pierce the veil of corporate entity"[22] in order to get at what another writer called "the human beings who are behind the entity."[23] The quarrel between Margaret and Alonzo is thus a quarrel between two different legal theories of the corporation: the theory of the corporation as one mode among others of organizing a "group of natural persons"[24] and the theory of the corporation as not simply a group but a "group" that "is recognized and treated by the law as something distinct from its members."[25]

In retrospect we can see that to characterize the dispute in this way is to miss its real point. The question of whether corporations existed independent of the persons who owned and operated them had already been decisively answered by the time *The Feud at Oakfield Creek* was written. In what legal writers characterized as the "leading case" of *Button v. Hoffman* (1884), the sole owner of all the shares in a corporation brought suit "to recover certain personal property which had been unlawfully taken from the corporation's possession."[26] The plaintiff thought himself entitled to recover the corporation's property because, as he put it, "I bought all the stock, I own all the stock now, I became the absolute owner of the mill. It belonged at that time to the company, and I am the company." The Wisconsin court, however, was unpersuaded by this Margaret Eldon–like account of corporate ontology. "The owner of all the capital stock of a corporation does not own its property," wrote the court, "and does not himself become the corpora-

---

[22] Ibid., 30.

[23] Arthur W. Machen, Jr., "Corporate Personality," *Harvard Law Review* 24 (1911): 265.

[24] John P. Davis, *Corporations* (1905; reprint, New York, 1961), 13.

[25] George F. Canfield, "The Scope and Limits of the Corporate Entity Theory," *Columbia Law Review* 17 (1917): 128.

[26] Wormser, *Disregard of the Corporate Fiction*, 17.

tion, as a natural person, to own its property and do its business in his own name. While the corporation exists he is a mere stockholder of it, and nothing else."[27] The man is not the company, and the company is not the man, because the company is, "by a fiction of law," another man. Royce's rhetorical doubling of the monster corporation (Davis calls it the "man in law") by the monster Alonzo Eldon (Margaret's "father-in-law") thus invokes the disconcerting possibility that the struggle between man and corporation at Mussel Slough can be transformed into a struggle between man and man not because the corporation is a veil concealing a man but because the corporation is itself a new kind of man.

But what kind? "The orthodox American lawyer," wrote Arthur Machen in his frequently cited "Corporate Personality," "would be apt to say, 'A corporation is a fictitious, artificial person, composed of natural persons, created by the state, existing only in contemplation of law, invisible, soulless, immortal.'"[28] According to Machen, however, this definition is nothing but a "*congeries* of self-contradictory terms" (257). It asserts both that a corporation is "artificial" and that it is "imaginary or fictitious," when, in fact, what is "artificial is real, and not imaginary: an artificial lake is not an imaginary one"; it asserts that a corporation is "created by the state" and "fictitious," whereas something that has been created must be "real"; and it asserts that a corporation is "composed of natural persons" and is "imaginary or fictitious," whereas "neither in mathematics nor in philosophy nor in law can the sum of several actual, rational quantities produce an imaginary quantity." All these contradictions revolve around what is said to be "fictitious" in the corporate identity, and since what is "fictitious" is the characterization of the corporation as a person, the way to eliminate the contradictions, Machen argues, is to try to hang on to the notion of the corporation's real and independent existence while getting rid of the idea that this independent existence is personal. He thus distinguishes between two "prop-

---

[27] Quoted in ibid.
[28] Machen, "Corporate Personality," 257. Subsequent page references are cited in parentheses in the text.

ositions" about the nature of corporations: "(1) that a corporation is an entity distinct from the sum of the members that compose it, and (2) that this entity is a person" (258). The first of these propositions seems to him true and the second false.

By way of argument for the real existence of the corporate entity, Machen adduces a series of analogies, from a bundle of faggots (the "bundle" being "something distinct" from the faggots) to a school ("something distinct from the boys that constitute it"[259]), to a "voluntary association" for doing business: "It is hard to convince a sensible businessman that when a senior partner gives his son on attaining majority a small interest in the firm, an entirely new firm is thereby created" (260). The "ordinary layman" can see that the identity of the firm is not changed just because a new owner has been added. Hence the identity of the firm is not dependent on the identity of its owners. And following this model, the existence of the corporate entity "is precisely as real as the existence of any other composite unit."

> If a corporation is fictitious, the only reality being the individuals who compose it, then by the same token a river is fictitious, the only reality being the individual atoms of oxygen and hydrogen. The only difference is that one of the essential elements of . . . a river, consists in juxtaposition in space of . . . the molecules of water, whereas the bond of union in the case of a corporation is less material. (261)

This real existence of the corporation as an entity does not, according to Machen, make the corporation really a person. He acknowledges that the two propositions have been "often confused" so that, for example, theorists in Germany, correctly asserting the real existence of corporations, have supposed that this assertion committed them also to thinking that corporations are real persons. They have actually carried this commitment to "grotesque lengths," describing the "corporate organism" as an "animal," claiming that "it possesses organs like a human being" and "even possesses sex" (churches are feminine, states masculine [256]). But, Machen points out, there is no logical connection between the claim that corporations are real and the claim that they are persons; rivers are real, but rivers are not persons. A "corporate entity," like a river, "is not a rational being, is not capable of understanding the law's commands, and has no will which can be affected by threats of legal punishment"—hence, "a corporation is not a real person" (265). It is "personified" (that is, "regarded as having rights and liabilities" [266]) only "for the sake of convenience"; in reality only "men of flesh and blood, of like passions with ourselves . . . enjoy the rights and bear the burdens attributed by the law to the corporate entity." Only corporate *entity* is real, then; corporate personality is a fiction.

By conceiving of the corporation as a real thing but not a real person, Machen suggests a difficulty with our earlier characterization of the corporation as a figure for intangible insatiability. Machen's corporation, because it isn't "flesh and blood," can experience no "passions"; and, although Cyclone Davis characterizes the corporation as "moved only by an exhaustless greed for lucre,"[29] for him too it is "without one human sympathy." Furthermore, its effect on the human beings who own it or who are employed by it is to recreate them in its own image—to deprive them of their "sympathy." These "natural persons" come to "feel no personal concern for the moral quality of the acts which produce money" and eventually cease to be persons at all. "The individual is merged in the money-machine of which he is an integral part."[30] So for Davis, as for Machen, the corporation is finally not a person but a thing—an "entity" or a "machine." But Davis goes one step further than Machen, conceiving of corporations not only as different from but also as threatening to "natural persons." And Norris's Shelgrim, the president of the railroad, goes further still, telling Presley that "when you speak of wheat and the railroads," "you are dealing with forces . . . not with men." Here what Mark Seltzer has called naturalism's "discourse of force"[31] not only

---

[29] Davis, *A Political Revelation*, 242.

[30] Ibid., 245.

[31] Mark Seltzer, "The Naturalist Machine," in *Sex, Politics, and Science in the Nineteenth-Century Novel*, ed. Ruth Bernard Yeazell (Baltimore, 1986), 116–47.

imagines a world of "entities" competing with men but imagines that men, properly understood, already have been reduced to the things ("brutes," "machines") they are said to be competing with.

In fact, following Seltzer's lead, we can say that the "discourse of force" not only undoes the opposition between body and machine but, perhaps more surprisingly, undoes the opposition between the body/machine and the soul, between something that is *all* body and something that is no body at all. Thus Davis can think of the corporation as simultaneously "intangible" (no body) and a "machine" (all body), not because he is inconsistent but because these two conditions are more like one another than either is like the alternative, a soul in a body. And much the same may be said about *The Octopus*. Norris's utterly idealized account of the production of wheat as the emergence of a spiritual body out of a natural one can coexist peacefully with an utterly materialist account of the growing wheat as a mechanical "force"; "indifferent, gigantic, resistless, it moved in its appointed grooves" (316). Furthermore, the problem of insatiability with which I began gets rather elegantly solved by this double reduction to ideal and to material. Insofar as men are really souls, they don't desire at all. To participate in the spiritual life of nature is to become, like the grain of wheat, like life itself, immune to loss. "Life never departs. Life simply *is*" (447). A world where nothing can be absent leaves nothing to be desired. And insofar as men are really bodies, they don't desire either; nothing can stop natural "forces," not because they are insatiable but—just the opposite—because they are "indifferent." Separating consumption from desire, the logic of material forces liberates men from the constraints of human embodiment just as surely as the logic of Pauline spirituality.

What Norris calls "human agency" is thus effaced by the double reduction to ideal and to material—which is to say, to a natural ontology of bodies and souls: "As if human agency could affect this colossal power!" (316). The point is not simply that human agents are less powerful than nature but that, reduced to the "forces" they really are, human agents are not agents at all. To recall Machen's terms, they are more like rivers than persons. His claim that corporations are "entities" appears now as simply a version of the more fundamental naturalist claim that "persons" too are really entities and hence that natural persons are as fictitious as corporate ones. From this standpoint, however, to characterize corporate personality as a fiction is not to dismiss it any more than to characterize numbers as imaginary is to dismiss imaginary numbers. American courts, more skeptical than German philosophers of the reality of corporate personality, had been "troubled" by the "old difficulty" of finding corporations guilty of "fraud, of malice, or of crimes involving a particular mental state"; since "a corporation has no mind and is therefore incapable of entertaining malice," how can it be capable of "contriving a fraud or of doing any other act involving a mental state?" But according to Machen, this reasoning is "illogical." The fact that corporate personality is imaginary constitutes no obstacle to treating corporations as if they had minds. On the contrary: "if the corporate personality is imaginary, there is no limit to the characteristics and capacities which may be attributed to that personality." In particular, "if you can imagine that a corporate entity is a person, you can also imagine that this person has a mind." And, having imagined that it has a mind, you can hold it responsible for "crimes involving a particular mental state." In fact, Machen suggests, with a flourish that might dazzle even a German philosopher, "to take the opposite view would be like arguing that Hamlet must have been insane, because he was a fictitious person and could therefore have no mind" (348).

What is dazzling here is the way in which the attempt to apply "sturdy common sense" (365) to the doctrine of corporate personality, denying the German theory that the corporate person is real and thus has real characteristics ("will," "sex"), has turned into the claim that because the corporate person is *not* real, we are justified in attributing to it any characteristic we like: a mind, a soul (Sir Edward Coke and Cyclone Davis to the contrary notwithstanding), even a body, although it may be that "to carry the metaphor so far would provoke a smile, and would serve no good purpose" (349). Common sense dictates that the "legal imagination" can attribute to corporations any characteristic of persons it chooses. The restraints lie not in any "logical" considerations but only in the demands of some-thing like good taste.

But why should we want to think of corporations as per-sons? If common sense tells us that corporate entities are real and corporate persons are not, why don't we just treat corpo-rations as things and forgo the fiction of personality? Machen's answer to this question is that it would be inconvenient and un-natural to do so. It is inconvenient because the law has given corporations as entities some of the powers of persons (the right to sue and be sued, for instance); thus the lawyer may think of the corporation as a person in the same way that a mathematician may call a "complicated expression such as $x^2 + 3ax + b^2$" y and then use y in his calculations "instead of the longer and more cumbrous expression" (353). It is unnatural because "the human mind is so constituted" that it finds it dif-ficult "not to personify" "close organization[s]": "We instinc-tively speak and think of [such an] organization as a person; and the law finds it difficult or impossible to refrain from doing the same" (349). As if he were parodying naturalism's reduction of persons to personifications, Machen identifies the desire to personify as itself one of those "instincts" that mark the re-placement of persons with brutes; the mark of the brute is his irresistible impulse to think of himself as a person.

Neither the appeal to convenience nor the appeal to nature is entirely satisfactory, however, for reasons having to do not so much with the distinction between (real) corporate entity and (fictitious) corporate personality as with the retroactive questions raised by such appeals about the nature of the cor-porate entity in the first place. For if a corporation created by the state is real and not imaginary, in the same way that "an ar-tificial lake is not an imaginary lake," and if that corporation is endowed by the state with many of the powers of persons, why isn't it a real, albeit artificial, person? The answer to this is pre-sumably that we find it more difficult to conceive of artificial persons than of artificial entities; indeed, our very notion of a person seems to require that it not be artificial. But why then is it more "natural" to personify a corporation than it is to person-ify another artificial entity like an artificial lake or river? If real persons are "men of flesh and blood, of like passions with ourselves," why is it natural to think of corporations as real persons?

The answer to this question is implicit in the account I noted earlier by Machen concerning the reality of the corporate entity. The corporate entity is real instead of fictitious, by analogy with a river or with an army:

> If a corporation is fictitious, the only reality being the individuals who compose it, then by the same token a river is fictitious, the only reality being the individual atoms of oxygen and hydrogen. The only difference is that one of the essential elements of an army, or of a river, consists in juxtaposition in space of the members, or of the molecules of water, whereas the bond of union in the case of a corporation is less material. (261)

The identity of a river, according to Machen, is a function of the "juxtaposition in space" of its molecules, but the "members" of a corporation, unlike the molecules in a river, are not juxtaposed in space; their "bond of union" is "less material." The relation between corporate entity and corporate person is understood along the same lines. "*In rerum natura* there is no distinction between a personified entity and an entity not personified" (349). The distinction between a personified entity and an entity not personified, like the bond of union between the members of a corporation, is immaterial.

In the case of corporate entity, Machen argues, the difference between material proximity and "less material" proximity is "not fundamental," but, as the parallel with personification suggests, it must by his own logic be at least as fundamental as the difference between a thing and a personified thing—indeed, between a thing and a person. The differences between persons and things, like the differences between personified entities and entities not personified, are not material. The transformation of thing into person involves, as it were, the addition of a certain immateriality. Conceiving this immateriality as fictional, corporate theorists repeat the naturalist gesture of imagining persons as personified things. But unlike rivers, the corporate entity requires the fiction of immateriality even to qualify as a thing. Without the "less material" "bond of union" that identifies the individual members of a corporation, there would be no body. Unless the individual members belonged to the same body, there would be no corporation. Hence the corporation comes to seem the embodiment of figurality that makes personhood possible, rather than appearing as a figurative extension of the idea of personhood. The corporation serves as a kind of model for personhood precisely because it finally makes no sense to think of it as a thing that has been personified (in the way that the ancients might have thought of a river, or in the way that naturalism might think of a human body). The corporation cannot be a personified thing because to be a thing at all it must already meet the conditions of being a person; its material identity as a thing is thinkable only in terms of the immateriality that constitutes its identity as a person.

"The doctrine of corporate personality is a natural though figurative expression of actual facts" (363). Machen opposes nature to figuration, conceiving the actual fact of corporate entity as ground for the legal fiction of corporate personality. But the commonsense difference between natural entity and fictional personality turns out to be unthinkable in the case of corporations, and the blurring of that difference turns out to be inevitable: "We do not need to be instructed to regard a corporation as an entity and to regard that entity as a person: our minds are so constituted that we cannot help taking that view." The point here is not, as before, that we instinctively personify but, more radically, that the possibility of personification depends on there already being persons.[32] In other words, corporations must be persons even if persons aren't. Or, to put it still another way, what I have described as the naturalist reduction to body and soul becomes impossible for the corporation, which, as an entity, must have a body, and which, to be the entity it is,

[32] I am led to this way of putting the point by Frances Ferguson's remark that the cottage girl in Wordsworth's "We are Seven" pushes personification "to such an extreme that it becomes a virtual anti-type to personification. This girl personifies *persons*" (*Wordsworth: Language as Counter-Spirit* [New Haven, Conn., 1977], 26–27).

must also have a soul. The scandal of the corporation, then, is not that it is a new kind of man; the scandal is that it is the old kind. If what seemed monstrous to Royce in *The Feud at Oak-field Creek* was the discovery that Alonzo Eldon's declaration—"a man isn't a corporation"—was only true because the corporation was *another* man, what seems monstrous now is the discovery that for a man to be a man he must also be a corporation—a man *is* a corporation. The monstrosity of the father-in-law, the monstrosity of the Land and Improvement Company, is the monstrosity of personhood, the impossible and irreducible combination of body and soul.

In *The Octopus*, the monster is the railroad, the "leviathan" (130), the "colossus" (42), the "ironhearted monster of steel and steam" (228). But the corporate moment, the moment when the nonidentity of material and ideal constitutes the identity of the person, is disseminated throughout *The Octopus*. When, for example, Vanamee, seeking to recall his dead lover, begins to exercise his telepathic powers, his "body" and "mind" come literally, if temporarily, apart as his "imagination" reshapes itself to encounter the "intangible agitation" (273) of Angele's spirit becoming the "tangible presence" of her daughter's body. By the same logic, Annixter's love for Hilma Tree involves what Norris characterizes as the fusing together of "things as disassociated . . . as fire and water" (258)—the "tangible, imminent fact" of Hilma herself and the "formless . . . abstraction" of marriage. On the night the wheat comes up, Vanamee calls Angele back, and the "tangible fact" and the "abstraction" are "melted into one" (259), turning Annixter from a "machine" into a "man" (329). The transformation from machine to man suggests here the customary opposition between mechanical and organic with the customary preference for the organic. But, as we have already seen, the sprouting seed makes a bad symbol of organic growth; what it emblemizes for Norris is the dispossession of the "natural body." And, following the same scenario, the machine becomes a man not because iron is made flesh (flesh can be the material of machines) but because the body acquires a soul. Just as the novel's chief symbol of organic materialism, the wheat, is made into the body of the immaterial, its chief symbol of mechanical materialism, the steam engine, is made into the site where material and immaterial intersect. Annixter, like the engine, is the place where the tangible and the intangible, "things as disassociated as fire and water," get mixed into one—steam. Reimagining the mixture of elements that produces thermodynamic energy as the mixture of tangible and intangible that produces human actions, Norris, like Machen, turns the emblem of the entity into the emblem of the person.[33]

Hence the monstrosity of the "ironhearted monster of steel and steam"; the point is not only that its heart is made of iron but also that its body has a soul. When Presley visits Shelgrim, it is not "a terrible man of blood and iron" (404) he meets, but "a sentimentalist and an art critic," a man as passionate as Royce's Land and Improvement Company. Expecting (perhaps hoping) to find a machine, something that is all body, Presley finds a body that, "enormous" though it is, is still not quite equal to "the head" of the railroad. Presley has never seen "a broader man" (402), but what really astonishes him is that "Shelgrim did not move his body. His arms moved, and his head, but the great bulk of the man remained immobile" (403–4). Eventually Presley begins "to conceive the odd idea that Shelgrim, as it were, placed his body in the chair to rest while his head and brains and hands went on working independently" (404). Reversing the charges of body and soul, it is tempting to see Shelgrim here as a figure for corporate disembodiment, his body even bigger than the "gross" S. Behrman's but at the same time more corporate, more truly "intangible." The railroad gets its way, after all, not by acts of physical violence but by changes in the freight rates, which, intangible themselves, can nevertheless leave as strong a man as the engineer Sykes—"a veritable giant, built of great sinews, powerful" (250)—"absolutely crushed" (252).

At the same time, however, even grain rates have a certain materiality; they are produced by "a turn of the hand" (251), "inscribed" on a piece of "yellow paper" (245). And in *The Oc-*

---

[33] For a different reading, emphasizing the "impersonal" and "indifferent" character of what he calls the "nature-machine," see Ronald E. Martin, *American Literature and the Universe of Force* (Durham, N.C., 1981), 146–83.

topus, it is Shelgrim, "the head" of the railroad, whose hands set the rates. In fact, like the octopus he heads, Shelgrim, his body placed in the chair to rest, is all head and hands, a cephalopod. With his "great bulk" set to one side, he is, like the corporation, something more than his body. But with his "head, brains and hands" all working, he is never—again like the corporation—independent of his body. Rather, everything that the corporation does must be done with its hands—from fighting for its property (the hired guns, Christian and Delaney, are "S. Behrman's right and left hands" [344]) to receiving that property ("Quien Sabe was in the hands of the railroad" [377]) to legitimating and consolidating its title to the property (by the time the "Supreme Court hands down a decision" [344], all political resistance will have been crushed by "the great iron hand" [379] of the trust). These metaphors, in their ordinariness, get at the causal connection between grain rates and bodies—no action can be performed without a body—and at the same time suggest—since as ordinary as they are they are still metaphors—that no action can be performed just by a body. The nonphysical notion of the person is required to make the bodies of Christian and Delaney, for example, the hands of the corporation. And Shelgrim, irrevocably in his body without being entirely of his body, embodies this constitutive discrepancy between material and ideal. Acting in the world with "a turn of its hand," the octopus embodies embodiment.

Versions of Dyke's complaint were, of course, traditional in populist attacks. Corporations "wield no weapon more alarming than the little pencil";[34] they destroy the farmers with "a single stroke of the pen."[35] Writing here is an emblem of the ideal, and as such, given the reversibility of material and ideal, it can easily be made mechanical. Cyclone Davis worries that because so much is published, "busy people are disposed to

[34] Edward Winslow Martin, *History of the Grange Movement* (San Francisco, 1873), 327.

[35] W. Scott Morgan, *History of the Wheel and Alliance* (1889), reprinted in part in Pollack, *The Populist Mind*, 274. Morgan here is actually quoting Jeremiah S. Black.

pass by a new book without stopping to even read the title."
They "would not be surprised to hear that some man had invented a machine for making books that dispensed with [the]
author . . . and ground out paragraphs by steam."[36] Tales of
"automatic writing" were common in the literature of psychology. Just as Shelgrim invokes the mechanical laws of supply and
demand ("forces" instead of "men") to describe the setting of
grain rates, so Norris flirts with automatism in his description
of Presley writing the poem that will make him famous, "The
Toilers": "For a time, his pen seemed to travel of itself; words
came to him without searching, shaping themselves into
phrases" (262).

But what we might call Shelgrim's mechanical alibi[37] won't
work. For one thing, the law of supply and demand is the law
that sets rates in a free market, but the railroad, as a monopoly,
doesn't operate in a free market. As Alfred D. Chandler, Jr., has
put it, "The operational requirements" of the railroads "had
made obsolete the competition between small units that had
no control over prices—prices that were set by the market
forces of supply and demand."[38] The whole point of mo-
nopolies, like the railroad (what makes them "monstrous"), is
that they transcend the mechanical laws of the market; they
are "no longer regulated by market mechanisms."[39] Furthermore, while business conditions were undermining the transposition of thermodynamic laws into economics, developments in physics seemed to be undermining the very notion of
a thermodynamic law.[40] Thus, in a paper called "The Mechani-

---

[36] Davis, *A Political Revelation*, 4.

[37] This phrase is adapted from Leo Bersani. Describing the turn toward the
family at the end of *War and Peace*, Bersani calls Tolstoy's appeal to "the obvious foundation of the family in nature" a "biological alibi for social confor-
mity" (*A Future for Astyanax* [Boston, 1976], 63).

[38] Alfred D. Chandler, Jr., *The Visible Hand: The Managerial Revolution in
American Business* (Cambridge, Mass., 1977), 203.

[39] Ibid., 204.

[40] Seltzer's description of the naturalist text as the naturalist "machine" and
his claim that the laws of thermodynamics constitute a "mechanics of power"
which "govern" that machine thus seem to me questionable. His appeal to De-

cal, the Historical, and the Statistical" (1914), Royce pointed out that recent work by Boltzmann and Arrhenius suggested the possibility of "the occasional if not the general reversal of the second law of the theory of energy," a reversal impossible in the mechanical view of nature but not in "the statistical view of nature."[41]

For Royce, the consequences of such reversals were profound: "Suppose an aggregate of natural objects which contains a very great number of members. . . . These objects may be things or events, at your pleasure. They may be molecules or stars . . . or literary compositions or moral agents or whatever else you will."[42] Such an aggregate is utterly indifferent to the apparently crucial distinction between the "vital" and the "mechanical." The laws of probability apply to it no matter what its members are. Hence, the statistical aggregate constitutes an entity quite distinct from an organic whole or a mechanical system. It is made up of natural objects—whether these objects be understood biologically or mechanically—but the laws of its behavior are neither biological nor mechanical, and, as a statistical aggregate, it is itself neither a biological nor a mechanical object.

This is not to say that for Royce the statistical aggregate independent of the identities of its members and indifferent to their status as "molecules" or "agents" is itself neutral with respect to agency. One of the "most widely applicable laws of nature," he thinks, "wholly indefinable in mechanical terms but always expressible in . . . statistical tendencies," is the "law that aggregation tends to result in some further and increasingly mutual assimilation of the members of the aggregate."[43] Thus, in what would seem a bizarre parody of naturalism's rhetoric of biological force were it not so clearly an earnest exten-

_____

leuze and Guattari's notion of the "desiring-machine" is illuminating in this regard, since the basic point of that notion is to do away with persons, and its ultimate effect (like that of the double reduction to body and soul) is to do away with desire itself.

[41] Josiah Royce, "The Mechanical, the Historical, and the Statistical" (1914), in *Basic Writings*, 2:726.

[42] Ibid., 728–29.

[43] Ibid., 729.

sion of that rhetoric, Royce speaks of the "law of the fecundity of aggregation" as expressing "what seems to be a sort of unconscious teleology in nature." Natural objects—moral agents or molecules—may or may not have their purposes, but nature itself, embodied not precisely in either the molecules or the moral agents but in the abstract principle of "statistical fecundity," has a purposiveness of its own, "a purposiveness whose precise outcomes no finite being seems precisely to intend."[44] It is thus the discrepancy between the behavior of individuals and that of aggregates that constitutes the personhood of nature, and the indifference of statistical laws to the question of whether *anything* really is a person turns out to be nature's way of guaranteeing that ultimately *everything* will be a person.

For Norris's Presley too, despite the touch of automatism in his inspiration, nature is a person. The "gigantic sweep of the San Joaquin" is a "mother" (39), like Royce's nature, "illimitable, immeasurable" (260). But as Norris describes it, the "romance" Presley wants to write in celebration of her, the "Song of the West," is "shattered" against the "stubborn iron barrier" (16) of the railroad. Dreaming of "things without names—thoughts for which no man had yet invented words, terrible, formless shapes, vague figures, colossal, monstrous," Presley is brought down to earth by the "realism" of the "commonplace" (15): "He searched for the true romance and, in the end, found grain rates and unjust freight tariffs" (16). From our perspective, however, it is easy to see how false this opposition between romance and realism, mother nature and the railroad, really is.[45] Dreaming of the "monstrous," Presley is already dreaming of the corporation. Imagining the valley as a "gigantic scroll" (260), he is already putting pen to paper, reproducing with the turn of the poet's hand the turn of the hand that sets the grain rates.

The poet, then, is the paradigm of the corporate person,

[44] Ibid., 731.

[45] For a different view, see Donald Pizer: "The monopoly is the soulless Force whose practices, spreading death and destruction, are opposed to the landscape" (*Realism and Naturalism in Nineteenth-Century American Literature* [Carbondale, Ill., 1984], 160–61).

writing the paradigmatic corporate act. When Vanamee urges Presley to "live" the "epic" life of the West rather than "write" about it, Presley responds that its "vastness" would "suffocate" him if he couldn't "record" his "impressions" (36). But Presley, unlike S. Behrman, is in no danger of suffocation. The wheat kills Behrman, forcing its way in from the outside just as Presley imagines himself "overwhelmed" by his "impressions." But the wheat is already inside Presley: "his mental life was not at all the result of impressions and sensations that came to him from without, but rather of thoughts germinating from within" (13). And when Presley *is* "all but suffocated," the cause is "the repression of his contending thoughts," and the cure is indeed literature—"he flung himself before his table and began to write" (262). Imagined simultaneously as consumptive (taking wheat in without losing his hunger) and productive (writing out his "germinated" thoughts), Presley and his "insatiable" desire "to write verse" (13) combine in one person the monstrous productivity of the valley and the monstrous appetite of the railroad.

In the Song of the West, the epic life doubles the corporate life, production doubles consumption, the "fecundated earth" (152) doubles the "fecundity of aggregation." They are all, as Royce and Norris variously put it, "immeasurable," "illimitable," "immortal," "infinite," "insatiable." The corporation, the "artificial person," incarnates (for better or for worse) this transcendence of the limits that make up "natural" persons. And in doing so, it represents what I take to be a central problem for naturalism, the irruption in nature of the powerfully unnatural. The rhetoric of "force" tries to solve this problem. Substituting machines for men, it resolves the anomaly of the corporate person by turning all persons, corporate and natural both, into entities. But just as Machen's commonsense reduction of person to entity turned out to involve an irreducible and immaterial fictionality that produced instead a dazzling legitimation of corporate personality, so the corporate fiction of Royce and Norris continually produces persons out of material as unpromising as statistical aggregates or the "limitless" "monotony of the . . . wheat lands" (229). It accomplishes this not by personification—treating the thing as if it were a person—but by seeing the immaterial in the material, seeing the person who is already there. While the word *monopoly* appears only once in the 450-odd pages of *The Octopus*, the word *monotony* appears over and over again, almost always describing the fields of wheat, "bounded only by the horizons": "there was something inordinate about it all, something almost unnatural" (48). What is "inordinate" and "unnatural" is the monopoly behind the monotony, the artificial person behind the natural one. Here is perhaps the deepest complicity between naturalism and the corporation. In naturalism, no persons are natural. In naturalism, personality is always corporate and all fictions, like souls metaphorized in bodies, are corporate fictions.

7. ACTION AND ACCIDENT: PHOTOGRAPHY AND WRITING

And then once more on the water again—about five hundred feet from shore, the while he fumbled aimlessly with the hard and heavy and yet small camera that he now held, as the boat floated out nearer the center. And then, at this point and time looking fearfully about. For now—now—in spite of himself, the long evaded and yet commanding moment.

Theodore Dreiser, *An American Tragedy*

What do we do when we press a button? This question arises in the context of the late-nineteenth-century debate over whether photography was an art, a debate that continues today, although today the question of photography's status as an art is more likely to be asked as a question about photography's "essence."[1] The question today is, what are the relations between photographs and the objects they are photographs of? In contrast, many writers in the late nineteenth century (and some into the twentieth) were more disturbed by the relations between the photograph and the photographer: they worried instead about how photographs were made. From this perspective, the debate over whether photography was an art focused above all on the difference made to our idea of action by that action's dependence on a machine—a machine that seemed to be something more than a tool, especially if one's model of a tool was, say, a painter's brush.

Here, according to the illustrator Joseph Pennell (writing in 1897) is what a painter does: having undergone years of "manual training," cultivating the union of "brain and eye and hand," he "sits down in front of his subject" and "makes a careful study of it with his unaided hands, which he is able to do because he . . . has the power to do it—a power in which the photographer is totally deficient."[2] Of course, his hands aren't utterly unaided, for he has a brush or a pen; they are unaided only by contrast with the kind of aid the photographer's tool offers him. For here is what the photographer does: hurrying out to Hampstead Heath or the Embankment on his "half-holiday," he "plants his machine in a convenient corner and, with the pressing of a button or the loosing of a cap, creates for you a nocturne which shall rank with the life-work of the master"

---

[1] I am thinking in particular of the claims made for and against the notion of the photograph as "document." For an important, if polemical, discussion of this question, see Joel Snyder, "Documentary Without Ontology," *Studies in Visual Communication* (Spring 1984): 78–95.

[2] Joseph Pennell, "Is Photography Among the Fine Arts?" *The Contemporary Review* 72 (December 1897); reprinted in *A Photographic Vision*, ed. Peter C. Bunnell (Salt Lake City, 1980), 50; all further references to this work will be included in the text.

(49). The photographer "prepares his camera; he focuses it . . . he puts in his glass plate or his film." But "who does the work? who makes the picture? Why, he does not as much as know whether there is a picture on it until he brings the plate or film home and develops it" (50). Whatever the photographer does when he presses a button, he does not make a picture. Perhaps one should say, following Pennell, that he starts a machine and the machine makes the picture for him. The machine, not the photographer, has the "power," which is why, "as photographers themselves say, anybody can make a good photograph" (53). Having set the machine in motion, the photographer becomes "anybody"; he gives up the control that would link him as a particular person to the photograph as a particular picture. The actual making of the picture is, on this account, not so much an action as an event, and the picture itself is best understood as the outcome of a series of mechanical interactions between the camera and nature.

Pennell, obviously, is attacking photography's claim to be an art, but it is essential to note that his description of photography—or rather, his account of the relation between pressing a button and making a picture—is accepted and even insisted upon by writers on the other side of the debate. In his famous essay "Pictorial Photography," for example, Alfred Stieglitz emphasizes the "plastic" as opposed to the "mechanical" character of photography, especially of the "development of a plate," and argues that skill in producing prints gives "almost absolute control of tonality, atmosphere, and the like . . . to the photographer, on whose knowledge and taste depends the picture's final artistic claim."[3] The photograph's artistic claim is here linked to the photographer's painterly skills. And with the advent of "straight" photography (the refusal to work with the print), creative control is transferred from the moment after the film is exposed to the moment before. Even as early as 1889, Peter Henry Emerson was asserting that the fundamental job of the photographer was to choose the picture he would take ("It

[3] Alfred Stieglitz, "Pictorial Photography," *Scribner's Magazine* 26 (November 1899); reprinted in Bunnell, *Photographic Vision*, 125; all further references to this work will be cited in the text.

is not the apparatus that chooses the picture, but the man who wields it"[4]—that is, cameras don't take pictures, people do); and as late as 1965, Edward Weston was claiming that "*the finished print must be created in full before the film is exposed.* Until the photographer has learned to visualize his final result in advance, and to predetermine the procedures necessary to carry out that visualization, his finished work (if it be photography at all) will present a series of lucky—or unlucky—mechanical accidents."[5]

For Stieglitz the making of the picture, the assertion of the photographer's "control," comes after the button has been pressed, for Weston it comes before; for both, however, the actual pressing of the button is fundamentally irrelevant to the photographic act. It is in this sense that Stieglitz and Weston can be said to share Pennell's view of art, his desire to minimize the mechanical and so reduce the possibility of accidents. But where for Pennell pressing the button—which has nothing to do with art—has everything to do with photography, for Stieglitz and Weston it has nothing to do with it. Thus Pennell jeers at the photographer whose "one ambition is to have you forget that his photograph is a photograph" (50), while Stieglitz proudly asserts "the claims of the pictorial photograph to be judged on its merits as a work of art independently, and with-

---

[4] Peter Henry Emerson, "Hints on Art," (London, 1889); reprinted in *Classic Essays on Photography*, ed. Alan Trachtenberg, with notes by Amy Weinstein Meyers (New Haven, 1980), 103. Emerson's commitment to the photographer's choice was so complete that when the chemists Hurter and Driffield "proved the unchanging ratio of exposure, density, and development," his "belief in the photographer's complete control over tonal relations in his works" was crushed, and, as Meyers puts it, he "felt compelled to denounce photography as a limited art form" (Trachtenberg, *Classic Essays*, 99–100). The problem as Meyers sees it is that "Emerson's narrow definition of proper photographic procedure did not allow the photographer to use more complex developing and printing methods to compensate for this limited flexibility." Thus, although she quarrels with Emerson's definition of photographic procedure, she assents to his definition of the photographic act, looking to "more complex developing and printing methods" to restore the choice that chemistry has taken away.

[5] Edward Weston, "Seeing Photographically," in *Encyclopedia of Photography* (New York, 1965); reprinted in Trachtenberg, *Classic Essays*, 172.

out considering the fact that it has been produced through the medium of the camera." (126).

For Stieglitz, then, the camera poses a threat to photography, or more particularly to the photographer; that is, the intervention of the machine makes it look as though the photographer either has not done anything (the machine does the work) or has not done what he meant to do (the picture is only an accident). In both cases, it is the photographer's "control" that is in question—his ability to make a picture and to make the particular picture he intended to make. What Stieglitz needs is a way of understanding the camera that will reduce it to the mere "medium" it really is. More broadly, he needs a way of understanding art that will reduce any particular means of artistic expression to just that, a means of expression, and he finds this way in a passage from the great English photographer Emerson:

> The painter learns his technique in order to speak, and he considers painting a mental process. So with photography. . . . The point is, *what you have to say and how to say it*. The originality of a work of art refers to the originality of the thing expressed and the way it is expressed, whether it be in poetry, photography, or painting. That one technique is more difficult than another to learn no one will deny; but the greatest thoughts have been expressed by means of the simplest technique, writing. (124)

For Emerson, the fact that almost anyone can take a picture is no more damaging to photography than the fact that almost anyone can write is damaging to poetry. The camera cannot tell you what to say, nor can it tell you how to say it, any more than the pen or typewriter can supply your thoughts or choose the words to express your thoughts.

Properly understood, then, photography is a kind of writing, and no one will deny that the writer has done something or affirm that he has done what he has done only by mechanical accident. To put the point this way, however, is immediately to suggest the vulnerability of this line of argument, for if the model of writing is to rescue photography from the machine, what becomes of photography when writing itself is understood as mechanical, "automatic"? The interest in automatic writing in this period was extraordinarily widespread, and any serious consideration of it would require an essay of its own. For my purposes here it is enough to point out that by 1900 the German psychologist G. Wundt had described writing as a "mechanical" obstacle between what we "will" to express and what we in fact express,[6] and that in 1901 Freud devoted an entire section of *The Psychopathology of Everyday Life* to what he called "slips of the pen." Indeed, by the 1920s a practice of photography had emerged—surrealism—that insisted on the centrality of automatic writing to the photographic project and that prided itself on incorporating chance or accident in the form of the found object. From this perspective, Stieglitz's vision of the photographer as deciding what he wants to express and then selecting the medium in which to express it begins to look as if it was outmoded even before it got itself expressed.

But it would be a mistake to see these developments as a repudiation of the idea of agency at work in the earlier discourse of photography. For there is a sense in which even as the Freudian assimilation of writing to technology compromises the agent's conscious control over his action, it simultaneously asserts the immunity of that action to mechanical accident. After all, the whole point of Freud's account of slips of the pen is that these slips are not accidents; on the contrary, they have a "hidden motivation" and are in this respect typical of most if not all "parapraxes and chance actions." Thus, in a famous comparison of psychoanalytic concepts to primitive superstition, Freud focuses on the interpretation of "chance events" as "actions and manifestations of persons" (259). "The differences between myself and the superstitious person," Freud writes, "are two: first, he projects outwards a motivation which I look for within; secondly, he interprets chance as due to an event, while I trace it back to a thought. But what is hidden from him corresponds to what is unconscious for me, and the compulsion not to let chance count as chance but to inter-

[6]G. Wundt, *Völkerpsychologie* (Leipzig, 1900); quoted in Sigmund Freud, *The Psychopathology of Everyday Life*, trans. Alan Tyson, ed. James Strachey (New York, 1960), 131; all further references to *The Psychopathology of Everyday Life* will be cited in the text.

pret it is common to both of us" (258–59).[7] The discovery of the unconscious thus problematizes agency only to extend it, finding actions where only accidents had been. And the radical nature of surrealist photography consists finally in its imperial commitment to Stieglitz's account of the photographic act rather than in its subversion of that account; according to surrealism, not only is it *possible* for a photograph to express the photographer's thoughts, it is impossible for it *not* to.[8] Where Stieglitz needed to repress the mechanical element in photography (the pressing of the button) in order to save photography as an expressive act, a Freudian discourse of action exploits the mechanical as a way of making visible what has really been repressed, and so what really needs to be expressed—the unconscious. The camera is returned to photography not as the tool it can never quite succeed in being but as the possibility of an accident that can never quite take place.

What are we doing when we press the button on a camera? We are writing—"giving expression to individual and original ideas in an original and distinct manner." The force of the question depends on our seeing the camera as a threat to our sense that we are doing something (that we are doing what we mean to do), and the point of the answer is to eliminate the threat. But what, then, are we to make of actions that seem to court the loss of "control" that photography represses and that psychoanalysis renders impossible? (Although the notion of control may seem inappropriate in a psychoanalytic context—don't Freudian slips show us that we're *not* in control?—the inappropriateness depends on a slippage in our use of *we*. We don't

[7]The power of the "compulsion not to let chance count as chance" should not be underestimated; Freud was prepared even to think of misprints as acts and so to regard them as "being in a very great measure [psychologically] motivated" (*Psychopathology*, 129).

[8]Thus Rosalind Krauss finds at the "core" of the surrealist aesthetic the concept of "convulsive beauty," which transforms "instances of objective chance" into messages "from the external world . . . informing the recipient of his own desire. The found object is a *sign* of that desire" (Rosalind Krauss and Jane Livingstone, *L'Amour Fou* [New York, 1985], 35). The transformation of random objects into speech acts represents a double extension of agency: the "superstition" of the savage combined with that of the psychoanalyst.

say what we meant to say [hence loss of control], but our unconscious says what *it* meant to say [recuperation of control]. Freudian slips are moments when the conscious cedes control to the unconscious, hence they suggest a transfer, not a loss, of control.)

What are we doing, for example, when we turn over a playing card, or when we roll dice? It would seem that the distinguishing characteristic of gambling—what makes it different from taking a picture—is, as John Bigelow put it in 1895, that "the fate of the game depends upon Chance or Luck." At least this is the "universal impression." But, again according to Bigelow, the universal impression is mistaken; in fact,

> There is no such thing as chance. What we commonly term chance or luck is simply a mode of expressing our ignorance of the cause or series of causes of which any given event is the inevitable sequence. No result can take place without a cause, and every proximate cause must operate in obedience to the exercise of some will. . . . There is nothing in the universe less accidental than the turn of a card, nor are any acts of our lives more inexorably providential than our gains or losses at the gaming-table.[9]

The psychoanalytic compulsion not to let chance count as chance finds its parallel here in the moralizing effort to make gamblers ethical agents. Thus Bigelow rejects the gambler's claim that he bets only in order to make the game more interesting. Such an interest would imply the suspension of "will"— the replacement of the desire to do something with the desire to see what will happen. Indeed, the very word *happen* seems deceptive to Bigelow, and the frequency of its use seems to him a morally unhappy consequence of the fact that "we have no words in popular use to express the occurrence of events that exclude the idea of their being fortuitous" (474). In a more enlightened culture with a more accurate language, nothing would ever "happen."

Furthermore, the transformation of gambling from a game of chance into an expression of providential will was by no

---

[9]John Bigelow, "What is Gambling?" *Harper's New Monthly Magazine*, February 1895, 473; all further references to this work are cited in the text.

means confined to antigambling propagandists. In fact, according to contemporary psychologists such as Clemens J. France, it was only such a transformation that made gambling attractive to gamblers. So strong is the gambler's belief in a "willing power" in the universe, and so strong is his desire to see how he stands with that power, that he must, France writes, repeatedly "enter upon the uncertain" in order to satisfy his "passion for certainty."[10] The gambler's overwhelming desire is to substitute "will" for "chance," to put "law in place of lawlessness" (142).[11] This is the function of his idea of "luck," an "inward divining rod" that, combining superstition and psychoanalysis, does duty for both the gods and the unconscious by telling the gambler the truth about his own acts. Thus the passion for gambling, as France describes it, is the "same great passion" for truth and certainty that provides the "cornerstone of science, philosophy and religion—the desire to put the element of chance out of the game" (141). This explains, too, the piety of the gambler. In Stephen Crane's remarkable story about poker dice, for example, no amount of "flaming ill-luck" can shake the New York Kid's faith in "the five white mice" ("if one was going to believe in anything at all, one might as well choose the five white mice").[12] In the gambler's wisdom, all things can be explained in terms of cause and effect. The chain of events set off by the New York Kid's losing at dice enables him to save himself and his drunken friends from murder. As one of the

[10]Clemens J. France, "The Gambling Impulse," *American Journal of Psychology* (July 1902); reprinted in *The Psychology of Gambling*, ed. Jon Halliday and Peter Fuller (New York, 1975), 141; all further references to this essay are cited in the text.

[11]Thus, for example, Dostoevsky, writing in 1866, represents gambling as a disease of the will, not because the gambler's will is weak but because his commitment to the power of his will (understood in *The Gambler* as absolute self-control) is total: "All it takes is to be calculating and patient just once in your lifetime—that is all! All it takes is to keep control of yourself just once. . . . Control yourself, that's the main thing" (Fyodor Dostoevsky, *The Gambler*, trans. Victor Terras, ed. Edward Wasiolek [Chicago, 1972], 198). The gambler's mistake is thus to imagine that his fate is entirely within his control.

[12]Stephen Crane, "The Five White Mice," in *Stephen Crane, Prose and Poetry*, ed. J. C. Levenson (New York, 1984), 762; all further references to this story are cited in the text.

friends puts it, " 'Kid shober 'cause didn't go with us. Didn't go with us 'cause went to damn circus. Went to damn circus 'cause lose shakin' dice. Lose shakin' dice 'cause—what make lose shakin' dice, Kid?' The New York Kid eyed the senile youth. 'I don't know. The five white mice, maybe' " (771). Crane's gambling philosophy repeats Bigelow's moral philosophy: "No result can take place without a cause." And the final words of his story—"Nothing had happened"—locates it in Bigelow's linguistic utopia; in what the New York Kid calls "the house of chance," nothing "fortuitous" can take place.

For those who wish to avoid the immorality of gambling, the difficulty, as Bigelow points out, is to establish "the ethical distinction between putting one's money on a wheel of fortune" and "underwriting a policy of insurance" or "buying shares in a corporation" (473). In a market society, a great many actions look like gambling; indeed, insofar as the value of commodities or services in such a society seems to be determined by factors over which the agent has no control (demand, for example), it might be argued that every businessman is perforce a gambler and that the distinction between gambling and "legitimate business" has disappeared. But if the first move of moralists like Bigelow is in this way to universalize gambling, their second move, as we have already seen, is to deny that it exists. In order to save some actions from accident, no actions will be allowed to remain accidental: in Crane's "house of chance," no chance; in Edith Wharton's *House of Mirth* (the nickname of a firm on the New York Stock Exchange), no gambling in stocks. Rather, in the hands of *The House of Mirth*'s great financier, the Jew Simon Rosedale, speculation is transformed into "patient industry,"[13] and making one's way on the social and financial markets of New York begins to look more like farming than gambling.

In this respect, *The House of Mirth* follows a by now familiar pattern of substitution: will for chance, law for lawlessness. Presenting as its utopian ideal a world of what its hero Lawrence Selden calls "personal freedom," freedom from "money,

[13] Edith Wharton, *The House of Mirth*, ed. R. W. B. Lewis (New York, 1977), 118; all further references to this work are cited in the text.

from poverty, from ease and anxiety, from all the material accidents" (65), it distributes at least one element of that world—
freedom from accident—everywhere. Thus the speculator
Rosedale doesn't gamble, and thus Lily Bart—to whom this "republic of the spirit" seems instead a "close corporation"[14]—
nevertheless behaves as if she were already a citizen of the republic. She has what Selden calls the "genius" of "converting
impulses into intentions" (65) so that actions identified precisely as unpremeditated (which is what makes them impulses)
can be converted after the fact into the expressions of some
plan. She embodies a commitment to causation so complete
that it can even run backwards.

But if there's a sense in which the republic of the spirit isn't
quite exclusive enough to count as a utopia (everyone seems
already to inhabit it), there's another sense in which it isn't
quite desirable enough: characters in *The House of Mirth* occasionally seem a little dismayed by the powers of premedita-
tion, and they find themselves exhibiting a certain ambivalence
toward the ideal of action implicit in the possibility of freedom
from accident. This ambivalence is perfectly illustrated in the
very first act Lily Bart commits in the novel: her decision to accept Selden's invitation to an unchaperoned tea. She begins by
blushing—"she still had the art of blushing at the right time"
(4), Wharton remarks, herself converting something like a reflex into something like a display of artifice—but she quickly
assents. "It's too tempting," she says; "I'll take the risk." And
Selden is pleased by the "spontaneity of her consent," by the
promise of figuring as the one "unforeseen element in a career
so accurately planned" (66).

Out of this moment one could, perhaps, construct an entire reading of *The House of Mirth*, insisting on the distinction
between the artificiality of Lily's normal actions—virtually every
one of them, as Cynthia Griffin Wolff puts it, "a deliberate piece
of acting"—and the genuine spontaneity of "those few impulses for which she pays so dearly."[15] In this reading, Lily's impulses embody her desire to escape the market, and the story

[14] I.e., a corporation whose shares are not publicly traded.
[15] Cynthia Griffin Wolff, *A Feast of Words* (New York, 1977), 128.

told by *The House of Mirth* is the story of her inability to do so. She is destroyed by the calculating commercial society of New York. The extent to which Selden, despite his protestations, participates in this destruction, the extent to which Lily herself collaborates in the suppression of her best self on behalf of the commodified self the New York social market demands, may remain objects of critical debate, but the moral seems clear: the "tragic implication" of such a society, in Wharton's own words, "lies in its power of debasing people and ideals."[16]

In the early chapters of the novel, no one embodies this society more than the ambitious Simon Rosedale, who, "with all his race's accuracy in the appraisal of values" (13), recognizes that even to be seen walking with Lily Bart in Grand Central at rush hour would be "money in his pocket." Thus it is Rosedale who produces an "irrepressible look of annoyance" on Lily's face; the look of annoyance, unlike the blush, is truly impulsive, and is accompanied by an "intuitive repugnance" that, "getting the better of years of social discipline" (14), causes Lily to snub Rosedale without calculating the social uses to which he might be put. But this snub, this intuitive display of contempt for the commercial, does not exactly put Rosedale off. On the contrary—in true Groucho Marx fashion—he is attracted by it. Thus, when a no longer fashionable and desperately poor Lily refuses even to accept his offer of a loan, the rebuff, as Lily herself notes, only serves to "strengthen her hold over him. It was as though the sense in her of unexplained scruples and resistances had the same attraction as the delicacy

---

[16]Edith Wharton, *A Backward Glance* (1934; reprint, New York, 1985), 207. Thus Blake Nevius understands *The House of Mirth* as trying "to calculate the expense of spirit that a program of material self-conquest entailed" (Blake Nevius, *Edith Wharton* [Berkeley, 1953], 56). And Cynthia Griffin Wolff takes it to be "about the psychological disfigurement of any woman who chooses to accept society's definition of her as a beautiful object and nothing more" (*Feast of Words*, 110). For an important reading of *The House of Mirth* as an attack on *both* capitalism and patriarchy, see Elizabeth Ammons, *Edith Wharton's Argument with America* (Athens, Ga., 1980). As the following pages make clear, I do not think *The House of Mirth* is a critique of market capitalism; moreover, I think that the terms in which it refuses the role of critique are also the terms in which it refuses a feminism that would identify its own social role as an essentially critical one.

of feature, the fastidiousness of manner, which gave her an external rarity, an air of being impossible to match" (294).

In making her rare, Lily's scruples and resistances also make her valuable, at least to the "real collector," who, as Selden has explained to Lily, "values a thing for its rarity" (9). Selden means here to put some distance between himself and men like Rosedale or Lily's other suitor, the collector of Americana, Percy Gryce; where Selden just likes to have "good editions" of the books he is "fond of," the "buyers of Americana don't sit up reading them all night." Yet Selden is more truly a collector, more like Gryce and especially Rosedale, than this distinction acknowledges. What he thinks of as "the real Lily Bart" (131), the one whose beauty shows forth in the *tableau vivant*, "detached from all that cheapened and vulgarized it" (132), appeals to him for the same reasons and in the same terms that she appeals to Rosedale. Rosedale loves her "exquisite inaccessibleness" (249); and Selden finally sees "deep into the hidden things of love" (320) only when death makes "the real Lily" "invisible and inaccessible" to him. In departing from the House of Mirth, Lily finally makes herself so rare, so valuable, that even a collector so refined as Selden wants her. She thus confirms that movement by which each gesture of "resistance" to the market serves only to augment one's value in the market.

But the most striking thing about Lily's relation to the market is not that she has a high value in it, or even that her desire to escape the market only increases that value; it is instead that those moments that seem to express her distaste for the commerce of Wall Street in fact express her complete commitment to the practices of speculation. This commitment makes a backhanded but significant appearance in a scene I have already mentioned, the walk with Selden at Bellomont where he initiates Lily into the "republic of the spirit." Defined by its freedom from risk, the republic is a world that, as we have seen, Selden imagines Lily (with her "genius" for producing "premeditated effects extemporaneously" [63]) already to inhabit. Indeed, their very walk together is understood by both Selden and Lily as an example of that genius, a "way of making use of [her] material"; she means "to use the accident of his presence as part of a very definite effect," that of disguising her interest in Percy Gryce. Turning material accident into intentional effect, Lily will make sure that in her world, as in Selden's republic, accidents don't happen.

In *The House of Mirth*, however, it turns out that accidents will happen and, more important, that the "risk" of such accidents is finally more attractive than the guarantee of freedom from them. Lily and Selden flirt with each other and carry their flirtation to the brink of a proposal by first asserting and then denying that they are "sure" of what the outcome of such a proposal might be; their erotic excitement reaches its height when Selden volunteers to "take the risk" (70) and Lily assures him of "how great" a risk it is. The interest of premeditating effects is here replaced by the charm of being utterly unable to do so, a charm that finds almost equally intense expression in what Wharton calls Lily's "passion" for bridge. If Lily's genius consists in turning accidents into intended effects, her passion is for situations in which the "terrible god of chance" (24) makes intentions irrelevant by turning all effects into accidents.

But the love of risk in *The House of Mirth* is not confined to speculating in stock, playing bridge, or even flirting with Selden; it appears also—most bizarrely—as the cornerstone of morality. When Rosedale offers to marry Lily if she will threaten Bertha Dorsett with her knowledge of that powerful lady's love letters to Selden, Lily finds herself momentarily attracted by his air of "business-like give and take"; her "tired mind was fascinated by this escape from fluctuating ethical estimates into a region of concrete weights and measures" (253). Compared to the unpredictable fluctuations of ethics, the business world has all the security of the republic of the spirit—which is why she rejects Rosedale's offer. The "essential baseness of the act"— and remember, the act in question is blackmail—"lay [not in the harm it might do Bertha or even Selden but] in its freedom from risk" (254). In other words, cutting a deal with Rosedale is immoral because it isn't enough like gambling; the passionate contingencies of the marketplace are here rewritten as the fundamental criteria of ethical choice, as if the only morally impeccable acts are those whose consequences are unforeseen.

This moral logic, like the book itself, culminates in Lily's death from an overdose of chloral and explains the resistance of that event to the question readers inevitably ask about it: did she or did she not mean to kill herself? It seems mistaken, though, to say either that she did or that she didn't, for the whole thrust of the novel has been to insist on the economic, erotic, and moral charm of actions marked by an irreducible discrepancy between intention and effect. The "action of the drug was incalculable" (316), Wharton insists; so, then, would be the action of anyone taking it. Whereas the skillful gambler seeks to minimize risk by exerting a certain control—indeed, the very idea of action seems to require some such idea of control, of an agent who intentionally causes something to take place—what Lily seems to love is the moment when agency is called into question. Her passion for gambling is a passion for giving up control, and her desire to do the right thing is a desire not to do anything at all. Insofar as the action of the drug that kills her really is incalculable, that drug is a figure for the House of Mirth itself, and Lily's decision to take it—meaning neither to live nor die, meaning only to take a chance—is an expression of her passion for the market.

The House of Mirth might thus be read as a counter to the discourse of action articulated in photography, gambling, and Wharton's own "republic of the spirit." At the same time, however, the freedom from accident that Wharton represents as the ideal of action—and against which her valorization of passivity seems to be directed—was elsewhere coming to be regarded as inimical to action and to freedom both. "The mere carrying out of predetermined purposes is mechanical,"[17] wrote Charles Sanders Peirce in 1892. By eliminating the element of "arbitrary spontaneity"[18] that Peirce thought crucial to human freedom, the discourse against accident transformed men into machines—not because purposiveness was dis-

---

[17] Charles Sanders Peirce, *Collected Papers*, ed. Charles Hartshorne and Paul Weiss, 8 vols. (Cambridge, 1935), 6:157.

[18] "The truth is, the mind is not subject to 'law' in the same rigid sense that matter is. . . . There always remains a certain amount of arbitrary spontaneity in its action, without which it would be dead" (ibid., 6:148).

carded, as is usually the case, but because it was imagined as all too pervasive. Only the presence in the universe of something like "absolute chance," with the corresponding presence of a certain irreducible even if minimal arbitrariness in all cause-and-effect relations, makes freedom possible. Thus where for Pennell and Stieglitz the camera as machine (instead of tool) constituted a threat to conceiving photography as human action, following Peirce we might say that it is only the mechanical nature of the camera that keeps photography from being mechanical. The camera saves photography by coming between the photographer and his "predeterminate" ends, by producing what Peirce calls "interference." And we might even extend this Peircian analysis to the rise of abstraction in painting. Here the saving interference is provided by the paint and by a brush imagined as a kind of camera. On this view, painting comes closest to achieving the condition of the photograph not when (as in super- or photorealism) it most resembles its object but when it resembles so little any object that it seems almost to have been produced by chance.[19] Resisting the mechanism of predetermined ends, abstract painting comes to court what Stieglitz called the "fatal facility" of photography, and Pennell's attack on photography in defense of painting comes to seem a rehearsal for his successors' attacks on painting: anyone could do it.

From this standpoint, to characterize Lily's love of the moment when intentions and effects come apart as a love of the moment when agency is called into question seems mistaken. It might instead be characterized as a love of that moment

[19]Thus, in a by-now-familiar gesture of compensatory redescription, Harold Rosenberg could insist on the primacy for abstract expressionism of the "will to paint." What Rosenberg called "action painting" was important to him not because it addressed the question of the medium as interference but because it seemed in a world of "depersonalizing" social machinery to provide the one escape from interference: for the abstract expressionists, the blank canvas "offered the opportunity for a doing that would not be seized upon in mid-motion by the depersonalizing machine of capitalist society, or by the depersonalizing machine of the world-wide opposition to that society. The American painter discovered a new function for art as the action that belonged to himself" (Rosenberg, *The Anxious Object* [Chicago, 1966], 39).

when agency is most purely itself, when the arbitrariness that makes freedom possible (the break in the chain of cause and effect) is most nakedly on display. And one can find support for this view in other texts of the period—in *The Octopus*, for example, where Norris identifies something like what Wharton calls Lily's "passion" for the "terrible god of chance" not with the desire to give up agency but with Magnus Derrick's desire to reclaim it, to "defeat the railroad, hold the corporation in the grip of his fist . . . regain his self-respect."[20] One of Derrick's "strongest instincts . . . was to be . . . the master," Norris writes, identifying this instinct with the "instinct of the old-time gambler": "Chance! To know it when it came, to recognize it as it passed fleet as a wind flurry, grip at it, catch at it, blind, reckless . . . that was genius."[21] The desire to be master, "controlling the situation," takes the form of the desire to put yourself in a position where, "blind, reckless," you have no control. As gambling becomes the paradigm for action, Magnus's desire to master and Lily's desire to be mastered begin to seem indistinguishable; they both express a desire for that break in the causal chain (the arbitrary "interference") that will make freedom possible.

Insofar as accidents help to make actions free, however, they also threaten to make them random and thus (just as the discourse against accident feared) not really actions at all. To give up agency for freedom seems a paradoxically heavy price to pay; in what sense is an agent free if he isn't free to act? But it may be that in a text like *The House of Mirth*, freedom is a little beside the point. For what Lily Bart sees in the possibility of accidents is something at once less grand and more compelling than the possibility of freedom; it is something like the ability to be interested, above all to be interested in oneself— which is to say, not only to be interested but to be interesting.

"There was nothing new about Lily Bart," Wharton says on the first page of the novel, yet Selden "could never see her without a faint movement of interest: it was characteristic of her that she always roused speculation, that her simplest acts

[20] Frank Norris, *The Octopus* (New York, 1964), 133.
[21] Ibid., 134.

seemed the result of far-reaching intentions" (1). Selden's speculative interest in Lily depends simultaneously on his realiza-
tion that everything she does is an act (not an accident) and on
his inability to know exactly what act it is. For Lily herself, however, as for any agent, such an interest may be harder to manufacture. On Selden's view, Lily always knows what she is
doing; for the agent herself, there is no epistemological gap
between intention and action. Hence, even "impulses" can be
"premeditated," but hence also they may not be interesting. It
is as if for Lily to be interested in herself, the relation between
what she does and what she means to do must be as mysterious
to her as it is to Selden. To "rouse speculation" *in* herself, she
must, as it were, speculate *on* herself, as when she plays
bridge, or as when (in what will turn out to be the moments
before her death) she takes a dose of the "incalculable"
chloral. What moves her to take the chloral is "immense wea-
riness," described by Wharton as a

> vivid wakeful fatigue, a wan lucidity of mind against which all the
> possibilities of the future were shadowed forth gigantically. She
> was appalled by the intense clearness of the vision; she seemed
> to have broken through the merciful veil which intervenes be-
> tween intention and action, and to see exactly what she would do
> in all the long days to come. (314–15)

There can be no doubt that Lily is appalled in part by what
she sees herself doing: "There was the cheque in her desk, for
instance—she meant to use it in paying her debt to Trenor; but
she foresaw that when the morning came she would put off
doing so, would slip into gradual tolerance of the debt." But
given Lily's love of risk, and given Wharton's extraordinary market psychology, it may be that the clarity with which she sees is
finally more appalling than the nature of what she sees. Chloral
restores the veil between intention and action. The "action of
the drug was incalculable" (316), Wharton writes; by transfer-
ring some of the incalculability of its own action to Lily's action
in taking it, the drug makes Lily interesting again. And only
speculative acts can guarantee this interest. For although the
consequences of any act may be unforeseeable (Lily takes

a sleeping potion and unfortunately dies), only the consequences of a speculative act have their unforeseeability built into the very identity of that act (Lily takes a sleeping potion and waits to see what she has done).

The conditions of speculative interest emerge with even greater clarity in Crane's "Five White Mice." Attempting to beat five queens at poker dice, the New York Kid rolls four aces and then for his last throw plants the cup "bottom-up on the bar with the one dice hidden under it." "Instantly," Crane says, "he was presiding over a little drama in which every man was absorbed" (761). When the Kid offers to bet another fifty dollars on whether the last die is an ace, the spectators begin to suspect he may be cheating, and perhaps their interest in the Kid's action may be said to depend, like Selden's initial interest in Lily Bart, on their sense that he has found a way to premeditate accidents. But the Kid's interest in his act depends on the fact that he is *not* cheating: the epistemological interference produced by the cup is just as real for him as for the other spectators. In this drama, then, he is finally neither just a performer (other men betting on what he does) nor a spectator (betting on what others do), but performer and spectator both, betting on himself, doing, and then betting on what he has done.

Another way of getting at this interest might be to note that the Kid's gesture in keeping the last die covered makes temporal, and therefore visible, a distinction that might otherwise go unnoticed: the distinction between rolling five dice and rolling, say, what he actually rolls—four aces and a "ten-spot." Perhaps this distinction could be expressed by saying that the Kid rolled the dice and that the consequence of his rolling the dice was that he got four aces and a ten—to speak, in other words, of the particular numbers you roll as a consequence of the act of rolling. But it seems a little odd to think of the particular numbers you roll as consequences of your rolling, because merely by rolling the dice you will necessarily roll some particular numbers, and, whatever numbers these are, the fact of your necessarily having rolled them makes them seem more a *part* of the act of rolling dice than a *consequence*. From this standpoint, rolling four aces and a ten is less a consequence of the act of rolling five dice than a different description of that act. But this account may be a little misleading also, since the difference in description does seem to reflect a more fundamental difference. After all, rolling four aces and a ten may be the same as rolling five dice; and rolling five aces may be the same as rolling five dice; but rolling four aces and a ten is not the same as rolling five aces. Thus, while it doesn't seem quite right to say that rolling four aces and a ten is a consequence of the act of rolling five dice, it doesn't seem quite right to say that rolling four aces and a ten is the same as rolling five dice either. Playing poker dice seems then to provide a kind of paradigm for intrinsically indeterminate acts. If Wharton's "republic of the spirit" images a world, free of "material accident," where all events are actions and all consequences intended, the game of poker dice, like the House of Mirth, images a world where not only the consequences of one's actions but the very identity of those actions may be unpredictable and unstable.

The temporal opacity introduced by the cup placed over the final die makes visible an opacity internal to the act of rolling dice itself, and it is this internal opacity—the fact that you cannot know exactly what you are doing until it is done—that makes the act interesting. As Bigelow says, gamblers "resent the imputation that they play for money," claiming instead that they "merely risk their money to give more interest to the game" (475). But Bigelow is skeptical of this claim: "who ever heard of two men playing at any game of chance with the understanding that what either won should belong to the loser, or should be shared with him?" Although Bigelow's point is that gamblers care only for money, his example does not exactly make that point. For if what makes gambling interesting is the difference between rolling dice and rolling some particular number, the money may be said to serve only as a reminder of that difference. If there were no stakes, it would not matter what numbers were rolled; the veil between intention and action would be lifted. Gambling without the chance to make money would be pointless, uninteresting. And, by the same logic, gambling as a way of making money—the mere fact of making money—would be equally uninteresting. For if rolling dice without caring how they come up is one way of lifting the veil, rolling loaded dice (and so knowing in advance how they will come up) is another. The moment of what Crane calls "drama"—waiting to see what you've done—is effaced both times: the first time because it doesn't matter what you've done, the second time because (like a good photographer) you already know what you've done.

And here we find ourselves at the site of a certain rapprochement between the compulsion to gamble and the Freudian compulsion not to let chance count as chance: the effect of both is to make actions interesting by making them at least temporarily indeterminate. Freud (like Lawrence Selden) does this by extending the range of actions, transforming "slips" into the expression of unknown intentions. By way of the unconscious, agents get to be Selden and Lily Bart at the same time, looking at what they have done and wondering what they meant by it. But if the unconscious is a technology for making acts problematic, it is also a technology for solving the problem; psychoanalysis produces the veil between intention and action only to remove it. Eventually one may discover what Lily Bart meant; eventually—through psychoanalysis—one may discover what one meant oneself.

In gambling, however, we can never know what we mean, not so much because the veil between intention and action is never lifted but because the intention itself is never quite there. Thus we can plausibly think of the New York Kid as *trying* to roll five aces, but it is not so plausible to think of him as *intending* to roll five aces. We might want to say instead that he is *hoping* to roll five aces, but this doesn't seem quite right either, for he isn't hoping to roll five aces in the same way that he might hope for rain or for someone to leave him a lot of money. If intending seems wrong because it gives the gambler too much causal control, hoping seems wrong because it eliminates the gambler's causal role altogether. The attraction of gambling is that it cannot be reduced to either intending or hoping. In gambling we are interested only in what we do, and it can never be a matter just of hoping, because then it would not involve doing; and it can never be a matter just of intending, because then it would not be interesting.

To put this another way, acts like rolling poker dice are not exactly unintended (for then they would not be acts), but they are, as John Berger says of photographs, "weak in intentionality."[22] Because, unlike paintings or novels, photographs are the products of a *"single constitutive choice,"* the "choice of the instant to be photographed" (89–90), and because the photographer contributes no more to the photograph than this choice of the instant, the "meaning" of photographs is intrinsically ambiguous. This "innate ambiguity," "if recognized and accepted as such," Berger writes, "could offer to photography a unique means of expression" (92), but instead, the history of photography is replete with efforts to control or deny it—from "positivist" attempts to use photographs as objective evidence of the real to "capitalist" attempts to use photographs to manipulate the real. Denying the ambiguity of the photograph, capitalism denies also what Berger calls the "social function of subjectivity," the potential for each viewer of a photograph (as a consequence of its weak intentionality) to construct a "personal relation" with it and to find for himself and share with others the photograph's "synchronic coherence."[23]

Berger thus identifies the weak intentionality of photography with resistance to the market, resistance to "commodification," whereas I have identified the weak intentionality of gambling—and, by implication, of photography too—with acts that take place in the market, such as speculating in commodities. But this apparent contradiction can be resolved simply by noting that for Berger the "innate ambiguity" of the photograph poses no real threat to the Selden-like integrity of the photographic act; rather, it is a consequence of that very integrity. For him, the *"single constitutive choice"* of the photographer makes the photograph an expression of the photographer's own subjectivity; at the same time (because it is only one choice that cannot constrain the choices of others), it leaves the photograph ambiguous, freeing it to serve as a vehicle for expressing the subjectivity of others. That's what it means to establish a "personal relation" with the photograph. In exactly the manner of Stieglitz and Weston, then, Berger manages to

[22] John Berger and Jean Mohr, *Another Way of Looking* (New York, 1982), 90; all further references to this work are cited in the text.

[23] The emphasis on the synchronic here might perhaps be understood as an attempt to get rid of the specifically temporal—Berger calls it "narrative"— aspect of photography, that is, as an attempt to get rid of the "suspense" inscribed in the gap between what one does and what is done.

eliminate accident from photography, imagining the camera as a tool for choosing instead of as a machine for problematizing choice.

This is not to say that photography must always respond to skeptics like Pennell ("And who does the work? who makes the picture?") by defending the integrity of the photographic act. Photography can be divided into three practices, writes Roland Barthes in *Camera Lucida*: "to do, to undergo, to look"—and Barthes immediately excludes himself from the class of doers because, he says, he is "too impatient." "I must see right away what I have produced."[24] If the photographer, according to Pennell, "does not as much as know whether there is a picture on [the plate or film] until he brings [it] home and develops it," Barthes here aligns himself with Pennell's phenomenology of the photographic act. His refusal to be a photographer follows directly from his recognition that the constitutive moment of photography is not the moment of "constitutive choice" but the moment in which—waiting to see how the picture comes out—the difference between choosing and hoping begins to blur. And it is precisely this moment that Barthes identifies when he speaks of his affection for "the sound of the camera," for the noise made by the photographer's finger, "what is linked to the trigger of the lens, to the metallic shifting of the plates." "I love these mechanical sounds . . . as if, in the Photograph, they were the very thing—and the only thing—to which my desire clings" (15). Barthes himself goes on to identify this love with his sense of the camera's history, tracing it back to the skills of the cabinet maker and imagining that what he hears in the "photographic mechanism" is the "living sound" of "wood." For me, however, the sound he loves is the sound of a button being pressed, and his love for it is the mark of his "impatience" (the impatience that keeps him from being

[24]Roland Barthes, *Camera Lucida*, trans. Richard Howard (New York, 1981), 9; all further references to this work are cited in the text. See also Stanley Cavell's powerful reminder that "you cannot know what you have made the camera do . . . until its results have appeared" and his insistence that Alfred Hitchcock's famed control over those results be redescribed as the ability to anticipate them, "the gift of photographic prophecy." Even Hitchcock (a movie Weston) cannot eliminate the "metaphysical wait between exposure and exhibition" (*The World Viewed, Enlarged Edition* [Cambridge, 1979], 185).

a photographer) eroticized. Impatience eroticized is transformed into suspense: waiting to see if you've taken a picture,
waiting to see if you've rolled five aces, waiting to see if you've
killed yourself. Loving suspense, the photographer loves the
presence in himself of an irreducible opacity, the presence in
himself of the market.

I began this essay by describing the efforts of certain photographers to save photography from chance by imagining it as
a kind of writing; I want to end by suggesting that it has recently become more common to think of writing as a kind of
photography. I mean by this that the market criteria of interest
established by such practices as speculation in commodities
and by texts like Wharton's *House of Mirth* have been extended
beyond the practices of the stock market itself, beyond the
more general speculative interest at work in virtually any market transaction, beyond even photography, to what Stieglitz
imagined as photography's salvation: writing. Indeed, the internal epistemological opacity of the act—its opacity not only
to the spectator but also to the agent—and the ontological indeterminacy of the act—the impossibility of determining exactly what act it is—have come to be regarded as almost
uniquely characteristic of writing. Hence the broadly formalist
claim that the meaning of a text exceeds its author's control; or
Paul de Man's more particular claim that there can be no use of
language that is not "radically formal, i.e. mechanical";[25] or
Jacques Derrida's more dramatic claim that the possibility of accident is an "essential risk"[26] of every speech act. Deconstruction, like poker dice, makes the speech act both undetermina-
ble and indeterminate, not only to readers but to writers as
well, and thus marks one of the deepest penetrations *into* the
market *of* the market. But it is perhaps more relevant to my historical argument in this essay—that is, to my attempt to characterize a certain moment in the appeal of indeterminacy—to
end by returning briefly to *The House of Mirth*.

Readers have long recognized the power in this text of the
tableau vivant scene in which Lily appears as Reynolds's "Mrs.
Lloyd," and they have in recent years tended to identify the

[25]Paul de Man, "The Purloined Ribbon," *Glyph* 1 (Baltimore, 1977), 41.
[26]Jacques Derrida, "Signature Event Context," *Glyph* 1 (Baltimore, 1977), 188.

power of this scene with its reduction of Lily to an ornamental victim of patriarchy and capitalism. This is not, however, how Lily sees it. Having chosen the Reynolds because it gave her a chance to represent herself without either the support or distraction of a "sumptuous setting," she finds herself fearing "at the last moment that she was risking too much in dispensing with the advantage" of that support—and then, when the crowd's murmur makes it clear that the risk was worth it, she experiences an "intoxicating sense" of "power" (133). The moment of the *tableau vivant* is thus a moment of speculation, and if Lily is a victim of patriarchal capitalism, so are Rosedale and Gus Trenor and all the other speculators. Only in the risk-free republic of the spirit can such victimization be escaped, and it seems a little odd for feminist readers to embrace as their own Lawrence Selden's utopia.

But the interest of the *tableau vivant* goes beyond the fact that Lily takes a risk in presenting herself as "Mrs. Lloyd." For if the moment of risk is the moment when intentions and actions may come apart, the *tableau vivant* is above all a depiction of that moment. Drawing upon the understanding of painting as a representation of action, it insists at the same time that painting suspends or interrupts the action in order to represent it. The fiction of the painting is that it represents one moment in the continuous series of moments through which any action must be performed, but, whatever Mrs. Lloyd is doing, Lily Bart is standing with attractively "poised foot" and "uplifted arm" to display not the action but the consequences of arresting it. Or, as Wharton puts it, "No other *tableau* had been received with that precise note of approval: it had obviously been called forth by herself, and not by the picture she impersonated" (133). The material interference with action produced by embodying the painting itself produces a Peircian display of personhood, what Wharton calls the "predominance of personality."

And yet the picture and the action it represents are not entirely irrelevant. For what Mrs. Lloyd is doing to get herself into that attractive position is carving her name into the trunk of a tree: she is writing. So if Lily herself and not the picture she impersonates is the object of interest, it may well be that Lily herself is only a stand-in for another person who is impersonating her, the person of the writer. It is this person who represents herself by representing Lily and who takes the risk that produces the power of dramatic interest. Writing here takes its place in the line of risky activities that begins with pressing a button and ends, if it ends, with taking chloral.[27] The figure of the writer thus becomes a figure for speculative self-interest— for the possibility of intention and action coming apart and, more generally, for a subjectivity constituted not by intentions or actions but by desires.

That writing should emerge as a paradigm for an exciting loss of self-control may be somewhat surprising, since for the essentially introspectionist psychology of the late nineteenth century (at least as exemplified in the work of by far the most influential American exponent of that psychology, William James), writing figured more often as an emblem of just the opposite: a self-control so absolute it seemed impregnable. Thus, in his chapter on will in *The Principles of Psychology*, James contrasts controlled actions like writing with apparently uncontrolled ones like sneezing: "I will to write, and the act follows. I will to sneeze and it does not."[28] But James's commitment to the "heroic" assertion of the will is so great that not even the will to sneeze may be thwarted. The real point of his example

[27] Michael Fried's insistence on the importance of Stephen Crane's handwriting and, in particular, on how *slowly* he wrote is relevant here. Fried suggests that "a manner of writing that shaped individual letters with extreme slowness would maximize the likelihood of diverting the writer's attention away from the larger flow of the meaning in his prose to the letters themselves. . . . It is as though below a certain speed of inscription the enterprise of writing threatens to become merely the drawing of letters" (Fried, *Realism, Writing, Disfiguration: On Thomas Eakins and Stephen Crane* [Chicago, in press]). The *tableau vivant* that represents someone writing does not merely slow the act of writing down, it brings it to a complete halt. But the point for the *tableau vivant* is not (any more than, in Fried's account, it is for Crane) that writing gets collapsed into complete materiality; the arrest of motion still functions, after all, in the service of representing the act. Rather, the *tableau vivant* insists on the tension between the intentionality that makes the act the act it is (writing) and the materiality that is both a condition of the act's possibility (without a body, no writing) and a threat to the act's identity (the body, its motion arrested, seems to have forgotten the intentions that impelled that motion in the first place). The *tableau vivant* thus suggests that the possibility of such a forgetting is intrinsic to the possibility of the act.

[28] William James, *The Principles of Psychology* (1890; reprint, Cambridge, 1983), 1165; all further references to this work are cited in the text.

is not finally to insist on the distinction between writing and sneezing but to assert a rather surprising identity between them, and between them and acts that are even less likely:

> I will that the distant table slide over the floor towards me; it also does not. My willing representation can no more instigate my sneezing center than it can instigate the table to activity. But in both cases it is as good and true willing as it was when I willed to write. In a word, volition is a psychic or moral fact pure and simple, and is absolutely completed when the stable state of the idea is there. The supervention of motion is a supernumerary phenomenon depending on executive ganglia whose function lies outside the mind. (1165)

Willing for James is entirely internal; external objects (including our own bodies, which, on this account, must be understood as at least partly external) pose no threat to the success of our willing, since our possible failure to do what we have willed must not be understood as a failure of the will itself. What actually does or does not happen when we will to move our hand across a page or a table across a room is "a mere physiological incident."

Like the psychologists of gambling or of slips of the tongue, James thus imagines the will as everywhere triumphant. No "sinister and dreadful" objects, "incompatible with wished-for things" can threaten it, precisely because such objects are by definition external and the will is not. At the same time, however, James realizes how implausible his description of the will may seem. In a footnote to the sentence that claims that willing to move a table is "as good and true willing" as willing to write, he acknowledges that "many persons say that where they disbelieve in the effects ensuing, as in the case of the table, they cannot will it." Knowing that they cannot in fact move a table, such persons find themselves unable to "exert a volition that a table should move." They find themselves at best in the position of wishing the table would move, since "when one knows that he has no power, one's desire of a thing is called a *wish* and not a will." But this obstacle can be overcome, James thinks, by "abstracting from the thought of the impossibility"— by, in effect, forgetting that you can't do what you're trying to do: "Only by abstracting from the thought of the impossibility am I able to imagine strongly the table sliding over the floor, to make the bodily 'effort' which I do, and to will it to come towards me."

It might still be objected, however (and the quotes around *effort* may indicate James's sensitivity to this objection), that this bodily effort remains unimaginable. For it would be one thing to will to move a table so heavy that moving it was obviously impossible; the *degree* of bodily effort required to move it might be unattainable, but the *kind* of bodily effort required would by no means be unimaginable. Converting this wish into a will would require only imagining oneself much stronger than one knew oneself to be. But what of imagining oneself moving a table across a room without touching it? What kind of bodily effort can one imagine without imagining that one is moving one's body? James doesn't say. On James's account, it seems, the idealization of the will is so complete that "good and true willing" is possible not only when you cannot in *fact* do what you will to do but also when you cannot in *principle* do what you will to do, that is, not only when you cannot do it but when you cannot even imagine how it could be done.

If, then, the difference between willing and wishing depends on the imagination of "power" (or, what comes to the same thing, the repression of impotence), and if power is always imaginable (impotence is always repressible), what is left of the difference between willing and wishing? The answer, on James's account, seems to be: nothing. Thus, wishing a table would move can be appropriately understood as willing a table to move, and inversely, willing to write can be appropriately understood as wishing that something would get written. Once the defining difference between the two terms ("power") has been elided, willing becomes as internal as wishing, and writing becomes as external as sneezing. The writer must now understand her *intention* to mean as a *desire* to mean and may thus come to regard her intentions as irrelevant in determining what she writes. Or, more rigorously, she may cease to think of herself as having intentions. In their article "Normal Motor Automatism," two of James's students, Leon M. Solomons and Gertrude Stein, describe a subject (apparently Stein herself) who, engaged in automatic writing, was able to get herself "in a condition where there was often an expectation of what would be written, but no *intention* to write it. One watched his arm with an idle curiosity, wondering whether or no the expected word would be written."[29] The writer here is not precisely a person but a person's arm, and although Stein's interest in what her arm will write amounts to no more than "idle curiosity," the structure of a more intense interest has been sufficiently established by the displacement of intention, which turns the writer into an observer of her own body and into a reader of the text that body writes.

This displacement makes our writing as interesting to us as, say, Lily Bart's body, displayed in the act of writing, is to "that experienced connoisseur, Mr. Ned Van Alstyne" (132): "Gad, there isn't a break in the lines anywhere" (131). Indeed, in a text where "to write" is, as often as not, "to write a line" (136), the "outline" (135) of Lily's body is sexy—and the display of that body is risky—in the same way that modern theory makes writing out to be. One's writing, like one's body, is beyond one's control; it belongs to oneself but only by belonging also to others. Or rather—like the "surrendered body" of Wharton's pornographic "Fragment of 'Beatrice Palmato,'"[30] and like the display of that body as written that constitutes the literal condition of a pornographic interest—the body of writing marks the possibility of a self-surrender (and hence a self-possession) that renders *other* others superfluous. Expressions of intention transformed into objects of desire, these lines become the site of speculative self-interest.[31] They are the "real Lily" (131) of the *tableau vivant*, the writing she represents and the writing that represents her.

[29]Gertrude Stein and Leon Solomons, "Normal Motor Automatism," *Psychological Review* (September 1896); reprinted in *Motor Automatism*, ed. Robert A. Wilson (New York, 1969), 22.

[30]Edith Wharton, "Fragment of 'Beatrice Palmato,'" in R. W. B. Lewis, *Edith Wharton* (New York, 1975), 548.

[31]It is no wonder, then, that arguments like those made by Steven Knapp and me in "Against Theory" meet with an intensity of rejection that seems to transcend the sense that we are merely mistaken. For in asserting that texts can only mean what their authors intend them to mean, such arguments seem to deprive us not only of the possibility of doing theory but also of the possibility of being interesting. And although many literary critics have begun to lose interest in theory, very few of us have begun to lose interest in ourselves.

Index

Agnew, Jean-Christophe, 15n
American Base Ball and Athletic Exhibition Co. v. Harper, 130
Amityville Horror, The, 89, 90
Ammons, Elizabeth, 227n
Associationism, 8, 121–22, 139–40, 155–56

Balzac, Honoré de, 46, 47
Barthes, Roland, 238–39
Bell, Michael Davitt, 87–88n
Berger, John, 236–38
Bersani, Leo, 46, 47, 48, 52–54, 209n
Bigelow, John, 223, 225, 235
Blackstone, William, 93
Bowlby, Rachel, 18
Boyer, Paul, 91, 92
Brecher, Edward, 115–16
Bryan, William Jennings, 139
Bryan Silver Club, 149
Button v. Hoffman, 197

Cavell, Stanley, 238n
Chandler, Alfred D., Jr., 209
Chase, Richard, 173n
Chevalier, Michel, 93n, 100, 101
Cleveland, Grover, 161, 162, 163, 172
Cochran, Thomas C., 62, 65n
Commodities, 20–21, 25–26, 67–68
Commons, John, 130

Consumption, 185–86, 201; culture of, 14–18; and production, 3, 11–13, 27–28. *See also* Desire
Cooke, Jay, 77
Corporation, 20; as Christian community, 193–94; as entity, 196–200; insatiability of, 48–49, 54–56, 185–87, 201; as person, 188–91, 195–96, 201–6; as monopoly, 209–10; as writer, 207–9, 211–12
Cowing, Cedric B., 63n, 67, 73
Crane, Stephen, 21, 224–25, 234–35, 236

Davis, James "Cyclone," 188, 198, 200, 201, 208–9
Deleuze, Gilles, 125n, 209–10n
de Man, Paul, 239
Derrida, Jacques, 28n, 239
Desire, 3, 20; and art, 45–46; and character, 2; in contract, 127–29; failure of, 43–44, 46, 183–84; feminine and masculine models of, 56–58; and insatiability, 35, 48–49, 53–58, 185–87, 201, 212; as self-betrayal, 107–108; as threat to social order, 46–47; and will, 241–44. *See also* Consumption; Corporation
Deutsch, Helene, 117

Dobb, Maurice, 31n, 50n
Doherty, Robert, 97, 98
Donnelly, Ignatius, 144–45, 186–87
Dostoevsky, Fyodor, 224n
Douglas, Ann, 14n, 16
Draper, John, 99
Dreiser, Theodore, 18, 19, 20, 27, 52;
    The Financier, 61–65, 67, 68, 70,
    73, 74–80, 82, 83; *The Genius*,
    80n; *A Selection of Uncollected
    Prose*, 80n; *Sister Carrie*, 17, 20,
    21, 22, 31–35, 41–46, 48–50, 54–58,
    184
Dreyfus, Hubert L., 179n
Dutoit, Ulysse, 53, 54, 56

Elias, Robert H., 47, 62n
Ely, Richard T., 125–35, 136n
Emerson, Peter Henry, 218–19, 220

Ferguson, Frances, 295n
Fitzhugh, George, 106
Foucault, Michel, 177, 178, 179
Fox, Richard Wightman, 14, 15
France, Clemens J., 224
Frankenstein, Alfred, 161, 162, 167n
Freedom, 101–2, 111–12, 130–33, 135–
    36; and accident, 230–32; of con-
    tract, 19, 126–36; of pleasure,
    124–26. *See also* Self-ownership
Freud, Sigmund, 9, 115, 236; *The Psy-
    chopathology of Everyday Life*,
    221–23
Fried, Michael, 21, 163n, 241n

Gambling, 77–78, 143–44, 223–25,
    232, 234–37. *See also* Speculation
Gates, Paul Wallace, 90
Genovese, Eugene, 104
Genteel tradition, 14–17, 50–53
Gilbert, Sandra, 4n
Gilman, Charlotte Perkins, 3, 16, 17,
    26; "Why I Wrote 'The Yellow
    Wallpaper,'" 4; *Women and Eco-
    nomics*, 3, 5, 13, 16; "The Yellow
    Wallpaper," 3–6, 9–13, 14, 27, 28
Gilmore, Michael T., 111–12n
Goodell, William, 93, 94n, 102–3, 104
Graham, Don, 166n
Green, T. H., 132
Greenberg, Clement, 163–65

Gubar, Susan, 4n

Haberle, John, 161, 164, 167n, 172
Harnett, William, 161, 164
Harvey, William H., 146, 147
Hathorne, John, 90, 91
Haupt, Ottomar, 139
Hawthorne, Nathaniel, 10; *The
    American Claimant; The House of
    the Seven Gables*, 87–101, 106–12,
    124
Hayden, Dolores, 13–14n
Haymarket Trial, 26, 172
Hofstadter, Richard, 147
Homestead Act, 94, 95
Howells, William Dean, 35, 42, 48, 50,
    51, 52, 83; "The Man of Letters as
    a Man of Business," 80–82; *The
    Rise of Silas Lapham*, 36–41, 45, 46
House Committee on Agriculture,
    58n, 66
Hysteria, 4, 23–26
Hume, David, 8, 9

Identity, 20–23; of acts, 217–21, 233–
    36; and idealism, 188–91, 201;
    and materialism, 162–67, 170–74,
    201; of persons, 7–9, 54–55; and
    representation, 167–69, 171–72,
    179–80; stability of, 40–41, 98–99,
    203–6; in statistics, 209–11
Imperialism, 49–50

Jackson, Andrew, 92, 101, 109, 110
James, William, 7, 10, 22, 154; *The
    Principles of Psychology*, 7–9,
    121–22, 139–40, 155–60, 170–71,
    241–43
Johns, Jasper, 164

King, Stephen, 89
Knapp, Steven, 244n
Krafft-Ebing, Richard von, 115–21,
    131, 135n
Krauss, Rosalind, 222n

Lears, T. J. Jackson, 14, 15, 16
Le Conte, Joseph, 170, 173
Lehan, Richard, 49, 62
Lenin, V. I., 50

Literature, 27; of corporations, 211–13; and the market, 81–83; and power, 52–54, 55–57
Lloyd, Henry D., 188
Longfellow, Henry Wadsworth, 105–6
Luxemburg, Rosa, 50

Machen, Arthur W., Jr., 197n, 198–205, 212
Macpherson, C. B., 102, 112
Maine, Sir Henry, 136n
Markels, Julian, 42
Martin, Ronald E., 207n
Marx, Karl, 20, 21, 26, 31, 32, 33, 48, 51–52
Masochism, 115, 121–22, 124–29; and contract, 124–29, 134–36; and hoarding, 120–23; and ownership, 117–20, 130–33
Mazzini, Giuseppe, 130–31
Meyers, Amy Weinstein, 219n
Miller, William, 62, 65n
Mimesis, 87–89, 156–60; as deception (trompe l'oeil), 160–65; and personhood, 171–72; and production, 95
Misers, 47–48, 120, 122–23, 139–41, 148–49, 153–54, 158–66
Mitchell, S. Weir, 4, 11, 26; "The Case of George Dedlow," 23–25; Characteristics, 25; Dr. North and His Friends, 6; Doctor and Patient, 6, 7; Hugh Wynne, 10; Lectures on Diseases of the Nervous System, 4, 6; Wear and Tear, or, Hints for the Overworked, 11, 25
Moers, Ellen, 34, 36
Money, 34, 35, 176–80; and aesthetics, 154–55; and commodities, 64–65, 67–68, 145–48; disappearance of, 144–45, 175; paintings of, 161–65; paper money, 146, 150–54, 160–61, 176; precious metals, 144–53, 174–77; value of, 31–34, 145–48
Mussel Slough, 191, 195

Nast, Thomas, 151, 160, 167, 168
Naturalism, 26–27, 172–80, 200–203, 205–6, 212–13
Nature, 3, 51–52, 71–72, 105–6, 123–24, 130–31, 208–11; and speculation, 174–77; unnaturalness of, 76–77; and work, 78–80
Nevins, Allan, 69, 70n, 71, 72
Nevinson, Henry, 126
Nevius, Blake, 227n
Nissenbaum, Stephen, 91, 92
Norris, Frank, 23, 131, 212; McTeague, 21, 119–21, 122–23, 135–36, 139–41, 146, 148–54, 158–59, 175–77; The Octopus, 21, 183–91, 200–201, 206–9, 211–13, 232; The Pit, 72–73; Vandover and the Brute, 142–44, 165–69, 174–75
Nugent, Thomas L., 146
Nurse, Rebecca, 90, 91

Olitski, Jules, 163n

Parrington, Vernon, 35, 36n, 151–53
Parsons, Albert R., 172
Peirce, C. S., 188, 230, 231
Pennell, Joseph, 217–18, 219, 231, 238
Photography, 96; as act, 217–20, 222–23, 236–39; and romance, 99–100
Physiocrats, 51
Pizer, Donald, 34, 35n, 61, 62n, 120n, 170n, 173n, 211n
Poltergeist, 90
Poor, Henry, 154–55
Populism, 176, 185, 208
Production, 3, 184; and consumption, 11–13, 27–28, 185–86; for exchange, 13, 17; and overproduction, 13, 73–74; of self, 5, 10–11; and speculation, 65–69, 70–71
Proffat, John, 55
Property, 92–93, 96–98, 102–4, 154–58, 178–79; and alienation, 93–94, 105–6, 112, 126–36; self as, 8–11, 109–12, 123–24, 130–33; title to, 89–93, 101–2, 110–11, 191–93

Rabinow, Paul, 179n
Realism, 26–27, 37–41, 46; and romance, 87–89; and sentimentalism, 45
Rest cure, 4
Reynolds, Mary, 11n
Ricardo, David, 31, 51

Rockefeller, John D., 69, 70, 71, 75, 83
Rockefeller, William, 69
Rodgers, Daniel T., 73, 74n
Rogin, Michael Paul, 110
Romance, 87–89, 95, 98–100
Rosenberg, Harold, 231n
Royce, Josiah, 23, 212; *California*, 190; "An Episode of Early California Life," 192–93; *The Feud at Oakfield Creek*, 191–98, 206; *Letters*, 193n; "The Mechanical, the Historical and the Statistical," 209–11; *The Problem of Christianity*, 190, 194; *War and Insurance*, 188–89; *The World and the Individual*, 190

Sacher-Masoch, Leopold von, 115; and slave contract, 125, 127; *Venus in Furs*, 124–29, 133–35
Scarry, Elaine, 26n
See, Fred, 42n
Self-control, 5–7, 107–8, 111–12, 222–23, 225–34, 240–41
Self-ownership, 8–11, 109–12, 123–24, 130–32. *See also* Property
Seltzer, Mark, 200, 201, 209–10n
Seward, William, 104
Shell, Marc, 151n
Simmel, Georg, 140, 141, 142, 144
Slavery, 101–2; and capitalism, 104–5; and contract, 124–27, 129–31; and masochism, 117–18
Smith, Adam, 31, 32, 51
Smith, Henry Nash, 62n, 94n
Smith-Rosenberg, Carol, 23
Snyder, Joel, 217n
Solomons, Leon M., 243–44
Speculation, 47–48, 100–101, 228–30; in futures, 57–58, 64–67; as gambling, 40–41, 66–67, 225; in real estate, 90; and self-interest, 232–34, 239–40; in slaves, 105
Spencer, Herbert, 76, 121, 155–56
Spendthrift, 141–44
Standard Oil Co., 69, 70n, 71
Stein, Gertrude, 243–44
Stieglitz, Alfred, 218–20, 222, 231, 237, 239
Stowe, Harriet Beecher, 83, 112, 134, 135; *The Key to Uncle Tom's Cabin*, 101, 105, 106, 108n, 109–10; *Uncle Tom's Cabin*, 101–5, 115, 116, 123–24
Strasser, Susan, 13n
Sumner, Charles, 108
Surrealism, 221–22

Tarbell, Ida M., 69, 71, 72, 75, 83
Thomas, Brook, 19n, 87–88n
Trachtenberg, Alan, 14n, 15, 16, 17

Value, 31–33, 51–52, 145–48, 227–28; and fluctuation, 40–41, 61–65
Veblen, Thorstein, 15, 51, 52

Watson, Tom, 186
Welling, James, 163n
Wells, David, 145–47, 149–51, 160–61, 167, 175
Weston, Edward, 219, 237
Wharton, Edith, 225–34, 235, 236, 239–41
White, Horace, 64n, 66–67n
Wilson, R. Jackson, 193
Wolff, Cynthia Griffin, 226, 227n
Writing, 3, 4–5, 21, 80–82, 167–70; automatic, 7, 209, 220–21, 243–44; and photography, 220–22; and risk, 239–44

Designer: Janet Wood
Compositor: Wilsted & Taylor
Text: 10/12 Optima Medium
Display: Optima Medium
Printer: Murray Printing Co.
Binder: Murray Printing Co.